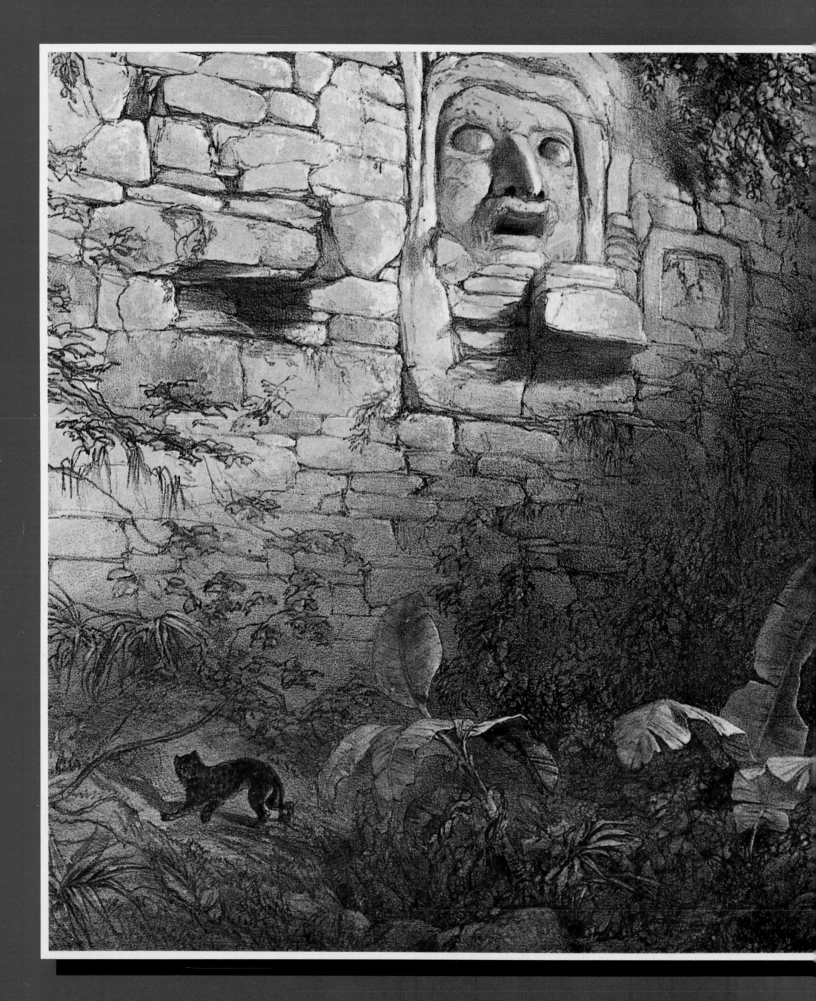

The ADVENTURE OF ARCHAEOLOGY

by Brian M. Fagan

NATIONAL GEOGRAPHIC SOCIETY

The ADVENTURE OF ARCHAEOLOGY

Published by
The National Geographic
Society

Gilbert M. Grosvenor
President

Melvin M. Payne
Chairman of the Board

Owen R. Anderson
Executive Vice President

Robert L. Breeden
*Vice President,
Publications and
Educational Media*

Prepared by
National Geographic
Book Service

Charles O. Hyman
Director

Ross S. Bennett
Associate Director

Staff for this book

Carol Bittig Lutyk
Editor

David F. Robinson
Assistant Editor

David M. Seager
Art Director

Linda B. Meyerriecks
Illustrations Editor

Jean Kaplan Teichroew
Chief Researcher

Louise Madison Washburn
Art Coordinator

Lynn R. Addison
Mary B. Dickinson
Edward Lanouette
Elizabeth L. Newhouse
Shirley L. Scott
Editor-Writers

Paulette L. Claus
Mary R. Lamberton
Mary Luders
Suzanne Kane Poole
Judy A. Reardon
Lise Swinson Sajewski
John G. Shaffer
Carol Skowron
Penelope A. Timbers
Editorial Researchers

Greta Arnold
Illustrations Researcher

Diana E. McFadden
Illustrations Assistant

Charlotte Golin
Design Assistant

Karen F. Edwards
Traffic Manager

Richard S. Wain
Production Manager

Andrea Crosman
Production Assistant

Georgina L. McCormack
Teresita Cóquia Sison
Editorial Assistants

John T. Dunn
David V. Evans
Ronald E. Williamson
Engraving and Printing

Maps by
John D. Garst, Jr.
Judith F. Bell
Peter J. Balch
Patricia K. Cantlay
D. Mark Carlson
Donald L. Carrick
Marguerite Suarez Dunn
James V. Mauck
Joseph F. Ochlak
Margaret B. Pierce
Martin S. Walz
Publications Art

Photographs by
Jonathan Blair
Ira Block
  and others

Paintings by
Thomas Blackshear
Michael A. Hampshire

Anne K. McCain
Indexer

George E. Stuart
*Staff Archaeologist,
National Geographic Society,
and Chief Consultant*

Werner L. Janney
Editorial Consultant

Thomas B. Allen
Elisabeth B. Booz
Andrew H. Brown
Louisa C. Clayton
Richard M. Crum
Caroline Hottenstein
Robert M. Poole
Peter L. Porteous
Deborah L. Robertson
Margaret Sedeen
Kim E. Shelsby
Susan E. Sidman
Jonathan B. Tourtellot
Contributors

First edition
260,000 copies

403 illustrations, 24 maps

Library of Congress
CIP data page 368

Pages 2-3: "Colossal Head, at Izamal,"
published in 1844 by Frederick
Catherwood, an early explorer of
Maya ruins in Mexico and
Central America.

CONTENTS

FOREWORD

"In the beginning. . . ." These words open the Scripture that is sacred to a fourth of the world's people. But they reflect an abiding curiosity that is shared by human cultures everywhere—a thirst for knowledge about our past. Every society has speculated about its origins. And many have dug into the earth in search of hard evidence.

One 18th-century British cleric shoveled into 31 ancient burial mounds in a single day. Today it can take weeks to uncover just a few square feet of an ancient city mound, and months more to preserve and study the finds. Digging up the past has become a sophisticated science that draws on experts in dozens of specialties.

The Adventure of Archaeology tells the story of how that science came into being—a compelling tale of tourists and treasure hunters, of strong-minded adventurers, of patient excavators laboring alone, of teams of scholars trekking into the desert or diving into the deep. In these pages you will witness the discovery of forgotten civilizations—the Assyrians and Sumerians of Mesopotamia, the Minoans of Crete, the Harappans of the Indus Valley, the Olmec of Mexico.

In words and images you will travel through time with the Leakey family to the earliest chapters of human existence in East Africa, and with Kathleen Kenyon to Jericho's 10,000-year-old walls. You will look over the shoulder of Howard Carter as he opens Tutankhamun's tomb, and dive with George Bass as he studies a Bronze Age shipwreck on the bottom of the Mediterranean.

Our journey also takes you to laboratories to witness the development of radiocarbon dating, to peer into a microscope at fossil pollen, and to discover what stone tools and bits of bone can tell us about the past. A fragment of pottery may reveal nearly as much as an entire bowl. A single coin in the proper context can yield more useful information than a golden trove ripped from the ground. Each clue, however small, adds to our knowledge of how our ancestors lived.

A century and a half ago, scholars assumed that humans had appeared on earth only six thousand years before and that the ancient Egyptians had created the first civilization. Today archaeologists study almost two million years of human existence and dozens of early civilizations, known to us from thousands of sites, large and small, on coastlines and mountaintops, in deserts and rain forests, deep below city streets, and even on the bottoms of rivers, lakes, and seas.

Unfortunately the triumph of archaeology lies in the shadow of tragedy. As archaeologists labor to record time's irreplaceable archives, eager collectors continue to buy anything they can for their own pleasure or profit. Housing developments, farms, factories, highways—these and more are obliterating archaeological sites every day. The Parthenon in Athens is crumbling, partly because of air pollution; Kampuchea's temples at Angkor were caught in the cross fire of war. The future of the past lies in our hands, a precious legacy to pass on to our descendants. But so much has been destroyed that, if we are not careful, there will be no past to leave them.

One day not long ago I visited the ancient beach at Herculaneum (opposite), a seaside Roman city buried by the eruption of Mount Vesuvius in A.D. 79. Beside me was Sara Bisel, a noted physical anthropologist. And before us lay the skeletons of Roman citizens who had died in the tragedy, fragile relics preserved for centuries in the mud. More skeletons would soon be unearthed—and, if not protected, would begin to deteriorate in the light and air.

The National Geographic Society had provided emergency funding to send Dr. Bisel to Italy for the painstaking task of preserving and reconstructing the skeletons. Nearly 140 have been excavated thus far, and some experts say that hundreds, even thousands, more may await discovery on the buried beach. For the first time, modern science will study human remains from the days of ancient Rome. Occupations, diseases, diet, appearance—the dead will tell many tales about life in Roman times. And the National Geographic will continue, as it has for nearly a century, to support such research in every corner of the world.

I sincerely hope that you will enjoy this true-to-life adventure story. If it shows you that archaeology is a science and not a treasure hunt, then it has helped ensure a future for our common heritage—the human past.

Gilbert M. Grosvenor

President, National Geographic Society

Syria, 1977: A full moon floats over the roofless walls of Ebla, a trade center 4,400 years ago and site of a dig since 1964.

THE ADVENTURE BEGINS

"We have here a completely new and unknown world.... An empire that alters forever our perception of ancient history." How many archaeologists have spoken words like these? How many have shared with Paolo Matthiae of the University of Rome the thrill of discovery that he felt as he gazed over the moonlit ruins of Ebla in Syria? Here in 1975 Matthiae hit an archaeological jackpot: the greatest archive ever unearthed from the third millennium B.C., more than 15,000 clay tablets and fragments inscribed in wedge-shaped cuneiform. Through the mists of time, they told of a kingdom whose rulers sat at Ebla and dominated much of the ancient Near East.

Such discoveries draw people to archaeology, to a profound fascination with the past. Every archaeologist hopes to feel, sooner or later, that thrill of discovery—and yet, for many, the find may be nothing more than a few grains of fossil pollen or a bit of graffiti on an ancient wall. Still, the very word "archaeology" conjures up grinning skeletons and cryptic inscriptions. People think archaeologists live in a world of lost cities, strange idols, and troves of gold. But do they? How did archaeology begin, and how did it get its aura of romance and adventure? These pages will trace the story of archaeology as it evolved from a glorified treasure hunt to a scientific study of human cultures in the past.

A century and a half ago an excavator would choose a site—perhaps a burial mound—and dig into it in hopes of a spectacular discovery. The modern archaeologist is concerned not only with the spectacular but also with the prosaic, from pottery fragments to cobs of prehistoric corn no longer than a fingernail. From such objects, archaeologists can often tell whether an ancient stoneworker was left-handed or calculate in what month a hunting camp was occupied.

Such information is only part of the complicated archaeological jigsaw puzzle. Many of its pieces come from other disciplines. Geologists re-create the ancient landscapes surrounding 50,000-year-old campsites in Europe. Botanists examine thousands of minute grains of fossil pollen to reconstruct the vegetation that carpeted the Bering Strait when it was a dry-land bridge linking Asia to North America. Metallurgists show that African smiths were welding iron more than 2,000 years ago.

9

An archaeologist once quoted a witticism from 1846: "That's Archaeology, *mon cher,* the Science of Rubbish." In some ways the quip is right, for archaeologists spend a lot of time delving into ancient garbage heaps. They gaze backward, working with the remains of both humans and ancestral hominids. To study human societies, they ponder the things left behind by peoples who lived and died throughout almost two million years of human existence. These material remains are called artifacts—any object made or modified by humans, be it as small as a pin or as big as a pyramid.

The focus of archaeology is changing today, away from questions of when and where to problems of how and why. Half a century ago Leonard Woolley excavated the ancient Near Eastern city that the Bible calls Ur of the Chaldees, with only a handful of European experts but several hundred diggers. Today an excavation at Ur would probably involve a long roster of archaeologists, architects, biologists, ecologists, language experts, geologists, and surveyors—and far less earth-moving. The swashbuckling archaeologist of yesteryear is nearly gone, replaced by slow-moving, multidisciplinary research teams who are involved as much in explaining the past as in describing it.

An early collector might delve into everything from American Indian artifacts to Roman pottery. His modern successors are specialists. Some are prehistorians and specialize in preliterate societies; within this group are paleoanthropologists, experts on the earliest human cultures. Historical archaeologists study societies that left written records; they work closely with historians on sites such as medieval European cities and American frontier forts. Then there are Egyptologists, Assyriologists, and classical archaeologists whose specialty is ancient Greece and Rome. Archaeology touches

The hard work of a dig absorbs an archaeological team at Monticello, Thomas Jefferson's 18th-century Virginia estate (above). After softening the soil with a water sprayer, a worker digs out a posthole, lying prone to reach the bottom. Others probe root cellars here on Mulberry Row, site of the estate's smokehouse-dairy, slave quarters, joinery, and a nailery with one of America's first nail-cutting machines.

Cups and cartons (opposite) keep the finds in order. Each box holds items from an exact spot on the site and a specific depth in the soil. Cups divide the contents by material: ceramic, metal, glass, bone, stone, and organic remains such as seeds and oyster shells.

As delicate items come to light, archaeologists switch to finer tools. At a dig in Crete, careful fingers select only a few bristles (left) to tease dirt from an emerging artifact.

12

There is more to a dig than digging. In this painting a team peels back the layers of a North American site—and combines in one afternoon a range of tasks that may span several years.

Surveyors (1) measure the layout and contours of the site. Other workers divide it into a grid (2) with stakes and strings. Maps are drawn of the site (3), and each feature or artifact is recorded exactly in its numbered square.

Heavy equipment (4) has stripped away layers that held no artifacts. Hand excavation follows (5) as workers with hoes and shovels watch for signs of human activity. Final excavation requires tools no larger than a trowel—and sometimes as fine as a dental pick—to free a small object (6) and expose a skeleton (7) with its grave goods. Sifting (8) sorts tiny items from the dirt.

Many finds cannot be dug up; they are part of the soil. Small pockets of darker earth (9) show where posts rotted or burned in their postholes; big pockets (10) may mark fire pits or even burials. Loaflike humps (11) show how Indians built this mound by dumping basketfuls of dirt upside down.

As the dig goes deeper, tags tacked to a vertical cut (12) identify the strata. And as the finds emerge, artists (13) preserve them on paper and photographers (14) record them—and the project's full scope—on film. Sheet plastic (15) waits to shield the fragile past from sun that can bake the soil hard as rock and from rain that can turn it to mud.

13

every era and every part of the world—from 3.6-million-year-old hominid footprints in Africa to Roman shipwrecks at the bottom of the Mediterranean Sea.

The beginnings of the science of archaeology lie in an abiding curiosity about humanity's origins. All societies have their own ways of explaining human existence and the world around them. "In the beginning there was only Ta'aroa, who had no forebears, who created himself and all other first beings and things," goes one Tahitian legend. The Old Testament contains some echoes of ancient Mesopotamian tribal lore—the stories of a sole creator and a great flood, for example. Most societies have been content with their legendary origins. Thus archaeology, the systematic inquiry into the past, has been until recently a special phenomenon of Western European civilization.

With a few notable exceptions. Back in the sixth century B.C., Nabonidus of Babylon unwittingly became one of history's first archaeologists. An undistinguished monarch with a passion for ancient religion, he dug deep into two city mounds. The aged king rebuilt the ziggurat, or temple-pyramid, at Ur. Searching for the temple of the goddess Ishtar at Agade, near Babylon, his workmen toiled in vain for three years. Then a torrential rainstorm cut a gully through the mound and revealed the foundations of the shrine. Nabonidus felt the thrill of discovery that every archaeologist dreams of. The find, says an ancient text, "made the king's heart glad and caused his countenance to brighten."

Nabonidus was not alone in his thirst for the past. A Babylonian tablet survives in which a son urges his father to look for buried treasure. "Dig it out of the ground wherever [such objects] are [found] and send it to me. I want it very much," he wrote. The Babylonians were well aware that history—and perhaps untold riches—lay under their feet.

The Greeks and Romans puzzled over the origins of human society. They thought of the Nile as the cradle of civilization. Roman tourists flocked to the great river to gaze at the colossal pyramids at Gîza and enjoy the fleshpots of Alexandria. The Roman emperor Hadrian adorned his garden with Greek statuary and with Egyptian sculptures as well.

These casual flirtations with archaeology petered out with the fall of Rome. Thereafter the story of the creation and of the Garden of Eden sufficed. People believed that their forebears had been banished from Paradise and had spread all over the world, which accounted for the diversity of humankind. History was short and simple. "Time we may comprehend," wrote English physician Sir Thomas Browne in 1643. "'Tis but five days older than ourselves." About the same time Archbishop James Ussher of Ireland used the long genealogies in the Old Testament to calculate that the world had been created on the evening of October 22 in 4004 B.C.

Both Browne and Ussher were steeped in knowledge of ancient Greece and Rome, for the Renaissance had reawakened classical learning and opened new gates to the past. The Renaissance was an age of collectors, of scholars and cardinals and nobles from all over Europe who journeyed to the Mediterranean to bring back antiquities for their homes. (Their acquisitive counterparts haunt archaeology to this day as affluent collectors bribe, smuggle, and flout protective laws to decorate their salons with antiquities.)

Soon it became fashionable to be an antiquary—a collector or student of ancient things. Only the wealthiest travelers could afford to collect classical treasures, so humbler collectors turned to the nearby countryside. In England they found Roman coins and inscriptions, and occasionally hoards of simple bronze and stone tools that seemed much older. Stonehenge on the uplands of southern England was the most famous curiosity, a place where—in the words of a 12th-century text—"stones of wonderful size have been erected after the manner of doorways."

Schoolmaster William Camden had been captivated by the past since childhood, by what he called a "back looking curiosity." After ten years of fieldwork and study of medieval chronicles, he published his immortal work *Britannia* in 1586, a straightforward topographic description of Britain and its ancient Celtic provinces. Camden's main interests were Celtic and Roman coins and inscriptions; he dismissed Stonehenge as "weatherbeaten and decaied."

Camden would never have dreamed of digging, but he was an acute field observer. When he visited Richborough,

14

A student archaeologist brushes away the centuries from the bones of an Indian in Arkansas. To ease such delicate work, field crews may cut away the soil to leave the skeleton on a pedestal.

Sketches and photographs record the skeleton's position and any offerings buried with it. Most skeletons are found in graves. Others may bear mute witness to wars or mishaps whose victims fell without the rites of burial—but sometimes with weapons or tools wielded in the last moments of life.

For almost two million years, humans have left a fragile testament to their existence: their bones. Skeletal remains, whether buried in a pharaoh's airtight tomb or a sailor's watery grave, yield a myriad of clues to the past.

Experts keep a sharp watch for cultural and physical traits, such as these head-to-toe tip-offs. Raised skull lesions (1) indicate a scalping, probably just after death. Flattened ribs and a fused breastbone (2) result from the fashionable constraints of the 18th-century girdle called stays. The shaded areas represent the normal curve of a rib cage. Twisted fingers with swollen and eroded joints (3) evoke the pain of rheumatoid arthritis.

Jagged knee spurs (4) form on horsemen too long in the saddle. Magnified 20 times, osteons—canal-like structures that feed nutrients to the bones—are more numerous in the bone of a middle-aged man (5, right) than in that of a young man (left). Grossly deformed foot bones (6) attest to a crippler fashionable in China until the mid-20th century—binding the feet of highborn ladies. Bone ravaged by a degenerative disease called osteoporosis (7, lower) looks more honeycombed than normal bone (upper).

Designed for childbirth, the female pelvis (8) is wider than its male counterpart. Tiny birth scars in the area indicated by arrows suggest the number of children a woman has borne.

The thick cortex of a leg bone (9, left) indicates a diet rich in high-protein foods such as meat; a narrower cortex (right) suggests a protein-deficient diet. Bony bumps or calluses (10) reveal broken bones. Fully mended bones leave only a trace of the fracture line. A scalloped bite (11) pinpoints the trade of the wool spinner who binds woolen strands by threading them through the teeth.

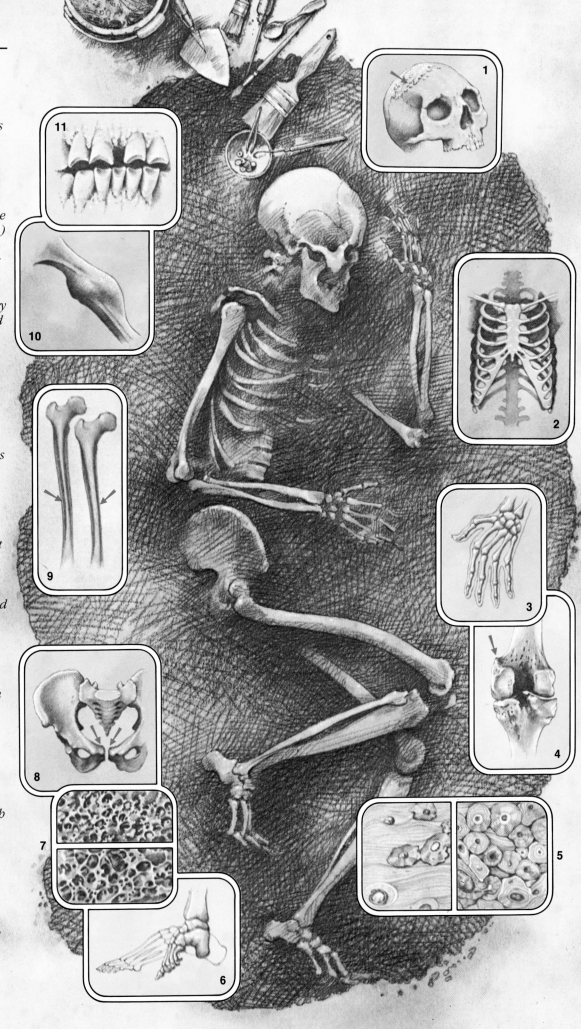

Coppergate Site
1. Modern (1750-present)
2. Post-Medieval (1550-1750)
3. Medieval (1200-1550)
4. Norman (1067-1200)
5. Viking III (975-1067)
6. Viking II (925-975)
7. Viking I (850-925)
8. Anglian (400-850)
9. Roman (A.D. 71-400)

the site of a Roman town, he found no remains of the ancient settlement. Then he noticed the stunted corn that grew in the shallow soil atop the foundations. "One may observe the draughts of streets crossing one another for where they have gone the corn is thinner," he wrote. Centuries later, archaeologists study such crop marks in aerial photographs.

Some eager antiquaries sent out questionnaires to the landed gentry. "Are there any ancient *Sepulchres* hereabout of Men of *Gigantick stature, Roman Generals,* and *others* of ancient times?" asked one such document. The responses produced plenty of burial mounds and stone circles—but no clues to their origin.

"These Antiquities are so exceeding old that no Bookes doe reach them," complained a curious scientist named John Aubrey in the late 1600s. He had first seen Stonehenge when he was eight. Fourteen years later a fox hunt took him by chance to the village of Avebury. He was "wonderfully surprized" to find it surrounded by a large ditch and bank and circles of massive stones. Neither Avebury nor Stonehenge looked like a Roman temple, so Aubrey decided that the only way to study them properly was by accurate surveys and comparisons with other stone circles in Scotland and Wales. These circles, he concluded, were the work of ancient Britons and probably "were Temples of the Druids." Since Julius Caesar and other classical writers had described the Druids as barbarian priests, the explanation seemed logical.

But what of the Britons themselves? Aubrey had seen the paintings of American Indians by Elizabethan artist John White. So, like modern archaeologists, Aubrey again made use of comparative data—and came up with an unflattering picture of the Britons, people "almost as savage as the beasts whose skins were their only raiment. . . . They were two or three degrees I suppose less savage than the Americans."

Half a century later a physician named William Stukeley spent his summers from 1719 to 1725 sketching and measuring Stonehenge and Avebury. He had a wonderful time striding over the springy grass, climbing up on the Stonehenge lintels with a ladder, and finding an area large enough "for a steady head and nimble heels to dance a minuet on." The energetic physician dug into the middle of Stonehenge to see

Time writes its own history in the pages of stratification—the name science gives to the buildup of layers in the soil. At York, England, archaeologists in the 1970s dug down 25 feet and found nine main strata of human occupation. Here an artist brings four of these layers to life.

Tourists fill the Coppergate shopping center (1). Two layers beneath their feet lie the cobblestones of medieval York (3), where a fair brings buyers and sellers into the street to haggle. Above the tourists' *heads swings a sign of earlier times: Jorvik Viking Centre. Under the shops, visitors find a museum at a level once settled by Vikings (6). There in Jorvik—whose name echoes in the name York—a Viking family of a thousand years ago gathers by a loom. Trade links their town with ports as distant as the Near East. Three strata and eight centuries separate them from ancient Eboracum (9), where a Roman soldier watches a burial near a Roman fortress founded here in A.D. 71.*

Floors stacked like flapjacks (above) emerge from the soil of Mesopotamia during a 1967 dig at Nippur, a cult center for Sumerians of the third millennium B.C. Where a structure once stood, a worker tags twelve floors, one atop another on a site peopled for centuries. Archaeologists have dug at Nippur since the late 1800s. Their labor has yielded thousands of clay tablets— and has awakened from the silence of centuries the poetry and literature of a people at the dawntime of civilization.

what he could find. Solid chalk lay a foot below the surface, and into it the builders had dug holes for the uprights. He found no clues to the identity of the builders.

Stukeley also excavated a nearby barrow, or burial mound. At the bottom of it he discovered a bronze bodkin, a stone spearhead, many beads, and a red clay urn containing burned bones "crouded all together in a little heap." Reverently he "recompos'd the ashes of the illustrious defunct."

Stukeley's archaeological notes and drawings were exceptional for their time. But he concluded that Avebury and Stonehenge were built by Druids, and the belief eventually became an obsession; he died convinced that he himself was a Druid. Cultists still espouse his beliefs. For some 80 years "Druids" have gathered by the mammoth pillars of Stonehenge on midsummer's dawn to act out rituals—processions, horn blowing, incantations, salutes to the rising sun.

The antiquaries were curious about places such as Stonehenge, but they were ardent collectors as well. Most vases, coins, and suchlike treasures ended up in private "cabinets of curiosities." There were a few museums—public displays of the exotic and bizarre. One of the best known was compiled by Ole Worm, a professor at the University of Copenhagen in the early 17th century. He collected almost anything. His museum was a strange jumble of exotica—American Indian weapons, stuffed armadillos and crocodiles, antiques, coins, and prehistoric tools.

Worm's venture was a great success. So was Tradescant's Ark, a museum in a private home south of London that eventually formed the nucleus of the Ashmolean Museum in Oxford. And when the wealthy British physician Sir Hans Sloane willed his vast library and fine collection of antiquities and other items to the nation, they became part of a general repository that, in 1759, became the British Museum.

Collecting antiquities was fashionable but hardly taken seriously. "What a cartload of bricks and rubbish and Roman ruins they have piled together," snorted author Horace Walpole in derision of London's Society of Antiquaries.

Many antiquaries turned from observation to excavation, a novel idea in the late 1700s. Some, such as wool merchant William Cunnington, became "barrow mad." Cunnington suffered from severe headaches, and to ease them he took to riding over the plain near Salisbury. During his rides he saw a lot of burial mounds, and curiosity prompted him to dig into them. By 1801 Cunnington had opened 24 barrows; he claimed that, with more practice, he could look at a mound and tell what it contained. Then he met Sir Richard Colt Hoare, a wealthy landowner and antiquary who lived about 20 miles from Stonehenge. The two made an excellent team: Colt Hoare paid the bills and searched for sites while Cunnington and his two diggers sank pits into the larger mounds and dug trenches across the smaller ones. In all, Cunnington opened 465 barrows, sometimes two or three in a day. Come evening, the two friends would toast the ancient Britons. "Amidst the desert [sic] of fruit [and] the sparkling glasses," wrote a guest, "stood the rude relicks of 2000 years."

Few of these relics have survived. Antiquaries wrote that often "on the slightest touch they mouldered to dust" or that

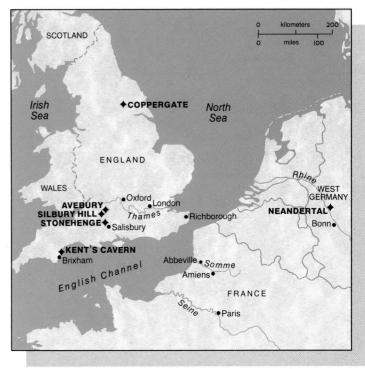

The stones of Stonehenge etch their ancient silhouette on Salisbury Plain in southern England (opposite). No one knows what beliefs inspired this roundel of ditches, banks, and massive monoliths begun about 2800 B.C. No one knows the rites it witnessed before it fell into disuse nearly 2,000 years later. Experts say it took some 30 million man-hours to build. And so did Silbury Hill, a man-made knoll (upper) of the same era. Rising 130 feet and covering more than 5 acres, the mound ranks as Europe's largest. British antiquary William Stukeley made this sketch of it in 1723. Several digs have tunneled into the mound, but none has solved its mystery: Is it a tomb, a boundary marker—or, as folklore says, a clod from the shovel of Satan?

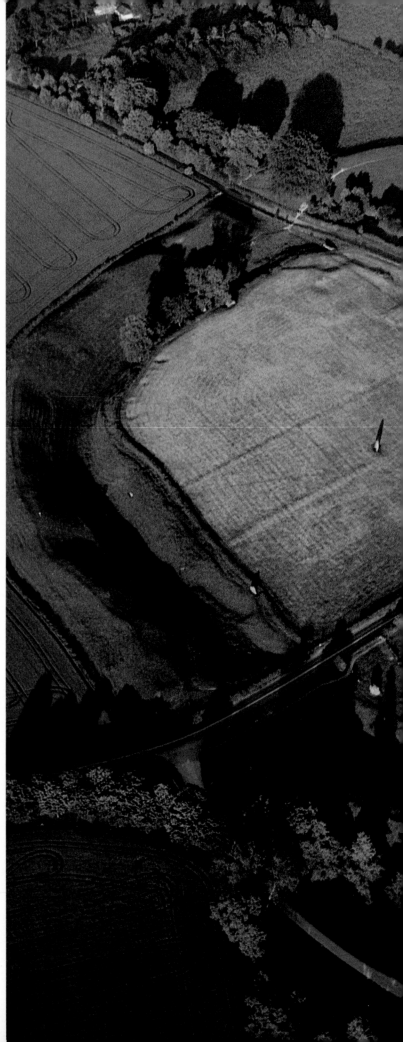

the tools of the "stout body of spadesmen" had crushed a burial urn. The quarryman's pick and the ditchdigger's spade became the trademarks of archaeology.

Cunnington and Colt Hoare have been called the founders of archaeological excavation in England. In truth, however, they belonged to the Stukeley era—collectors of curiosities set haphazardly in country-house cabinets. The first part of Colt Hoare's *The Ancient History of Wiltshire* appeared in 1810, a painstaking catalog of artifacts from hundreds of barrows. But there is no sense of order in his random assemblage of clay urns, iron swords, gold ornaments, glass and amber beads, and bone artifacts. After 25 pages on Stonehenge, Colt Hoare seems to have thrown his hands up in dismay. "HOW GRAND! HOW WONDERFUL! HOW INCOMPREHENSIBLE!" he wrote.

Colt Hoare was not alone in his confusion. Danish antiquary Rasmus Nyerup started a small museum but despaired of putting anything in chronological order. "Everything which has come down to us from heathendom is wrapped in a thick fog," he complained. He was sure his artifacts were older than Christianity, "but whether by a couple of years or a couple of centuries, or even by more than a millennium,

"With awe and diffidence, I enter the sacred precincts of this once hallowed sanctuary ... the wonder of Britain," wrote British antiquary Sir Richard Colt Hoare in an 1812 study of Avebury. Stone Age hands 4,000 years ago built this earthen ring and its circles of more than 150 monoliths, as re-created in a drawing (above) from Colt Hoare's treatise. Few of the stones remain (right); village folk in centuries past broke up the rest to make building stone or to clear farmland.

MUSEI
WORMIANI
HISTORIA

LUGD · BATAVORUM
EX OFFICINA ELSEVIRIANA
Acad: Typog · 1655.

we can do no more than guess." His chaotic collections formed the nucleus of the National Museum of Denmark, founded in 1807. Its first curator was Christian Jürgensen Thomsen, a merchant's son with a penchant for order.

Thomsen found himself amid utter confusion. But he had read the works of Danish historians and scholars, who speculated that early Scandinavian cultures could be divided into a Stone Age, a Copper Age, and an Iron Age. Thomsen adapted the idea and organized the prehistoric displays of his museum in three separate rooms: one for the Stone Age, when "very little or nothing at all was known of metals"; a second for the Bronze Age; and a third for the Iron Age. Thus was born the Three Age System, a classification still used today for subdividing the prehistoric past.

Thomsen knew that his cherished classification was mere theory. One of his assistants at the museum, a young law student named Jens Jacob Worsaae, had been excavating barrows since his teens. Worsaae took the Three Age System out of the museum and applied it to archaeological sites. In burial mounds and stone tombs he found Stone Age artifacts that underlay Bronze Age sites that were, in turn, succeeded by Iron Age settlements.

23

Collections of curiosities launched many a modern museum. Exhibits crowd the shelves of Danish physician Ole Worm (left). In this 1655 drawing, artifacts share the space with natural history specimens. On a sill stands a narwhal skull—proof, said Worm, that such horns did not come from unicorns. Fellow savants helped gather exhibits. "I beg of you," Worm once wrote to a friend, "have posterity and opportunities of enriching my Cabinet of Naturalia at heart."

Still more wonders jammed Tradescant's Ark, a family residence in England. In this 17th-century painting (above), John Tradescant the Younger, at left, regales a visitor with shells from a collection that included "Two feathers of the Phoenix tayle," a "Dragon's egge," and "A Bracelet made of thighes of Indian flyes."

Length 5"

At last Nyerup's "fog" was dispelled. The prehistoric past—which, by Archbishop Ussher's reckoning, comprised only a few millennia—could be roughly divided into three broad stages that reflected humanity's increasing skill with metals. The Three Age System was in widespread use by the 1860s. Just then another group of experts showed that humans had lived on earth much longer than 6,000 years.

The industrial revolution of the 18th century had spawned a new class of engineers and surveyors whose work required a detailed knowledge of geological layers. One of these engineers, William Smith, was so obsessed with the earth's layers that he was nicknamed "Strata" Smith. As a boy this self-taught observer had collected fossils in England; as a man he put both fossils and geological time in order. He realized that natural processes—erosion, weathering, sedimentation—had shaped the earth's strata, with the lowest

layer being the oldest. The layers had accumulated slowly over long periods of time—and were still accumulating. Thus the world and its creatures could have been around much longer than the time calculated by the theologians.

In many layers Smith found dozens of distinctive fossils that could be used to correlate a layer exposed here with another many miles away. The same approach, using artifacts instead of fossils, is widely employed in archaeology today.

Smith's contemporary, the French anatomist Georges Cuvier, also used fossils as geological markers. A genius at anatomical reconstruction, he pieced together the fossil bones of prehistoric reptiles, such as the pterodactyl, and studied the extinct Ice Age elephant, the mammoth. He used fossil animals to lay out a series of geological epochs by associating each period with distinctive species. But how had the animals become extinct—and where did humans fit in?

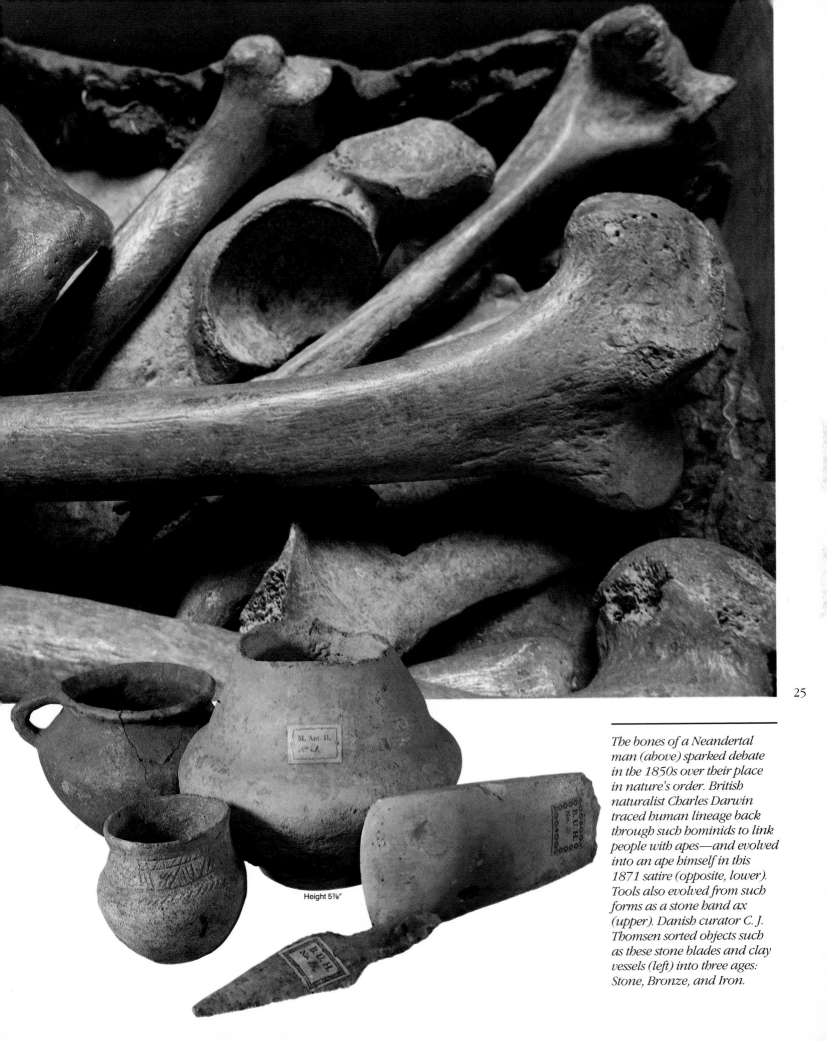

25

Height 5⅞″

The bones of a Neandertal man (above) sparked debate in the 1850s over their place in nature's order. British naturalist Charles Darwin traced human lineage back through such hominids to link people with apes—and evolved into an ape himself in this 1871 satire (opposite, lower). Tools also evolved from such forms as a stone hand ax (upper). Danish curator C. J. Thomsen sorted objects such as these stone blades and clay vessels (left) into three ages: Stone, Bronze, and Iron.

Cuvier held that floods had wiped out each successive group of animals. Since humans were not associated with these early layers, he reasoned that people must not have appeared until about 6,000 years ago, when the last major floods occurred. His idea conformed nicely with theology.

Cuvier was wrong; humans had indeed lived in Europe at the same time as extinct animals. Evidence had been turning up for years, but no established scientist took it seriously. In the late 1600s a stone ax and some bones thought to be those of an elephant came to light at a construction site in London; antiquaries assumed that both dated from Roman times. In the 1820s a Catholic priest found stone tools and fossil bones under a layer of stalagmite at Kent's Cavern in southern England. But a geologist told the priest that the ancient Britons had dug pit ovens down through the stalagmite, and some of their tools had fallen into the underlying strata.

In 1837 customs officer Jacques Boucher de Perthes started examining gravel pits in the Somme River Valley of northern France. He was surprised to find dozens of stone axes alongside the remains of extinct animals. He argued that the axes were left behind by a human race wiped out by a flood much earlier than the biblical Deluge. Most scientists shrugged and ignored him; even Charles Darwin examined his first book and "concluded that the whole was rubbish." Few respectable scholars felt like bucking the church.

The scientific establishment finally took notice in 1858, when quarrymen exposed a sealed cavern at Brixham in southwestern England. A blue-ribbon committee of the Geological Society of London probed the cavern's floor and found more than a dozen stone artifacts sealed in layers that also contained the bones of mammoths, rhinoceroses, and cave bears. The next year a steady parade of British geologists and archaeologists crossed the English Channel to view Boucher de Perthes' stone axes. One British scholar compared such ancient cutlery to the pocketknives being turned out in the factories of his homeland: "The flint hatchets of Amiens and Abbeville seem to me as clearly works of art as any Sheffield whittle." The experts finally accepted the association of artifacts and extinct animals; the great antiquity of humankind was at last acknowledged.

That same year, 1859, saw the publication of Charles Darwin's *Origin of Species,* the pivotal scientific essay of the 19th century. Ever since his expedition to the Southern Hemisphere a quarter century before, Darwin had been mulling over a theory of evolution by natural selection—the idea that species evolve or disappear in response to natural factors, so that only the fittest survive. He sat on his ideas for years, realizing that the concept of evolution would unleash a storm of controversy about human origins. He was right.

While Darwin stayed quietly in the background, British biologist Thomas Henry Huxley and others declared that evolution by natural selection provided a theoretical framework for early human history. They also argued that humans had apelike ancestors—a horrifying notion to pious Victorians. As the controversy raged, archaeologists began the long search for human ancestors, a search that continues today.

In 1857 quarrymen working in a cave near the German village of Neandertal had found—and discarded—an assortment of old brown bones, including an odd-looking skull. A local physician later heard of the bones and retrieved them. What he saw were the bones of a human—and yet not quite a human. An elongated dome and massive, beetling brow ridges made the skull a real curiosity. Some scientists dismissed it as the skull of an idiot who had lived as a hermit in the cave; others thought it had belonged to a savage from pre-Roman times or even to a Cossack renegade.

Thomas Huxley disagreed. He examined the skull and in 1863 pointed out that it had apelike characteristics. The modern world at last stood face-to-face with a possible ancestor—Neandertal man—and with scientific evidence that humans have some evolutionary links to the apes.

Charles Darwin developed the theory of evolution and Christian Thomsen the Three Age System; together these ideas provided a firm foundation for archaeological research for most of the late 19th century. Their insights climaxed a time of momentous discoveries—not only in northwestern Europe but also in the lands of the Bible, the temples of Athens, and the realms of pharaohs who worshiped in great shrines and went to their tombs amid treasure untold.

Antiquities both near and far lured the gentry of Europe to admire and the adventurous to acquire. A "Group of Englishmen at Rome" lolls before the ruins of the Roman Empire—the Colosseum and a triumphal arch—in this scene from the mid-1700s (left). Nearly a century later, French collectors brave the Preah Khan marshes of Cambodia to harvest ancient sculptures (opposite). Such looting erased much from the human record, yet from these roots grew the science of archaeology.

Egypt, 1817: Giovanni Battista Belzoni pauses amid mummies of ancient Egyptians as he ransacks their burial caves for treasures.

THE TREASURE HUNTERS

"What a place of rest! surrounded by bodies, by heaps of mummies in all directions; which . . . impressed me with horror. The blackness of the wall, the faint light given by the candles or torches for want of air, the different objects that surrounded me, seeming to converse with each other. . . ."

Egyptians dead for thousands of years crowded in on Italian adventurer Giovanni Battista Belzoni as he shattered their solitude on a stifling day in 1817. Stripped nearly naked in the heat, the former theater strongman had squeezed his huge frame into their burial caves at Qurna on the Nile.

"Nearly overcome," he wrote, "I . . . contrived to sit; but when my weight bore on the body of an Egyptian, it crushed it like a band-box. . . . I sank altogether among the broken mummies, with a crash of bones, rags, and wooden cases, which raised such a dust as kept me motionless for a quarter of an hour, waiting till it subsided again."

To modern scientists these mummies could have told of the lives they led and the ills they suffered. But in Belzoni's day there were no archaeologists; he and his Egyptian guides—"naked and covered with dust, themselves resembling living mummies"—had come to look for papyrus scrolls. For in the 18th and early 19th centuries, fashionable collectors, and even countries, vied in a ruthless scramble for the past. Two collectors loom large: Belzoni, showman extraordinary, and the British nobleman Thomas Bruce, seventh Earl of Elgin. While Belzoni looted Egypt, Elgin carried away masterworks of Greece. Yet each left a rich legacy, not only of priceless objects but also of paintings and narratives that have been of enduring value to modern archaeologists.

Lord Elgin was only one of many aristocrats with an acquisitive interest in the Mediterranean. While some British collectors dug into ancient burial mounds at home, others traveled or sent agents to Italy to gather antiquities. In time British mansions became some of the finest repositories of classical statuary in the world.

In 1732 a group of British gentlemen had founded the Society of Dilettanti, a social club that met once a month and drank toasts to "Grecian taste and Roman spirit." Many members had taken the Grand Tour, a leisurely journey through Europe that was an essential part of a gentleman's education.

29

His future wife Emma Hart at his side, British collector Sir William Hamilton admires the loot from a day of robbing tombs near Naples, Italy, in 1790. In this engraving from a book on his "ancient vases mostly of pure Greek workmanship," men hack at a tomb to harvest its treasures. Some tombs, he wrote, held "Earthen Vases of beautifull forms, with Elegant figures." But yields varied, "probably according to the dignity of the Personage for whom the sepulchre was made."

The Dilettanti encouraged "a taste for those objects which had contributed so much to their entertainment abroad."

In 1751 two members, painter-architect James Stuart and architect Nicholas Revett, went to Athens. For three years these talented men measured and sketched temples and sculptures. Their work, published as *The Antiquities of Athens*, caused a sensation and helped turn British architects from copying Roman styles to imitating the Greek instead.

The Dilettanti included many influential diplomats, men like Sir William Hamilton, British minister in Naples from 1764 to 1800. Remembered now as the husband of Lord Nelson's mistress Emma, Hamilton was celebrated then as a collector of antiquities. In just seven years he amassed 730 ancient Greek vases and more than 6,000 coins and other artifacts, which he sold to the British Museum. His lavish folio volumes on the collection influenced a generation of artists.

Hamilton's second collection of vases was even finer; it included the Portland Vase, a Roman masterpiece on which the artist had carved a cameo from layers of blue and white glass. The famous British potter Josiah Wedgwood marveled at the vase and spent four years copying it in ceramic. Unfortunately some of the Greek vases from this second collection, dispatched to England in 1798, sank with H.M.S. *Colossus* on the rocks off the Isles of Scilly. Not until 1975 did divers begin to salvage the 35,000 vase fragments tucked into pockets of sand and weeds around the rocks. Guided by detailed engravings made in the 1790s, technicians are slowly piecing some of Hamilton's vases back together.

Like many antiquaries, Hamilton wanted to increase the public's appreciation of the arts as well as to collect antiquities. But his efforts paled alongside the activities of Lord Elgin.

In 1798 Elgin was appointed British ambassador to the sultan of Turkey in Constantinople, during the era when the Turks ruled Greece. When a British architect proposed that plaster casts be made of Greek sculptures, Elgin saw a chance to make his diplomatic mission "beneficial to the progress of the Fine Arts in Great Britain." At his own expense he sent Italian artist Giovanni Battista Lusieri and a team of draftsmen and mold makers to Athens.

Athens was a dilapidated provincial town of some 1,300 houses. But high on a rocky hill called the Acropolis soared its greatest treasure—the battered but still imposing Parthenon, glistening amid the ruins of lesser temples. More than 2,000 years before, Athens under the statesman Pericles had raised this white marble temple to the city's patron goddess, Athena. Inside, the sculptor Phidias had fashioned in gold and ivory a 40-foot-high statue of the goddess. Outside, artists had adorned the building's pediments, or gable ends, with sculptures of Athena's birth and struggle with the sea god, Poseidon. Reliefs showed warring gods, Greeks, and giants, and a frieze around the walls portrayed Athenians in a great religious procession held every four years.

Lusieri found the Acropolis strewn with bits of marble. Generations of Greeks had quarried the temples for building stone or lime. When Venetians besieged the Acropolis in 1687, a cannon scored a hit on the Parthenon, then serving as a powder magazine. The building exploded and the roof fell

Bud vases take on classical motifs in the hands of skilled ornamenter Roy Pugh at the English pottery of Josiah Wedgwood & Sons Ltd. Designs from this famous factory in Staffordshire pay homage to the potters of ancient Greece and Rome— and to Sir William Hamilton, whose collections of vases inspired Josiah Wedgwood two centuries ago. To make copies in ceramic, Wedgwood borrowed a masterwork that Hamilton had brought to England: the Portland Vase (left), blown and carved about the time of Christ from white glass laid on blue. The artist remains unknown; so does the story his languid figures tell.

"Is it yours? Will you sell it?" asked an eager Hamilton at first sight of the vase in Rome. Its owner named a price that drove Hamilton into debt: a thousand pounds sterling, a huge sum in the 1780s. In 1845 the vase lay in fragments in the British Museum, smashed on impulse by a visitor. Now the vase stands restored, a treasure beyond price.

Height 9¾"

in. When Lusieri arrived, Turkish troops were living among the ruins and pounding down the marble to make mortar.

Turkish authorities had made only one concession: No one was permitted to remove any of the Parthenon's sculptures. But the Venetians took pieces as souvenirs, and the Turks sold some on the sly to travelers and ambassadors. Such was the zeal to own even a tiny piece of Phidias's art that bits of his sculptures were soon scattered across Europe.

Lusieri intended to draw and make casts on the Acropolis, but the Turkish governor stopped him; foreigners, he said, would climb on the buildings and gaze down on Turkish women. So Elgin appealed directly to the sultan in Constantinople and got a permit allowing Lusieri to sketch and make casts on the Acropolis. The permit included a statement that "when they wish to take away any pieces of stone with old inscriptions or sculptures thereon, that no opposition be made thereto." Nothing gave Elgin's agents explicit permission to remove anything from the Parthenon itself— but nothing forbade them either.

Lusieri immediately hired a large crew. They gathered up all the inscriptions strewn about on the Acropolis but stopped short of the Parthenon. Meanwhile Elgin's emissary plied the Turkish governor of Athens with gifts and pressed him for clearance to work on the temple itself. Finally the governor interpreted the permit to include the Parthenon.

Sweating, shouting, coughing in the dust, Greek laborers swarmed over the Parthenon on a hot July day in 1801. A ship's carpenter rigged windlasses and tackle beside the magnificent ruin. Workmen high overhead passed ropes around a stone decorated with reliefs. Laborers below swabbed their brows and leaned into the windlass cranks. The ropes went taut; slowly the block swung free and settled onto a wooden gun carriage. The carriage groaned down the steep path to town. The task of removing the best of the Parthenon sculptures and shipping them to England had begun.

"I should wish to have . . . everything in the way of sculpture, medals, and curious marbles that can be discovered by means of assiduous and indefatigable excavation," wrote Elgin to Lusieri. By year's end the statues from the Parthenon's west pediment had been taken; the following year

32

Ruined temples from a brilliant past brood over Athens in a painting from the early 19th century. Before then, few Western Europeans visited the seedy village where ancient Greece rose to greatness. Some who did brought back sketches of the Parthenon atop the rocky Acropolis. There they saw some of the temple's sculptures still in place despite wars, earthquakes, lightning, and vandalism. By 1812 few sculptures remained; the best had been shipped home by Britain's Lord Elgin.

the east pediment was emptied. Elgin's men took away about half the building's frieze, along with sculptures and architectural details from other temples on the Acropolis.

The man behind it all sat far away in the British Embassy in Constantinople. But Elgin had won perhaps the greatest archaeological prize of his era—the marble sculptures of the Parthenon, known ever after as the Elgin Marbles.

He had spent heavily to acquire them; now he would spend heavily to ship them to England. The task took ten years and involved more than a score of ships. One was Elgin's own brig, the *Mentor*. Two days out of Athens in 1802, the ship ran into a storm and sank in 70 feet of water. It took two years and still more expense to salvage the antiquities.

To exhibit the marbles, Elgin built a large shed on the grounds of his house in London and displayed them inside. People bombarded him with requests for passes. The exhibits awed artists who flocked to the shed. The figures portrayed idealized humans, their faces and forms refined to perfection, their garments draped as if made of gauze. Yet, unlike the ideal beauty that artists strove for in Elgin's day, the marbles showed great naturalism and detail. Prize-fighters were brought in to pose naked in various stances so visitors could compare their anatomy with that of the statues.

Roman imitators had sculpted stock copies of such Greek originals, with heads portraying their clients. British artists had been doing much the same, portraying clients in a neoclassical style based on the copies from Italy. Now artists crouched for hours in the chilly shed, sketching, measuring, contemplating a cultural miracle—and redefining the neoclassical style in terms more clearly Greek.

Elgin, now in desperate financial straits, tried to sell the marbles to the British Museum, but the government offered only 30,000 pounds sterling—about half what they had cost him. He had to sell his London house and move the marbles to a friend's residence, where some were crowded into an outbuilding and the rest stacked in the open air. To add to Elgin's woes, several critics charged that the statues were Roman imitations. Others complained that the ambassador had gone too far and had ravished the most beautiful building in the world—though the priceless works would probably have been destroyed or dispersed had he not removed them. Even the Society of Dilettanti snubbed him. Elgin was puzzled and hurt, for his motive in acquiring the marbles had been to enhance appreciation of the arts.

Finally he sold the sculptures to the government for 35,000 pounds sterling. While artists and celebrities crowded the British Museum to see them, Elgin returned to his native Scotland. In 1831 the Dilettanti relented and elected him to membership. Elgin declined the honor, saying it was too late. His efforts to improve the arts were long over. Still struggling with debt, he died in Paris in 1841.

Nine years earlier the Greeks had overthrown the Turks and almost at once began restoring the Acropolis. At intervals ever since, Greece has asked the British government to return the marbles. "They are the symbol and the blood and the soul of the Greek people," said Melina Mercouri, Greek Minister of Culture, after yet another overture in 1983. But the British keep refusing, and the marbles remain in London.

Though many Englishmen made the Grand Tour, few ventured to the Nile. Until the end of the 18th century, Europeans had viewed ancient Egypt largely through the eyes of Herodotus, the Greek historian of the fifth century B.C. He had toured Egypt, and though he was sometimes a gullible observer, his curious mix of fact and fiction stood for centuries as the definitive account of Egyptian civilization. He described how ancient embalmers drew out the brains of the deceased through the nostrils with an iron hook—and 25 centuries later, researchers have proved him right. But when told that the Great Pyramid of Khufu at Gîza was built by a daughter of the pharaoh with her earnings as a prostitute, he wrote down this absurdity as well. He saved himself with a masterful disclaimer: "Such as think the tales told by the Egyptians credible are free to accept them for history."

Sundown strikes a spark on the columns of the Parthenon (opposite), even in ruin a sublime marriage of sculpture and architecture. Completed in 432 B.C., the marble temple honored the goddess Athena Parthenos—Athena the Virgin —for 800 years. In the early 19th century, remnants of its sculptures received homage anew as crowds flocked to see them in the British Museum. In 1819 artist A. Archer included himself at lower right among dignitaries in the museum's first Elgin Room (above).

Ht. 3' 11"

In ancient times Greeks and Romans toured the ruins along the Nile. Even then, most of the royal tombs in the Valley of the Kings at Thebes had been looted. Today visitors can still read the names of Roman tourists who crept into the empty sepulchers and scrawled on the walls by torchlight. Roman emperors vandalized on a larger scale, carting off hundreds of statues and other artifacts for their capital. Now there are more Egyptian obelisks in Rome than in Egypt.

When Rome fell, so did tourism to Egypt. Travel to the Nile revived with the Renaissance, though few visitors ventured upriver beyond Cairo. In the 17th century, as now, Europeans bought amulets and scarabs in Cairo bazaars. Some brought back an odd treasure: mummy powder, the crushed bodies of mummified Egyptians. Physicians prized it as a cure for an astonishing variety of ills, including fractures, rashes, paralysis, ulcers, and liver disorders. King Francis I of

France never traveled without it. The demand for the powder was insatiable and the profits could be enormous, for Egyptian relics of any kind were rare in Europe.

Egypt's greatest attraction was the complex of pyramids at Gîza. Scholars since classical times had identified them as the tombs of kings, but the old myth persisted: They were the granaries of Genesis, built by a king on the advice of Joseph the Hebrew. Whatever they were, no serious tourist would omit them from an itinerary. Visitors would strip near-naked and crawl into the narrow, bat-infested passages of the Great Pyramid of Khufu, sometimes fainting from heat or even fear. Now and then one got stuck in a passageway and had to be extricated like a cork from a wine bottle.

Cairo under Turkish rule was a commercial center and hub of caravan routes. It had become a debauched, disorderly city, seething with crime and violence, religious strife, and

Ht. 5′ 7″

political intrigue. Egypt's Turkish overlords had little tolerance for European visitors. "Begin by dressing yourself in the Turkish manner," advised a Danish artist and sea captain who visited in the 1730s. "A pair of mustachios, with a grave and solemn air, will be very proper companions by which you will have a resemblance to the natives."

A European bent on collecting Egyptian antiquities found the search was not easy. He had to know, as a French diplomat put it, the "use of tact, manoeuvre, and money"—tools that were to become only too familiar in the 19th century. But he could sell anything Egyptian to eager buyers all over Europe. Imagine the sensation in 1763 when Professor John Hadley displayed a complete mummy—few Europeans had ever seen one—and proceeded to dissect it in his London home before an enthusiastic crowd. As the onlookers stood agog, Hadley sliced through the bandages and the

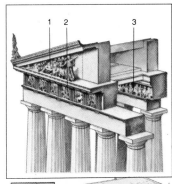

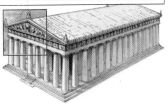

Sculptures from among the Elgin Marbles reveal by their shapes the positions they held on the Parthenon. In the east pediment (1), one of these figures reclined, two sat, and another stood to fit into the angle where roof and cornice met. Time has erased the paints that once brightened these ancient deities. Panels called metopes (2) decorated the lintels. On one of the 92 metopes (inset), a Greek hero battles a centaur. Reliefs encircled the inner walls as a frieze (3) some 525 feet long.

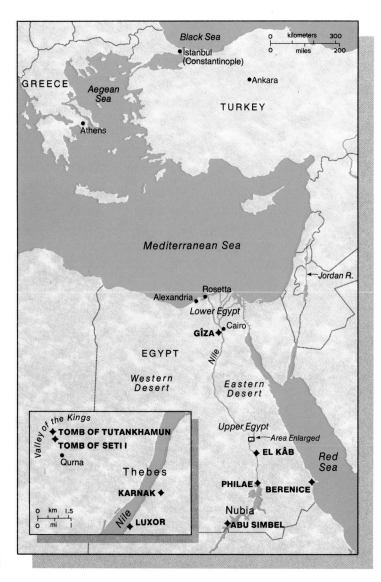

Camels and riders paint a timeless tableau across the pyramids at Gîza in Egypt. A casing of limestone still clings to the top of the Pyramid of Khafre, ruler of Egypt 40 centuries ago. Behind it looms the Great Pyramid of Khufu, originally taller than Khafre's by about ten feet. Both served as tombs for kings who ruled soon after the dawn of a civilization that endured for 3,000 years. Treasures once filled humbler tombs that dotted the Nile (map), luring plunderers through the ages.

desiccated skin. The resin used by the embalmers had damaged the tissues so badly that little flesh remained.

The ancient Egyptians were a mystery, partly because no one could read their hieroglyphic writing. They might have remained so had not Napoléon Bonaparte dreamed of a great Eastern empire based in India with Egypt as its gateway. When he sailed for the Nile in 1798, he took with his army a team of scientists, civil engineers, writers, and artists. Their task: to collect artifacts and learn all they could about Egypt.

The immensity of the Gîza pyramids alone was an intoxicating surprise. The travelers climbed on the Sphinx, a colossal human-headed lion. They measured its features, peered into painted tombs near Cairo, and admired the brilliant works of a civilization unlike any they had ever seen. When the troops sighted the temples at Luxor and Karnak on the way up the Nile, they spontaneously presented arms.

One artist, Baron Dominique-Vivant Denon, wanted to sketch every temple he saw, yet "felt ashamed of the inadequacy of the drawings" he made of "such sublime objects." Even engineers started sketching. When the supply of pencils ran out, they melted down lead bullets as substitutes.

The team collected numerous artifacts, including an incised basalt tablet that would provide the key to ancient Egyptian writing. The Rosetta Stone bore a decree of 196 B.C. in three scripts: hieroglyphic, an informal script called demotic, and Greek. Napoléon himself examined the stone and ordered ink impressions sent to scholars all over Europe.

A British fleet doomed Napoléon's Nile adventure in 1798, and in 1801 the victors sent the French home. The British let the scholars keep their drawings but appropriated the Rosetta Stone, which ended up in the British Museum. Denon and his colleagues labored for many years on their

Its body all but buried, the Sphinx at Gîza faces another windstorm in this lithograph of 1846. The artist has turned the colossus southward; actually it looks east. Torches light the gloom in Khufu's pyramid (opposite, upper) as visitors clamber into the Grand Gallery that slopes up to the king's burial chamber. Thus a British book portrayed in 1801 a mighty monument few Europeans had ever seen. Today electricity lights the Grand Gallery (opposite, lower) for throngs of tourists.

24-volume *Description de l'Égypte*. Temple by temple, pyramid by pyramid, artifact by artifact, the savants created a wondrous panorama. They also triggered a ruthless scramble for Egyptian antiquities that was not to abate for nearly a century.

In 1803 the British handed Egypt back to the Turks. A shrewd opportunist named Muhammad ʿAlī seized power and ruled as Egypt's pasha for 43 years. Eager for the fruits of Western technology, including new irrigation methods, the pasha encouraged foreigners to come to his country. If they wanted to hunt for antiquities and take them away, that was fine. He used archaeology as a diplomatic lever, a means of charming powerful visitors who had exotic hobbies. All sorts of adventurers came to the Nile in search of quick fortunes.

Nationalism had already entered archaeology. The *Description de l'Égypte* was seen by the French as a triumph. The British and French began to compete for antiquities on a scale far larger than earlier collectors ever had.

The French consul general in Egypt was Bernardino Drovetti, an intense man who looted tombs and pursued antiquities with unflagging zeal. In 1816 a rival reached Cairo: British consul general Henry Salt, whose quiet ways set him in stark contrast to the mercurial Drovetti. While the Frenchman flitted about the Nile, courting village headmen and local tomb robbers, the Englishman usually stayed in Cairo and paid others to dig. Since both enjoyed favor with the pasha, they were able to obtain excavation permits and carve up the Nile into treasure-hunting fiefdoms. Woe betide the stranger who tried to muscle in. "Those were the great days of excavating," wrote Egyptologist Howard Carter a century later. "Anything to which a fancy was taken, from a scarab to an obelisk, was just appropriated, and if there was a difference with a brother excavator, one laid for him with a gun."

The freebooters who came to Egypt were no archaeologists. A talent with gunpowder, a knowledge of weights and levers, infinite patience, and flexible morals were all they needed. Few fitted the mold better than Giovanni Belzoni.

The son of an Italian barber, Belzoni had eked out a living as an itinerant trader in religious relics and later as an actor. In 1803 he appeared as the "Patagonian Sampson" at a London theater. The rowdy audience cheered as the gaudily

Height 3′9″

Napoléon overwhelmed Egypt with his army—and Egypt overwhelmed the general with wonders from its past. In this 1798 painting (opposite), scholars he brought with him fly a kite to gauge the height of Pompey's Pillar in Alexandria, an ancient city of learning. Crusaders in the 15th century misnamed the column; an inscription honors another Roman emperor, Diocletian, who crushed an uprising here in A.D. 297.

Artists with Napoléon drew everything they could. One portrayed a comrade sketching in a tomb at El Kâb (upper) in native regalia. Another scene shows Napoléon watching as his troops unwrap a mummy (lower) at Gîza. "From these pyramids," he had told his men, "forty centuries look down upon you."

Napoléon's campaign in Egypt was a military flop but a scholarly success. For near the town of Rosetta, his troops found an inscribed basalt slab (left) now called the Rosetta Stone, the key to deciphering Egyptian hieroglyphs.

Overleaf: *Graceful cotton sails catch the prevailing wind to waft Egyptian feluccas up the timeless Nile. Napoléon would recognize these boats; their design has changed little since his artists sketched them as his army advanced upriver. Boats have made the Nile a highway since before the pharaohs ruled; some vessels sailed with the dead into eternity as tomb paintings and boat models.*

dressed Belzoni strode the stage shouldering 12 actors on a 127-pound iron frame. For nine years he made a living as a strongman and also learned about hydraulics by working on stage spectaculars featuring fountains and pyrotechnics.

Belzoni had a perpetual wanderlust. In 1815 he turned up on the Mediterranean island of Malta, where a chance encounter with one of Muhammad ʻAlī's agents changed his life. Trading on his skill with hydraulics, Belzoni talked his way into an assignment to design a waterwheel that would revolutionize Egyptian agriculture. The venture failed, and he found himself, penniless, in Egypt.

About this time he met Henry Salt, who had just arrived in Cairo as British consul general. Belzoni soon had Salt interested in a colossal granite portrait of Pharaoh Ramesses II at Thebes. Known as the Young Memnon, the seven-and-a-half-ton head had been much admired by Napoléon's troops, who had tried to haul it away but had failed. Belzoni, with his skill at lifting weights, was the ideal man to achieve the impossible. "This is a godsend indeed," cried Salt as he looked over that imposing six-foot-six-inch frame.

Belzoni sailed up the Nile to Thebes with only a handful of men, fourteen poles, four palm-leaf ropes, four rollers, and very little money. The locals were skeptical as he rigged four huge levers, but doubts vanished as the massive head rose easily and settled onto a crude wooden frame. It took sweat and labor to roll Ramesses nearly three miles to the Nile. On the way the workmen went on strike. Belzoni, livid with rage, pinned the local chief to a wall, then shook him. In a calmer mood he plied the district governor with a gift of a pair of pistols. The men were back at work the next morning, and the head reached the river a few days later.

Success whetted Belzoni's appetite. With beads, looking glasses, and other gifts, he bribed his way upstream into Nubia, where he cleared 20 feet of sand off the Great Temple of Ramesses II at Abu Simbel. Then he continued his journey through Upper Egypt and assembled one of the largest hoards of antiquities ever shipped to Cairo. Drovetti's men were furious at the sight of his loot. From that moment Belzoni was a marked man. As he returned to Thebes, the French consul's agents bedeviled him every mile of the way.

"They thought in terms of men 100 feet tall," wrote Jean-François Champollion in awe of the temples at Karnak. There the great Hypostyle Hall thrusts its columns skyward (opposite); some top 73 feet. By 1822 this French savant could read Egyptian hieroglyphs— and the texts inscribed on temples such as this. The pillars once blazed with color, as in a fanciful scene (upper) by one of Napoléon's artists.

Another view (lower) shows French collector Bernardino Drovetti and agents at Thebes.

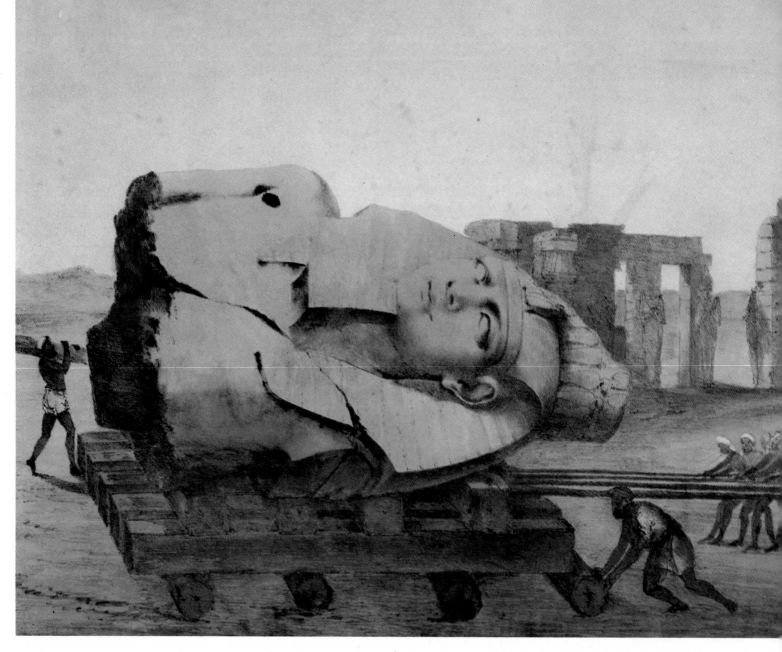

They bribed local headmen, bought antiquities from under his nose, and even threatened to cut his throat.

They made it nearly impossible for Belzoni to work at the great temples at Karnak on the Nile's east bank, so he tried Qurna on the west. For centuries the villagers had been robbing tombs and selling a seemingly endless supply of mummies and papyri to the highest bidder. The Qurnis, wrote Belzoni, were "superior . . . in cunning and deceit."

The Qurnis lived in burial caves and burned mummies instead of firewood. Belzoni soon became blasé about the ancient "hands, feet, or sculls" strewn around their caves. He got on well with these robbers, paid them handsomely, and went with them into the cramped and stifling honeycomb of tombs in the rocky hills. Stripping off most of his clothes, he squeezed through the narrow passages, squirming, sweating, choking on dust that stank of mummies. The Qurnis

gave their friend a virtual monopoly on their finds. Drovetti's agents retaliated by wangling an official ban on sales to Belzoni. The Italian threw up his hands in disgust and returned to Abu Simbel with two Englishmen to finish digging out the Great Temple of Ramesses II.

Two weeks later the rising sun shone through the entrance for the first time in untold centuries. Belzoni gazed wonderingly on eight huge figures of Ramesses II in a lofty pillared hall. He examined painted reliefs of the pharaoh and his army in battle. Much to his dismay, almost nothing portable remained. But he compiled detailed plans and drawings of the temple's interior—no mean feat in a torrid, rock-hewn chamber 30 feet high. "The heat was so great," he wrote, ". . . that it scarcely permitted us to take any drawings, as the perspiration from our hands soon rendered the paper quite wet." It is this concern for recording his discoveries

"I found it . . . with its face upwards, and apparently smiling on me, at the thought of being taken to England," recalled Italian strongman Giovanni Battista Belzoni after viewing a granite head of Pharaoh Ramesses II at Thebes. In 1816 he made the thought a reality as his men (above, left) trundled the head to the Nile en route to the British Museum. Belzoni's drawings and records shaped the science of Egyptology. In a tomb he discovered at Thebes, he gazed at painted reliefs of Pharaoh Seti I standing before the seated god Osiris. Belzoni preserved the scene (above) in one of his many paintings of the wonders he had seen.

In 1817 he dug his way into Ramesses' temple at Abu Simbel. Soon after, his British sponsor, Henry Salt, hired a crew (left) to clear the sands of centuries from the shrine.

that sets Belzoni apart from most of his rapacious peers.

Again Belzoni returned to Thebes. He set up camp in the desolate Valley of the Kings, the resting place of some of Egypt's greatest pharaohs. There he battered or dug his way into several newly discovered tombs. Once he was only 60 yards from the treasure-filled tomb of Tutankhamun.

At one point in Belzoni's search for tombs, his men told him he was in the wrong place. He ignored them. The very next day they uncovered an entry to a long passage covered with painted reliefs. Stairs led down to another decorated corridor with a deep pit in its floor.

The following day Belzoni used stout beams to bridge the 12-foot-wide pit. Robbers had holed the wall at the other side, so he squeezed through—and into a series of elaborately decorated rooms. Paintings, drawings, and hieroglyphs covered almost every inch of the walls and ceilings. Six massive columns stood in one chamber. In an adjoining hall Belzoni gazed up at a dark blue, vaulted ceiling that glistened as if painted the day before. Here his flickering candle shone on the sarcophagus of Pharaoh Seti I. Its translucent alabaster glowed softly in the gloom as Belzoni admired on its interior an image of the goddess Neith waiting to receive the king. Seti's sarcophagus stood empty, but the tomb and its vivid paintings—serpents, demons, vultures hovering on a ceiling, the god-king Seti and his fellow deities—were as great a treasure as the mummy might have been.

Always a showman, Belzoni saw a chance for fame and fortune: He would prepare a model of the tomb and exhibit it in Europe with the sarcophagus. But first he showed his arch-rival, Drovetti, through the sepulcher—with superficial cordiality, as always. Drovetti stood in speechless admiration.

Soon Belzoni resumed his treasure hunt. A month's arduous digging through sand and rubble took him inside the Pyramid of Khafre at Gîza. Thieves had broken into it thousands of years before; the burial chamber held only an empty sarcophagus. Next Belzoni crossed the Eastern Desert to the ruins of Berenice, an ancient Egyptian port on the Red Sea, only to return almost empty-handed. But back at Thebes a challenge waited for him: A British collector wanted him to

Portraits hewn in sandstone at Abu Simbel repeat the face of Ramesses II. Each tops a seated statue—four in all—looming 67 feet from crown to toe. In text and temple Ramesses looms larger than life. Some scholars identify him as the pharaoh of the biblical exodus. His name recurs up and down the Nile, often chiseled over another name on monuments Ramesses never built. Here his face bears its own share of graffiti—as do many of Egypt's monuments, marred by the scratchings of centuries of visitors.

remove a 22-foot-high granite obelisk from among the temples at Philae, an island that today lies submerged in the Nile.

By chance Belzoni met Drovetti in Thebes and casually mentioned his new assignment. Belzoni arrived at the island to find that the Frenchman's agents had claimed the obelisk. So he placed one or two timely bribes, then moved the obelisk by levers and rollers to the riverbank. As it was being loaded onto a stout boat, it fell into the river. Belzoni and his crew fished it out, built a bridge of palm logs, and finally hauled the ponderous obelisk aboard.

When the boat reached the nearby cataract, Belzoni's genius for improvisation again came into play. He tied the boat to a stout tree upstream, then rigged ropes from the boat to workers on either side of the rapids. The captain had been paid handsomely for his craft, but he now begged in tears for its return. Belzoni took no notice, so the captain, in

Belzoni's words, "threw himself with his face to the ground."

Belzoni gave the signal to slacken the tether. The boat lurched ahead. As it careered downstream, the men on either side pulled or slackened their ropes to hold the boat on course. It was all over in a few hectic moments. The captain, his tears forgotten, came up to Belzoni wreathed in smiles. Back in Thebes the crew moored the laden boat right under the noses of Drovetti and his men. "It irritated them," recalled Belzoni with considerable understatement.

Belzoni reveled in his coup during a quiet Christmas spent in a royal tomb with his wife, Sarah, as much a wanderer as he. "We spent the solemnity of that blessed day," he wrote, ". . . undisturbed by the folly of mankind."

The very next day Belzoni was accosted on the street by two of Drovetti's agents and about thirty Egyptians, some of them armed. The angry men surrounded Belzoni's small

party and beat his servants. Why, they demanded, had he taken Drovetti's obelisk? One pointed a loaded gun at him, but he calmly stayed on his donkey, regarding his attackers with contempt. "My situation was not pleasant," he later wrote.

Drovetti arrived with more armed Egyptians. Belzoni complained about the discourtesy shown him. Drovetti ordered him to dismount. Then someone fired a pistol behind Belzoni's back. Belzoni dismounted in a fury. By now a crowd had gathered, so Drovetti, realizing he had gone too far, tried to smooth things over. But Belzoni was badly shaken. He packed up Seti's sarcophagus and the wax impressions and drawings of the tomb and sailed for Alexandria. In 1819 he left Egypt forever—without his precious sarcophagus. Henry Salt had claimed it, to take to England himself.

Belzoni arrived in London an overnight celebrity. He wrote a book about his adventures and in 1821 organized an

Like an islet in time, Philae Island holds a treasure of temples above the Nile in this lithograph of 1838 (above, left). Gone is the island's granite obelisk; Belzoni had hauled it away 20 years earlier. Today the island itself is gone, drowned not by the annual flooding of the river (above) but by a permanent lake behind a new dam. In the 1970s engineers ringed Philae with a cofferdam to hold the waters back, then moved some of the ancient buildings to a higher island nearby.

exhibition of his finds. The displays featured a 50-foot-long model of Seti's tomb decorations, full-size copies of its two most impressive rooms, a model of the Abu Simbel temple, a cross section of the Pyramid of Khafre, and what the *Times* of London called "a multitude of collateral curiosities." The book sold briskly and the exhibition was a success.

Afflicted again by wanderlust, Belzoni embarked on a search for the source of the Niger River. But the man who had defied almost superhuman odds in Egypt succumbed to dysentery only a month after landing in West Africa—alone, ever the outsider, a driven but gentle man in a giant's frame.

Belzoni died a pauper—one of the few tomb robbers who made no money from his ventures. Salt netted a tidy sum from Belzoni's work and his own collections. Drovetti sold his collections to the king of Sardinia, the Louvre, and the Prussians. Though Belzoni, Salt, and Drovetti became fierce rivals, parts of their collections ended up gracing the museums of each other's countries: Belzoni, an Italian—the British Museum; Salt, an Englishman—the Louvre; and Drovetti, a Frenchman—the Egyptian Museum of Turin.

Elgin, Belzoni, and their contemporaries turned archaeology from a sport into a treasure hunt that pitted museum against museum, collector against collector, nation against nation. The dual threads of nationalism and greed became inextricably entwined. Men like Sir William Hamilton and Lord Elgin collected vases or sculptures for the loftiest of motives, but others sought only fame, fortune, and hard cash.

Archaeology as a science did not exist. There were no excavation procedures, no university courses, no archaeological manuals. Belzoni shoveled his way into fame, but his careful record keeping stood well above the standards of his peers. He was no archaeologist, yet this ambitious expert in stagecraft was one of the founders of Egyptology.

Elgin and Belzoni pillaged temples and tombs that had been famous for centuries. A generation later, in 1840, the French took archaeology a step further. They appointed a consul in Mesopotamia to look for the lost city of Nineveh. All he had to dig into were dusty mounds of moldering mud brick. Here large-scale excavation began.

54

Stylish Londoners of 1821 loll amid the grandeur of the tomb of Seti I in a copy of one of its painted chambers (right). Giovanni Belzoni, the tomb's discoverer, surrounded his reproduction with what the Times *of London called "mummies, papyri, medals, and female ornaments." He watched thousands pay to see it all in the Egyptian Hall— a museum for "The New & The Wonderful!" heralded a poster (left). Although Belzoni died penniless, he lives on as one of the founders of Egyptology.*

Persia, 1847: A Kurdish lad dangles from the Rock of Bīsotūn to make paper molds of Babylonian texts, while Henry Creswicke Rawlinson yells advice.

IN SEARCH OF BURIED CITIES

"The boy's first move was to squeeze himself up a cleft in the rock. . . . He drove a wooden peg firmly into the cleft, fastened a rope to this, and then endeavored to swing himself across to another cleft . . . but in this he failed owing to the projection of the rock. It then only remained for him to cross over the cleft by hanging on by his toes and fingers to the . . . almost smooth perpendicular rock in a manner which to a looker-on appeared quite miraculous. . . . Driving in a second [peg], he was enabled to swing himself right over the projecting mass of rock. Here with a short ladder he formed a swinging seat [and] took under my direction the paper cast of the Babylonian translation of the records of Darius."

History remembers the lad only as "a wild Kurdish boy," as Henry Creswicke Rawlinson described him after that heart-stopping cliff-hanger in 1847. But when the boy came down from the sheer face of the great Rock of Bīsotūn in western Persia, he handed the British military officer the "squeezes"—wet-paper impressions—that were the key to the ancient writings of Mesopotamia, the land between the Tigris and Euphrates Rivers. Soon Rawlinson, with his great aptitude for languages, would decipher the strange cuneiform (wedge-shaped) characters, the script most widely used by cultures of the ancient Near East. And soon the Persian king of 25 centuries before would boast again, "I am Darius, the great king, the king of kings. . . ."

Moments of high adventure, years of patient study—these were the ingredients of Mesopotamian archaeology in Rawlinson's day. Adventurers journeyed into strange lands, negotiated with local rulers, and eventually carried off tons of antiquities from some of the oldest cities in the world. Scholars sat for endless hours in book-lined rooms or under the broiling Mesopotamian sun, copying and poring over cuneiform characters that would bring to life some of the kings and cities and events described in Scripture.

Until the 18th century, Europeans rarely visited Mesopotamia. The few travelers who reached it had to brave harsh deserts and marauding bandits to get there. And when they did, the sites of the biblical Garden of Eden, of the great cities of Nineveh and Babylon, came as a shock. The fertile lands of the Old Testament were a shriveled desert, the famous cities little more than crumbling bricks and dusty mounds. What had become of Nebuchadnezzar's dazzling capital at Babylon, of the bloodthirsty Assyrian kings who had deported entire cities? "He will stretch out his hand ... and destroy Assyria," the Old Testament prophet Zephaniah had written, "and will make Nineveh a desolation, and dry like a wilderness."

In 1616 an Italian nobleman, Pietro della Valle, wandered into Mesopotamia during an eight-year journey undertaken after "a disappointment in love." He returned to Rome with a remarkable collection of curiosities, including a few inscribed bricks from the ruins of Babylon and sketches of inscriptions from Persepolis. Scholars flocked to see these first specimens of cuneiform. The curious script, produced by pressing a stylus onto wet clay, held secrets of civilizations lost since biblical times. But their message was a mystery.

And so it remained 150 years later as Europeans began to trickle into this backwater of the Turkish Empire. Carsten Niebuhr, a German mathematician and surveyor, visited the ruined Persian capital of Persepolis in 1765 and surveyed the royal palace. Alone in the blistering heat, often blinded by the sun's glare on the white marble walls, Niebuhr filled page after page with copies of intricate inscriptions. He identified 42 symbols but could not interpret them or identify the authors. Still, his lonely weeks at Persepolis gave Europe's scholars their first good look at cuneiform.

Then, in 1798, Napoléon Bonaparte invaded Egypt, the first stage of his plan to gain control of Mesopotamia and, thereby, an overland route to India. Alarmed, the British government strengthened its presence in Arabia, upgrading its agency in Baghdād to a full-fledged consulate. In 1808 Britain appointed 22-year-old Claudius James Rich as consul, a choice that proved fortunate for both politics and archaeology. A superb diplomat, Rich brought style and forcefulness to the British presence. In his spare time he pursued his interest in antiquities, collecting manuscripts and artifacts. He also visited Babylon, taking along his "own troops of Hussars, with a galloper gun ... [and] about seventy baggage mules." Rich studied and sketched the ruins, collected bricks inscribed with cuneiform, and made a rough survey of the

58

A lunging lion sinks fang and claw into the haunches of a bull (right) in a stone bas-relief at Persepolis, the capital in Iran where kings of Persia ruled 25 centuries ago. In the 1760s Carsten Niebuhr, a German surveyor, sketched such carvings (opposite) in his study of cuneiform, the wedge-shaped script used throughout the ancient Near East. Niebuhr isolated 42 symbols, realized that they represented three separate languages, and laid the groundwork for the later deciphering of cuneiform.

verschiedene Buchstaben der ältesten persisch

Dignitaries by the dozen climb a monumental staircase at Persepolis (above). Most carry flowers; some turn to help the next man on the ascent to a palace gate called the Triple Portal. Buried under centuries of debris, this stairway was excavated in 1932 by German archaeologist Ernst Herzfeld.

Living processions mounted such stairways as monarchs were crowned or buried in this ancient ceremonial center. Here too came envoys from all parts of the Persian Empire to present tribute to the king.

city. When he published two monographs about the ruins, European scholars took notice; perhaps such dusty mounds would add insight to the Old Testament.

In 1820 Rich went looking for Nineveh, that infamous city of Scripture where the Assyrian kings had reigned. Perhaps both history and treasure waited there. But where? Local Arabs pointed to two tells, or mounds, across the Tigris from the town of Mosul. There Rich surveyed the higher tell, 43-foot-high Kuyunjik. Potsherds and bricks, some with cuneiform inscriptions, littered its flat top. This, Rich surmised, "formed only a part of a great city, probably either the citadel, or royal precincts, or perhaps both." But he never had a chance to excavate Kuyunjik. A year later he died of cholera.

With his maps and accounts, Claudius Rich began a new chapter in Mesopotamian studies, one based not on travelers' tales but on careful description. Napoléon's invasion of Egypt had not only initiated the science of Egyptology but also, though inadvertently, sparked the beginnings of Mesopotamian archaeology. Rich's sizable collection of cuneiform samples and copies, sold by his widow to the British Museum, was eagerly welcomed by scholars throughout Europe who were struggling to decipher this mysterious script.

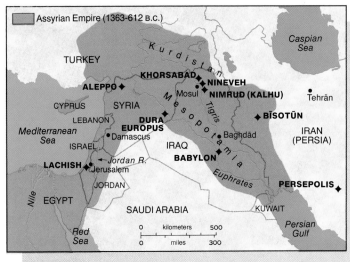

Perched on its own history, the 13th-century citadel of Aleppo looks down on Syrian plains long dominated by a great trading center here. Goods were flowing through the portals of a settlement on this site more than 3,000 years ago. As mud-brick buildings crumbled, new structures were built atop the old. Layer by layer the town rose on its own ruins, gradually piling up a mound known in Arabic— and in archaeology—as a tell.

Modern Aleppo, a city of more than a million people, *encircles the ancient tell. The medieval citadel now serves as a historical museum. But the unexcavated tell may hold greater treasure—ruins and remnants of the earliest settlement here, of the Hittites and Egyptians who fought over control of the city, and of the fierce Assyrians whose empire (map) swallowed the entire Fertile Crescent.*

Slowly, piece by piece, the puzzle would finally be solved—one of the greatest scientific feats of the 19th century.

Much of the credit goes to Henry Rawlinson. In 1835 military duties took him to the area near the Rock of Bīsotūn in Kurdistan, a remote region of Persia. He stared 400 feet up at the rock's trilingual inscription—in Old Persian, Elamite, and Babylonian—and realized it held the key to cuneiform. Scholars were already able to read many characters in Old Persian writing. A translation of the Old Persian text at Bīsotūn would aid in translating the other two languages.

The task of copying the carvings would have daunted even an expert mountaineer. But with makeshift scaffolding Rawlinson clambered all over the steep wall during visits over the next 12 years. He copied nearly the entire inscription, which covered about 1,200 square feet. Once he nearly plunged to his death when a ladder he was using to span a chasm gave way. When only the most inaccessible lines remained, Rawlinson sought help from Kurdish climbers. They protested that overhangs blocked the way. Then, enticed by "a considerable reward," the Kurdish boy with nerves of iron clung to the cliff to bring Rawlinson the missing lines.

By now Rawlinson was British consul in Baghdād and had time to work on the texts. Like other experts, though he was probably unaware of it, Rawlinson began by deciphering the kings' names in the Old Persian text. He was then able to compile an alphabet and translate sentences and whole paragraphs. But in the Elamite and Babylonian scripts, the signs seemed to represent syllables rather than letters. Rawlinson realized that he needed more texts to work with—and he could get them only by digging for them.

Rawlinson had a rival. In 1840 the French government, prodded by interest in Claudius Rich's monographs about

King Ashurbanipal skewers a lion in an alabaster bas-relief from a palace at Nineveh, capital of the Assyrian Empire in the seventh century B.C. With plunder and tribute won in war, the kings of Assyria embellished their palaces with carvings flaunting their own strength and fearlessness.

More than a century ago, archaeologists sought Nineveh in the tells of Nimrud (left) beside the Tigris River. Instead they found Kalhu, an Assyrian city resplendent with palaces, temples, and a citadel.

Babylon, appointed Paul-Émile Botta as consul in Mosul. Ostensibly his job was to look after French political interests, but this obscure town had no diplomatic importance. Botta's real assignment was to dig into the mounds and find the remains of Nineveh. His work, the French expected, would yield new treasures for the Louvre and uphold the traditions of French scholarship in the Near East.

A quiet, introverted man, Botta had traveled the world and spent several years in Egypt. He had never excavated a site, but he knew the monuments of ancient Egypt and spoke fluent Arabic. Now he found himself in a land where nearly every antiquity had to be dug up, not simply carted away as in Egypt. Late in 1842 he began digging into the Kuyunjik mound, which Claudius Rich had surveyed two decades earlier. But Botta dug no deeper than the top layers, and the results—fragments of alabaster and a few inscribed bricks—disappointed him. He listened with interest when a man from Khorsabad, a hamlet 14 miles north, rhapsodized about the riches in the mound under his village. Even his own stove was built of ancient bricks, the man cried. The consul finally sent him off with a couple of workmen.

A week later one worker rushed back to tell Botta of walls decorated with carvings of strange animals. Botta jumped on his horse and galloped to Khorsabad. He gasped at the bas-reliefs: winged, human-headed animals and processions of men with long beards and rich robes. In 1843 Botta moved his crew to the mound and soon found more reliefs—a rich reward after the letdown of Kuyunjik. Could it be possible that Nineveh lay here instead?

The discoveries at Khorsabad made banner headlines in Paris. Archaeologists and theologians alike exulted; Botta had found Nineveh! The French government sent money and an artist, Eugène Napoléon Flandin, to draw the sculptures. Botta purchased the village that stood on the mound and hired more than 300 workers to dig.

The lost cities of Mesopotamia were not like other archaeological sites. Greeks and Egyptians built in fine marble and granite; Babylonians and Assyrians built with clay. The bricks were sun dried, not baked in a kiln, so they gradually

64

Scourge of the desert, a dust storm roils toward Dura Europus. This ruin in Syria began as a Babylonian village and ended as a large Roman fortress sacked by invaders in the third century A.D. At such sites the desert's dryness can preserve much that might perish in other climates: wood, fabrics, food scraps, human remains. But desert hazards bedevil archaeologists who must cope with heat, the sun's glare, the scarcity of water, and the scorpions that crawl into their boots at night.

dissolved in water, eroded in wind, and crumbled under pressure. Buildings were often rebuilt atop their own rubble. Thus a city rose on a growing mound of its own debris.

Early excavators had few guidelines for such a dig. Unable to date pottery or read cuneiform, they could only sink their picks and see what turned up. Botta knew little about stratigraphy, about how tells formed, or about how to trace a mud-brick wall long since gone to dust. The workmen simply exposed the few stone buildings and bas-reliefs.

Even so, six months of digging uncovered unprecedented treasures. Winged, human-headed lions and bulls flanked the gates of a royal palace. Reliefs of gods, humans, and mythical animals emerged from the soil. In mind-numbing heat Flandin crouched over the slabs, tracing figures and copying cuneiform. Botta gazed at scenes of a king besieging cities, hunting game, and sacrificing to the gods. But what king? Not until 1845 would scholars decipher his name: Sargon II, King of Assyria in the eighth century B.C.

Meanwhile Botta faced the formidable task of removing the reliefs from the palace. Most slabs were so heavy that Botta had to instruct his workers to saw them up. Then his crew loaded the pieces onto a huge cart, to be hauled by 300 straining men over 14 miles of rough country from Khorsabad to the Tigris. There the slabs were moved onto crude wooden rafts supported by inflated goatskins. The rafts could not be controlled in rough water. The first load capsized and was lost, but another made it to port and to Paris.

The first exhibit of these Assyrian artifacts opened at the Louvre in 1847 under Botta's supervision. Curious citizens mobbed the bas-reliefs. In 1849 and 1850 the French government published five lavish volumes of Flandin's art and Botta's notes, *Monument de Ninive*. But politics dictated that the French consulate in Mosul be closed; Botta was transferred to Lebanon and never took up archaeology again.

To the French the Khorsabad excavations symbolized their nation's abiding commitment to the fine arts. Their British rivals in Mesopotamian archaeology simply thought such excavations were worthwhile. One of these was Austen Henry Layard, a restless 25-year-old fleeing his dull British life by riding overland toward Ceylon, where he planned to pursue his career in law. Layard and a friend, Edward Mitford, set out in 1839, "careless of comfort and unmindful of danger." At times they survived on a simple diet of carob beans, fish roe, and unleavened bread. "Our arms were our only protection," wrote Layard, "a valise behind our saddles was our wardrobe, and we tended our own horses."

Arriving in Mosul in April 1840, Layard wandered spellbound over the nearby mounds, enthralled by the dusty earthworks. He also got his first look at Nimrud, a high mound 30 miles downstream from Mosul. Layard resolved then that someday he would excavate Nimrud.

Five years of adventure and intrigue passed before Layard achieved this ambition. While Mitford rode on to India, Layard stayed in Persia and wandered the rugged mountains with local nomads. He was robbed and robbed again; he was adopted by a tribal chief after curing the chief's son of a fever. Eventually Layard arrived in Constantinople and became

"When not otherwise occupied, I made drawings of the bas-reliefs...." Thus did British archaeologist Austen Henry Layard describe his days at Nineveh—and thus did a visiting cleric, S. C. Malan, portray him in 1850 (above).

Into the mounds of this ancient capital Layard and his crews dug a honeycomb of tunnels. Workers excavate the palace of King Sennacherib (opposite) in a scene painted by artist Frederick Cooper, a member of Layard's team. In such passageways, Layard

later recalled, "my guests, choosing some convenient place underground ... spread their carpets beneath the crumbling sculptures.... The temperature in the dark tunnels was cool and agreeable." But the stifling heat outdoors was not. "One by one," Layard wrote, "we dropped off with fever."

68

Pen, brush, and camera record the 1847 odyssey of two masterworks—a winged, human-headed bull and a lion-bodied counterpart— from Nimrud to a gallery in the British Museum. From his perch on a wall (above, left), Layard watches his work gang ease the bull onto a cart, "a moment of great anxiety." A stout raft and ample crew (opposite) bear one of the ten-ton alabaster treasures down the Tigris River for the journey by ship to London. There a framework steadies the lion as a crew winches it up a ramp and into the museum (left). Today the lion stands in a portal (above) as it did in the palace at Nimrud, where pairs of such beasts guarded the chambers of Assyrian kings.

an unofficial agent for the British ambassador. By then Layard had an impressive command of Arabic and Persian, and he had not lost his interest in archaeology. He corresponded regularly with Botta in Mosul and with Rawlinson, who was hard at work in Baghdād deciphering cuneiform. News of Botta's discoveries at Khorsabad spurred Layard to seek funding for the excavation of Nimrud. At last, in 1845, the British ambassador agreed to sponsor the work.

"Visions of palaces underground . . . floated before me," Layard later wrote. But when he arrived in Mosul, he found the French fiercely protective of their archaeological interests. The resourceful Layard announced he was on a boar hunt, had some excavating tools made in secret, and slipped downriver to Nimrud with six Arab workmen. They unearthed two Assyrian buildings on the first day. One of the chambers yielded carved tablets and ivory ornaments with "traces of gilding," including a king and a crouched sphinx —just the kind of sensational finds Layard needed to excite popular interest and generate financial support.

A grant from the British Museum, which expected a steady flow of fine sculptures in return, enabled Layard to continue his work at Nimrud. A modern archaeologist would be appalled by Layard's methods. His diggers simply tunneled into the mounds at various spots; the site soon looked like a moonscape. The men kept going until they came upon a sculpture or a stone wall. Then they worked along the walls or friezes, shoring up their tunnels with timbers and occasionally digging an air hole to the surface. Layard spent hours in the hot tunnels, sketching each slab as it emerged.

Visitors trooped in to see the wonders that were being revealed. "The portly forms of kings and [viziers] were so lifelike . . . that they might almost be imagined to be stepping from the walls to question the rash intruder on their privacy," wrote a London newsman.

By now Layard was like a tribal chieftain, ruling his crew with both sensitivity and firmness. He arranged a marriage, settled quarrels, and took ruthless action if the need arose. When bandits stole some packing materials, Layard rode to their camp, clapped handcuffs on the startled sheikh, and dragged him away. The materials were promptly returned.

Layard built a mud-brick house for himself, complete with "wallpaper" of grass that sprouted when it rained. Rice and vegetables made up his monotonous diet. Tents and huts teemed with vermin. Rains made the site a quagmire in winter—and a few weeks later everyone baked in shimmering heat and the ground was like concrete. Violent sandstorms occasionally swept through.

Rising at dawn, Layard supervised the dig all day, then recorded inscriptions and bas-reliefs well into the night. The Nimrud excavations were so productive that he had to spend more and more time on packing and transport. Often in temperatures above 110°F, his men swathed the precious slabs in felt, then loaded crate after crate onto rafts. One night marauders tried to steal the felt packing from a winged bull. They were repulsed with gunfire. The bullet-scarred bull stands today in the British Museum.

Over French protests Layard turned in 1847 to Kuyunjik,

70

Height 2¾"

From an artist's exuberant imagination springs a Nimrud as it never looked in reality (above). This romantic view of the royal Assyrian city, painted by James Fergusson, was published by Layard in 1853.

Layard was the first archaeologist to excavate at Nimrud, but not the last; the dusty mounds have rewarded his successors too. In 1949 a British team directed by Max Mallowan—shown opposite in hat and vest—began to probe the ancient city. There they found thousands of carved ivory ornaments and plaques. A winged sphinx Mallowan unearthed struts amid stylized plants on the plaque shown at left. Many Assyrian ivories were originally gilded, but invaders stripped off the gold and tossed the ivory aside.

the tell abandoned by Botta. He realized Botta had not dug deep enough. In one hectic month Layard uncovered nine palace rooms with large bas-reliefs of a king besieging a city and returning in triumph. The British Museum's money had run out, however, so Layard left for London.

There he received a hero's welcome. He dined in great houses, lectured to learned societies, and wrote "a slight sketch of the history of Nineveh"—for Rawlinson had told him that Nimrud, rather than Khorsabad as the French believed, was in fact Nineveh. In 1849 *Nineveh and Its Remains* became an immediate best-seller. The *Times* of London called it "the most extraordinary work of the present age."

Despite Layard's fame, the British Museum gave him only a niggardly sum for more excavation. "My private resources are far from considerable," said Layard, "but, such as they are, they shall be devoted to the undertaking." He returned to Mosul and a warm welcome from his workmen. Excavations at Nimrud and Kuyunjik resumed at once.

One morning at Nimrud, Layard found Henry Rawlinson asleep in one of the excavated chambers, exhausted after a long ride from Baghdād. Rawlinson had come to explain that his cuneiform studies now convinced him that Nimrud was not Nineveh after all. Rawlinson, along with another cuneiform expert, an Irish parson named Edward Hincks, had deciphered the name Sennacherib, King of Assyria, from finds at Kuyunjik. Later discoveries, compared with Old Testament passages, confirmed that Kuyunjik was Nineveh. Nimrud was the ninth-century B.C. city of Kalhu, the Assyrian capital until Sennacherib built at Nineveh his "palace without a rival." The long-debated question was settled at last.

Layard spent two busy and productive years at Nineveh and Nimrud. With more than a hundred workmen he tunneled into Nineveh's palace and bared a facade stretching more than 180 feet. It opened, wrote Layard, "into a wide portal, guarded by a pair of winged bulls, 20 feet long and . . . more than 20 feet high." Elsewhere his diggers uncovered limestone slabs that bore ruts made by chariot wheels.

Layard was stunned to discover bas-reliefs of military campaigns that, if placed side by side, would have reached 73

The Roman city of Pompeii meets its doom as the wrath of Mount Vesuvius descends on it in A.D. 79. Russian painter Karl Bryullov in the 1830s imagined the gruesome scene; so did scores of other artists, authors, and archaeologists as discoveries began to lay bare this city sealed in volcanic debris and all but forgotten through the centuries. The eruption also smothered seaside Herculaneum (map) and smaller hamlets on the volcano's flanks, each now a time capsule of Roman life.

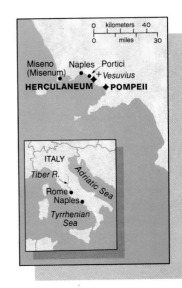

almost two miles. Two slabs depicted the Assyrian army besieging and capturing a walled city. In another scene the king sat in judgment over the prisoners. Layard was delighted when Rawlinson deciphered the inscription over the king's head: "Sennacherib . . . king of the country of Assyria, sitting on the throne of judgment, before the city of Lachish. I give permission for its slaughter." Layard remembered words in the Old Testament: "Now in the fourteenth year of king Hezekiah did Sennacherib king of Assyria come up against all the fenced cities of Judah, and took them." And one of those cities was Lachish. Layard now had an actual record of this campaign. With such vivid confirmation, historians could link Layard's Assyrians with Old Testament kings.

The excavation of Sennacherib's palace could have occupied Layard for a lifetime. But, impatient and impulsive, he returned to Nimrud and, even there, dug only briefly, finding a room full of copper vessels and jars, bronze bells with iron tongues, cups, dishes, cauldrons, and trappings for horses and chariots. There were also exquisite ivory ornaments, bronze weapons, glass bowls, and many smaller treasures. Layard's main interest, however, was in reliefs and large sculptures that would satisfy the British Museum. So he left much of the room's contents alone. In the 1950s Max Mallowan, a British archaeologist, would recover a rich harvest of delicate ivory carvings from Nimrud.

Ironically Layard's humblest discovery was his greatest legacy. At Nineveh his men tunneled into a palace chamber where thousands of clay tablets and fragments lay a foot deep on the floor. But time and money were running out. Layard bundled up the tablets for Henry Rawlinson to examine. Rawlinson identified grammars, histories, hymns, and commercial records that filled in the vague picture of Assyrian life outlined in the grandiose inscriptions on palace walls. Layard had broken into the royal library, a discovery that laid the foundation for scientific study of the Assyrians and revealed the rich cultural legacy of Mesopotamia.

Layard left Mesopotamia forever in April 1851. His assistant, Mosul-born Hormuzd Rassam, took charge. Hungry for recognition as an archaeologist, Rassam sought spectacular discoveries. Because the French had digging rights on the

Five dapper visitors and a dog look on as workers haul away rubble from the Temple of Isis at Pompeii (left). The fluted pillars of the once magnificent temple dwarf them all in this fanciful painting from the late 1700s, when diggers unearthed the temple. In 1908, armed with the insights of archaeology, a French architect named Léon Jaussely drew the city's forum (below). His view cuts the basilica down the middle to show Pompeians milling among the columns of this center for public gatherings.

north side of Nineveh, he dug on the south. After a fruitless year, one moonlit night he took a few trusted workmen to the French area. In three nights of feverish digging they uncovered a relief of King Ashurbanipal in his chariot, hunting lions. Discovery meant possession, so Rassam started digging in daylight, disregarding French protests. He was so engrossed with the reliefs that he almost ignored the hundreds of crumbling clay tablets strewn on the hall floor. He had his workmen stuff them into baskets and crates, unaware that he had stumbled upon the main body of Ashurbanipal's personal archives. The palace had burned, and the tablets had fallen through the ceiling from above. From this and Layard's discovery, more than 25,000 tablets of Ashurbanipal's archives eventually reached the British Museum.

The French were not so lucky. In 1855 all their finds, including 240 crates from Nineveh and Khorsabad, started downriver on boats and rafts. Robbers attacked and tipped the treasures overboard. Only 78 crates were recovered.

Meanwhile Layard had written *Discoveries in the Ruins of Nineveh and Babylon.* Now he had enough deciphered texts to write an account of the Assyrian kings. They lived, he wrote, in perennial warfare. Nonpayment of tribute meant siege, slavery, and exile for entire populations.

Layard's work generated immense public interest. Visitors to the British Museum could see the living Scriptures for themselves. They could meet Assyrian kings seated in judgment, watch them hunt lions in a royal park, and see boatmen crossing the Tigris in round boats like those still used in Layard's time. He had brought the past and the Bible to life.

Today Austen Henry Layard ranks as one of archaeology's immortals. Visitors to the Assyrian rooms at the British Museum marvel at what Layard accomplished with scant resources. Sadly, much was lost, for his huge gangs of unskilled workers did irrevocable damage as they dug away with no notion of stratigraphy or proper record keeping. And of what he did find, only a small portion could be shipped home. The rest is known only from his sketches.

At 36 Layard retired from archaeology. Only once more did he visit an excavation, when a trench at Pompeii was

Death scene in a basement laundry room intrigues visitors to Pompeii in an engraving (right) published about 1830. British antiquary Sir William Hamilton, famed as a collector of Greek and Roman antiquities, painted the same scene in words in 1777: "The washerwoman... seems to have been shut up in this vault, the staircase having been filled with rubbish, and to have waited for death with calm resignation, and true Roman fortitude." Hamilton left the bones untouched.

opened in his honor. It was a fitting gesture, for at this buried Roman city on Italy's west coast, archaeology was taking a dramatic turn from treasure hunt to science.

The ancient cities of Pompeii and Herculaneum had died within a few short hours, victims of Mount Vesuvius. With a blast like a monstrous cannon, a huge, fountainlike column of ash, rocks, and smoke burst from Vesuvius on August 24, A.D. 79, and turned daylight into darkness. The Roman Pliny the Younger witnessed the catastrophe from the nearby town of Misenum: "You could hear the shrieks of women, the wailing of infants, and the shouting of men." A snowfall of ash and pumice slowly buried Pompeii. About midnight a glowing avalanche of superhot gases, mud, and rocks slid down the fractured mountain and roared through both Herculaneum and Pompeii. Herculaneum vanished from sight. At Pompeii only the eaves of larger buildings protruded above the volcanic debris. Eventually topsoil and vegetation covered them. Then only a large, grassy mound revealed the presence of a long-forgotten city.

More than 16 centuries passed before anyone disturbed the buried cities. In 1709 a peasant dug a well shaft over Herculaneum, found some fragments of sculptured marble, and sold them to a dealer. A prince heard about the sculptures and bought the land. Workmen were lowered into the shaft and told to dig horizontally. Though the ground was full of noxious gases, the men were able to recover fragments of sculpture and three intact female statues. By chance the shaft had penetrated into Herculaneum's theater.

Still no one realized what lay below this fertile farmland. No further excavation took place at Herculaneum until 1738, when Italy's King Charles III decided to dig for statues, frescoes, and other works of ancient art. He hired Spanish engineer Rocque Joaquin de Alcubierre, who began by using gunpowder to blast down through some 60 feet of rock-hard volcanic debris. Tunneling sideways into underground galleries, his diggers recovered jewelry, statues of eminent Herculaneans, and fragments of bronze horses. Here was buried treasure indeed—a whole city full of it!

Though the king insisted on secrecy, rumors of the excavation percolated throughout Europe. A few distinguished

Pompeians sprawl in a grim tableau (above), their final moments locked in plaster in a technique developed in the 1860s by Italian archaeologist Giuseppe Fiorelli. The diagram at right explains his ingenious method. Here pumice and ash bury a victim and, after soaking rains, dry hard as rock. Over the years the body decays, leaving a hollow. Archaeologists come upon the hollow and inject plaster into it. After the plaster hardens, the pumice and ash are chipped away from the fallen form.

visitors were allowed into the mile or so of tunnels. Smoking torches lit the theater, marble-columned houses, and frescoed rooms. The workers removed everything portable—statues, frescoes, jewelry, furniture—for the king's personal museum at Portici, near Naples.

Alcubierre sank haphazard pits in likely places and abandoned them when nothing turned up. His assistant, Karl Weber from Switzerland, was more systematic. Weber drew a floor plan of the Villa of the Papyri in Herculaneum, an enormous private home that held nearly 1,800 texts written on papyrus scrolls, along with bronze busts and statues, including copies of Greek masterpieces that are now lost. Hundreds of men, including some prisoners, labored below ground to dig out these treasures. Work on the villa was never completed; toxic gases, slime, and collapsing tunnels forced the crew to quit. But they did recover all the scrolls—

Teams of diggers burrow into Pompeii (above) in the late 1800s. Archaeologists have labored at intervals for more than a century to free the buried city from its shroud of volcanic debris, in places as deep as 15 feet.

Three-fourths of Pompeii's 160 acres have now been cleared (right), including two theaters (foreground) and the civic forum (the large open space left of center). The rest of the city still lies buried below today's houses and gardens. A broad avenue points to the *ragged remnant of Vesuvius, whose slopes once rose to a majestic cone before the volcano blew its top off and entombed the towns at its base. Now about 4,200 feet high, Vesuvius can still threaten when lava wells up in its crater. The last major eruption took place in March 1944.*

a complete private library. The secretive king locked all these priceless works away in his museum.

Most 18th-century antiquaries were collectors and connoisseurs of art, interested not so much in the buried cities themselves as in what came from them. Seldom did antiquaries spend any time systematically investigating such places as Pompeii and Herculaneum. Johann Joachim Winckelmann was an exception. The son of a German cobbler, Winckelmann began his career as a schoolteacher and librarian and soon earned a reputation as a brilliant antiquary. In 1758 he became librarian of Cardinal Albani's celebrated collection of antiquities in Rome. Five years later Winckelmann was appointed supervisor of antiquities. He decided to see for himself the excavations at Herculaneum and Pompeii.

The king's secrecy shocked Winckelmann. He gained reluctant permission to see the king's museum but was

forbidden to visit the excavation site. Nevertheless, Winckelmann studied as much as he could about the Herculaneum finds. He placed them in the context of Greek mythology and tried to produce order from hundreds of isolated sculptures and frescoes. His letters and his great book, *History of the Art of Antiquity,* published in 1764, contained the first systematic descriptions of Greek and Roman art. Winckelmann was murdered by a robber before he could confirm his theories with further study of excavations. But his writings kindled a new awareness that excavations were not merely treasure hunts but sources of knowledge about ancient civilizations.

Winckelmann's brilliant work had little effect, however, at Pompeii and Herculaneum. Chaotic treasure hunting continued through the rest of the 18th century. Pompeii's Temple of Isis came to light in 1765, complete with the bones of an animal about to be sacrificed on the altar. British

minister Sir William Hamilton witnessed the discovery and complained about the careless, muddled excavations. He was incensed at seeing frescoes removed from the temple and mixed indiscriminately with other loot. During the Napoleonic Wars of the early 19th century, when France ruled Italy, French excavators dug trenches, stripped ancient buildings of their contents, and left the buildings to decay. Pompeii seemed doomed to a second destruction.

The turning point came in 1860, when King Victor Emmanuel II ascended the Italian throne. Fired by the glorious Roman past, he encouraged excavations at Pompeii as a matter of national prestige. Giuseppe Fiorelli, a professor who had written a history of Pompeii, set to work. By 1861 more than 500 men were laboring on the excavations.

Fiorelli was ahead of his time in many ways. Inheriting a site covered with trenches, tunnel openings, and rubble

A jet of water exposes a skull (opposite) at Herculaneum, a city that fell to Vesuvius in A.D. 79. Almost 140 skeletons have been found here since 1982, one still with bracelets and earrings of gold (above). Preserved by groundwater seeping into the volcanic ash, the bones will deteriorate rapidly when exhumed. In a project sponsored by the National Geographic Society, physical anthropologist Sara Bisel (center) cleans and dries bones at Herculaneum, then dips them into an acrylic

preservative. Her studies of reconstructed skeletons reveal the age, sex, and health of these ill-fated ancient Romans.

Overleaf: A death embrace still links victims of the volcano's fury on Herculaneum's beach, where townsfolk fled in vain for rescue or shelter.

dumps, he cleaned it up, numbered the buildings, and kept a journal, which he eventually published. He looked for layers in the soil and excavated the city block by block.

Fiorelli even set up a training school where other archaeologists could learn his methods of stratigraphical excavation. Repeatedly he reminded his students that the goal was not merely to find art objects but to reconstruct a long-dead Roman city. The houses of the wealthy might yield spectacular artifacts, but those of the poor, with their crude furnishings, were just as important. Nothing, however humble, should be discarded or overlooked.

The observant Fiorelli noticed cavities in the pumice that seemed to have a human shape. He filled some of them with liquid plaster, let it dry, then excavated the molds—complete body casts of Pompeians sprawled in the positions in which they had perished.

Fiorelli's careful excavation was a far cry from the rough-and-ready methods of Layard at Nimrud, for Fiorelli was among the first of a new breed: the professional archaeologist. Only a handful of men could claim such distinction in the 1860s. They were pioneers of a new type of excavation—a quest for information rather than treasure.

Two bronze athletes from Herculaneum stand poised in the Naples National Archaeological Museum (right). Behind them spreads a floor plan, drawn by Swiss engineer Karl Weber, of the house where they were found in the 1700s—the luxurious Villa of the Papyri, named for its well-stocked library of papyrus scrolls. More than 90 statues decorated the villa, possibly the home of Julius Caesar's father-in-law. But noxious gases lingering from the eruption that had buried it *forced excavators to abandon their work in 1765.*

More treasures wait to be found at Herculaneum. On its beach a Roman boat long since turned to fragile carbon (above) awaits a slow and painstaking journey to the museum, where specialists will begin its reconstruction. Under the boat may lie clues to how it was used and steered.

England, 1844: Chic Victorians brave a drizzle to open an Anglo-Saxon burial mound at Breach Down.

FROM SPORT TO SCIENCE

FROM SPORT TO SCIENCE

*S uch draggling of skirts! such giggling of flirts,
As you see in a storm in Hyde Park;
With no end of umbrellas, to shelter the Fellows,
Who seemed bent upon digging till dark.*

Not even rain could dampen "this very enjoyable day" in September 1844, when some 200 ladies and gentlemen of the British Archaeological Association stepped from their carriages at Breach Down near Canterbury to watch the final opening of eight partly excavated Anglo-Saxon barrows, or burial mounds. Though some members wrote soberly of skeletons and artifacts, one partygoer caught the spirit of the outing—"It was ten times as good as a play"—in this romping rhyme. Afterward the association president hosted a reception at his nearby mansion. As a final treat three days later, one member removed the wrappings from an ancient Egyptian mummy after dinner.

No present-day dig would be turned into such a social splash, for archaeology has become a systematic search for information as well as artifacts. The momentous years of discovery in the latter half of the 19th century saw a gradual improvement in excavation methods and the transition of archaeology from a treasure hunt to a fledgling science. But in the late 18th and early 19th centuries, archaeology was still chiefly a sport, a hobby of country gentlemen.

While Belzoni labored in Egypt and Layard in Mesopotamia, hundreds of British antiquaries dug into Roman villas and Anglo-Saxon graves at home. (Germanic tribes now called Anglo-Saxons had settled in Britain in the fifth century A.D.) Some of these diggers could not afford to visit classical sites on the Grand Tour; others, influenced by current literary and artistic thought, pursued a romantic interest in Britain's ancient history. A new generation of middle-class collectors joined in—merchants, craftsmen, and farmers with spare time for probing the past.

They were an industrious lot as they shoveled out urns, swords, beakers, and sometimes gold ornaments among the human bones. One 18th-century parson opened 31 barrows in a single day. On another occasion, after supervising the opening of nine mounds, he reported: "We finished our business in little more than two hours." Canon William

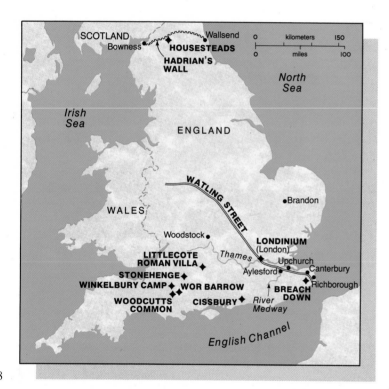

Greenwell, a noted 19th-century antiquary, once dug with six inches of snow on the ground; at twilight he knelt in his trench and examined his finds by flickering candlelight.

In August 1844 a small party of ladies and gentlemen gathered near Aylesford in southeastern England for the opening of a Roman barrow. While laborers dug for four days, the onlookers spent their time "at intervals between digging and pic-nicing, in games of various descriptions—not exactly such as those which the builders of the mound celebrated when they laid the deceased on his funeral pile."

That dig yielded little. But four centuries of Roman occupation had left its imprint across much of Britain. Hadrian's Wall guarded the northern frontier. Long, straight roads such as Watling Street bisected southern Britain and were still in use. Farmers plowed through Roman earthworks and uncovered colorful mosaic floors. The discovery of a Roman

floor near Woodstock in 1712 set landlord and tenant to quarreling over the profits from showing it to visitors. In a fit of rage the tenant ripped up the pavement. Hundreds of similar floors vanished during the 19th century, destroyed by plowing or by the building boom.

Archaeologists can only guess—and lament—what has been lost in London alone. Founded by the Romans around A.D. 43 at a vital crossing place on the Thames, Londinium grew into a major city. Today it is an archaeological puzzle. Yellow bricks of a Victorian foundation may rest on the red bricks of a house razed in the Great Fire of 1666, standing in turn on a medieval chalk wall atop the stone and tile of a Roman footing. Like a Mesopotamian tell, the city rose on its own ruins. Cellars, water pipes, sewers, subways—all punch through the accumulation of centuries. Nineteenth-century antiquaries haunted building sites to see what might turn up.

But some of the richest Roman finds came from the Thames and its tributaries. The river had been the scene of battles, shipwrecks, drownings, and trash dumping for thousands of years; its protective mud had become a storehouse that preserved metal, wood, and leather far better than did the aerated soil on land. Professional salvagers called mudlarks combed the Thames foreshores for anything from medieval buckles to bright red Roman pottery. The mudlarks learned to recognize artifacts and had a regular clientele interested in buying them.

Some collectors went mudlarking on their own. In 1846 one group explored the refuse from Roman potteries by the River Medway, about 30 miles from London. The best finds lay in the mud, so they donned high wading boots and slogged in. Probing with sticks, they found plenty of pottery but spent half their time pulling each other out of the mud

Hadrian's Wall, a legacy of Britain's occupation by the Romans, rambles the ridgetops of northern England near the Scottish border. Built in the second century A.D. as a bastion against the warlike "barbarians" to the north, the wall reached 73 miles across the narrow neck of Britain from Wallsend to Bowness (map). This section, the longest remaining stretch, runs east to a well-preserved Roman fort at Housesteads and has been a major tourist attraction since Queen Victoria's day.

and roaring with laughter. They thought it was all good fun, but it did irreversible damage to the record of the past.

Such destruction was nothing new. William Stukeley, famed for his work at Stonehenge, had complained in the 1720s that roads in Scotland were being built of stone from Hadrian's Wall. Even religious fervor had taken its toll; he railed against "the desolation . . . of Roman works, owing to the delusion and abominable superstition of cloyster'd nuns and fryers, what the fury of wars could not demolish, their inglorious hands have destroyed." Now, more than a century later, antiquaries too were ravaging important sites.

Not all were thoughtless hobbyists. Charles Roach Smith took his antiquarian pursuits seriously. A pharmacist by trade, Smith became an insatiable collector of Roman coins, bronze statues, and other antiquities. Haunting London construction sites and the banks of the Thames, he assembled a magnificent collection. He worked closely with the mudlarks and paid them well, so he usually got first refusal on anything that they found in London.

Smith was more than a collector. He wrote prolifically about archaeology—not adventure books like those of Belzoni and Layard, but catalogs of his discoveries, volumes on prehistoric and Roman remains, and pleas for accurate records. He realized that artifacts out of context meant little. "Coins stand well by themselves," he scolded, "but how deplorable 'tis to see . . . disintegrated works of art, severed from their birthplaces, to perplex the intelligent in the jumbled collection of some rich indiscriminating gatherer!"

A much respected man, Smith was one of a new breed of antiquary—the collector-turned-archaeologist. His descriptive researches led to the detailed artifact reports written today, and his personal collection formed the nucleus of the Roman-British collection at the British Museum.

Looking for Roman ruins at home became almost as popular as seeking classical antiquities in Greece and Italy. British antiquaries had a field day, aided by a recent invention: the railroad. As rails were being laid, work crews might uncover a new site. And as trains rolled, antiquaries climbed aboard to see distant sites or meet with their fellows.

In 1843 Smith helped organize the British Archaeological Association, a group of amateur archaeologists who joined together to promote antiquarian activities throughout Britain. The next summer the members visited sites in and around Canterbury, attended the opening of some Anglo-Saxon barrows at Breach Down, and toured Roman ruins at Richborough. Theirs was one of the first of dozens of archaeological societies that sprang up throughout the British Isles in the 19th century, a tradition of amateur archaeology that flourishes in Britain to this day.

One member of the association was John Evans, a paper company owner and amateur geologist and collector. He made his house a museum of coins, stone tools, ancient bronzes, and Roman jewelry and glassware. Evans spent thousands of pounds sterling on his collections over a long lifetime. He too published reports of his discoveries and went beyond Smith to even broader inquiries about the past.

Evans traveled far afield. In southwestern France he found the local people quarrying away at prehistoric caves and selling tools and weapons made of flint, bone, and antler to the French authorities, the British Museum, and all other comers. So he too dug, in the Stone Age rock-shelter of La Madeleine—a cliffside protected by an overhanging rock beside the Vézère River. "We had a few hours' digging and found several reindeer horn barbed darts, and as usual no end of flints, some of which I was constrained to keep."

In 1859 Evans had helped verify the extreme antiquity of the Stone Age hand axes from the Somme Valley in northern France. This won him the sobriquet "Flint" Evans and linked him with contemporary archaeologists and a small group of amateur biologists and geologists who shared his interest in archaeology and paleontology. Some were doctors, others merchants, lawyers, or bankers; few had formal academic training in the subjects of their hobbies. Yet together they altered the course of sciences such as geology and biology by their observations in the field. Naturalist Charles Darwin, a prominent figure in this revolutionary decade, published his *Origin of Species* in 1859, and Darwin's ardent champion, biologist Thomas Henry Huxley, applied the theory of evolution to humans.

Diamonds and rubies from India, turquoise from Persia, and emeralds from Colombia, fashioned into ornaments by London goldsmiths: The Cheapside Hoard, found at a building site in the Cheapside district in 1912, reflects the burgeoning foreign trade of Elizabethan England. The jewels, now in the Museum of London, probably graced a jeweler's shop around 1600.

Seeking profit rather than knowledge, Victorian mudlarks (left) grope for Roman pottery in a marsh near Upchurch.

An emerging breed of self-trained archaeologists began to puzzle over the murky vistas of prehistoric time in northern Europe. At one end of the time scale stood crude stone axes, at the other the Romans. But what lay in between?

Jens Jacob Worsaae, a Danish archaeologist, took the Three Age System—a scheme for dividing the past into the Stone, Bronze, and Iron Ages—out of the museum and applied it in the field at Danish barrows and stone tombs. Many people, he wrote, "assume that the bronze objects, which are distinguished by their beauty of workmanship, may have been used by the rich; while the iron objects belonged to those less wealthy, and those of stone to the poor." On the contrary, Worsaae found varied types of architecture, funeral customs, and workmanship associated with the three technologies. He concluded "that the often-named division of antiquities and barrows into three ages, is founded not on probability alone, but on positive facts. . . ."

The broad time scale of the Three Age System provided a rough chronology for the hand axes of northern France but was too general for the variety of lifeways then coming to light throughout Europe.

For years fishermen on the lakes of Switzerland had

Site director and students at Littlecote Roman Villa in southern England seem to listen (right) as Orpheus strums his lyre amid a circlet of goddesses and prancing beasts. In 1727 the steward on the estate found the mosaic floor while digging postholes. Reburied but discovered again in 1978 and restored, it now mirrors its former glory.

Volunteers scrub Roman tableware (above) discovered at Littlecote. Potters' names help date these bowls and vases to about A.D. 100.

spread tales about submerged forests. Then a drought in the 1850s shrank the lakes and exposed some of the "forests" as wooden pilings set into the mud. Antiquaries investigated. By 1869 they had confirmed more than 200 sites.

Ferdinand Keller, a well-known Zürich archaeologist, dug in the dried-up bed of Lake Zürich near Obermeilen. There he found the mud had preserved perishable objects—animal bones, wooden ax handles, even hazelnuts—that gave a more detailed picture of ancient lifeways than stone tools and potsherds could. His task was daunting, for no one had ever excavated a site containing such perishable items, let alone found a way to date the dwellings. Keller's methods were rough at best. He dug around the pilings, uprooting some for study, and recovered anything he could.

Some lake sites yielded Roman artifacts and thus could be dated fairly accurately. Most offered a varying mix of stone, bronze, and iron implements and could only be ranked in the Three Age System according to which artifacts predominated. It was clear, though, that the Swiss lake dwellers had lived long after the hunters of the Somme Valley, for they left behind remains of domesticated plants and animals as well as those of wild beasts. But Keller could only guess that the dwellings were "of very high antiquity"; other archaeologists estimated them to be thousands of years old.

Keller wrote lengthy descriptions of his discoveries and of how the villagers had lived. He mused over a striking analogy. Remembering stories of Pacific islanders who lived in stilt houses over the water, he concluded that his villagers had inhabited similar dwellings and dropped their refuse into the lake beneath their homes. His stilt-house theory was widely accepted until the 1920s, when Keller's successors used sophisticated digging methods to show that the lake people had built their dwellings on dry land at the water's edge; gradually the lakes had risen and flooded the sites where the houses had once stood.

Keller's villages were soon added to what could be called the Grand Tour of newfound prehistoric sites in northern and western Europe. Other prime stops were the caves in southwestern France, where a French lawyer and a British banker had made some astounding finds.

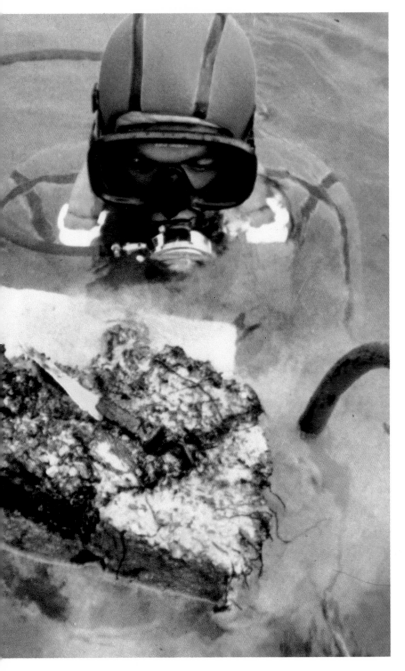

Édouard Lartet was a small-town lawyer in southern France, but his real love was collecting fossil bones. Chance launched his archaeological career in 1852, when a road worker pulled a human bone out of a rabbit hole near the village of Aurignac in the Pyrénées foothills. The worker dug out the hole and found a cave containing the bones of 17 people, perforated shell disks, and mammal teeth. Amid rumors of foul play, the skeletons were interred in the local cemetery. The road superintendent sent some of the other contents for paleontological study, and Lartet had a chance to examine them. Intrigued, he visited Aurignac in 1860. Digging inside the cave and in a hearth outside, he found tools made from flint and antler together with the bones of extinct mammals. These and the absence of metal artifacts led him to believe that the Aurignac people had belonged to "the remotest antiquity"—the early Stone Age.

In 1862 Lartet found a box of bones and flint tools in the store of a Paris collector. They came from Les Eyzies in the Vézère Valley in southwestern France. A visit to the village revealed dozens of caves and rock-shelters awaiting excavation. Lartet devoted the rest of his life to this pursuit.

He joined forces with a friend, Henry Christy, a wealthy British banker with a love of travel and antiquities. The two men made an effective team: Christy bankrolled the research; Lartet supervised the digs. At rock-shelters near Les Eyzies in 1863-64, they unearthed thousands of stone tools and fragments of animal bone, as well as antler tools and large pieces of antler engraved with extinct animals.

Lartet identified different levels of human occupation more by their animal remains and artifacts than by careful observation of stratigraphy, which relies on detecting variations in soil color and texture. Lartet and his crew—and Christy too—shoveled their way through abundant deposits of tools, weapons, and bones. The diggers found the remains of reindeer, long-haired elephant, and arctic fox—evidence that the rock-shelter people had lived during periods of intense cold. Over tens of thousands of years they had eaten a profusion of game animals and probably wild plants.

These hunter-gatherers neatly filled a gap in the Three Age System. They were well ahead of the Somme Valley

Length 7½"

Relic of the Stone Age, a flint dagger emerges (above) from a lake bottom in southeastern France, its wooden haft still intact (left) after 5,000 years. A severe drought in 1921 exposed the remnants of an ancient settlement (opposite) on the bottom of Lake Paladru near Lyon. Similar sites had led 19th-century scientists to describe villages of lake dwellers whose houses rose above the water on tall stilts.

But archaeologists working on the submerged site since 1972 have confirmed that the *inhabitants built their houses on dry land—on a shoreline that flooded as the climate changed and lake levels rose. The Stone Age farmers of Baigneurs, as the village is now known, grew wheat and barley, kept livestock, hunted deer, and fished with nets. Inundation created a natural time capsule, preserving nuts, seeds, animal bones, wooden spoons and ax handles, house timbers, fragments of cloth, and other fragile clues to the daily lives of these ancient lakeside dwellers.*

axmakers but not as advanced as the Swiss lake farmers. After a few seasons Lartet was dating one cave later than another by the fineness of its flint tools, the use of bone and antler, and the artistry of its craftsmen.

A group of superbly crafted artifacts came from La Madeleine, a rock-shelter beside the Vézère River. Here Lartet found reindeer antler harpoons with curved barbs. Ancient artists had decorated bone fragments and tools with engravings of the game they hunted; one sculpture of an extinct bison was so detailed that the tear duct of its eye could be seen. Even casual onlookers gasped with amazement. Who were these hunters, so far ahead of the Stone Age axmakers?

The answer came in 1868, when railroad workers discovered a rock-shelter at a large rock near Les Eyzies called Cro-Magnon. At the back of the shelter, Lartet's son Louis unearthed what has been cited as one of archaeology's first murder mysteries: the remains of a fetus and several adults, including a woman who may have been killed by a blow on the head. The small band lay amid a scatter of shell beads and ivory pendants. These hunter-gatherers, named the Cro-Magnon people after the site, were of modern appearance and used a tool kit far more elaborate than that of the Neandertals. Modern methods date the Cro-Magnon from about 35,000 years ago, the Neandertals from about 100,000.

In 1879 a Spanish nobleman named Don Marcelino Sanz de Sautuola was digging at Altamira cave in northern Spain. His young daughter Maria, tagging along, wandered off into a low side-chamber. Suddenly her father heard her cry out "Bulls, bulls!" Grabbing a lantern, he crawled into the chamber and peered up at bison and other wild creatures painted in vivid reds, browns, and black on the ceiling. He was convinced that he had discovered Stone Age paintings, for the Altamira scenes resembled Stone Age engravings he had seen at a Paris exhibit the previous year. Other scholars expressed skepticism; some even accused him of commissioning a forgery. Not until the end of the century did the discovery of other cave paintings near Les Eyzies and in the Pyrénées prove him right.

More clues about prehistoric hunters came from kitchen middens—grass-covered mounds of seashells and stone tools—rising from ancient beach lines now above the modern level of the sea. Danish scientists dug into the Mejlgård midden in eastern Denmark and found ancient hearths and fossilized animal bones—the remains of an eating place. Zoologist Johann Japetus Steenstrup analyzed three-foot-wide cores cut from another midden. Various clues—the bones of wintering swans, stag antlers shed in the spring or autumn—indicated that people had probably lived there most of the year. The remains of a grouse species that feeds on pine tree buds suggested that evergreens once blanketed the area.

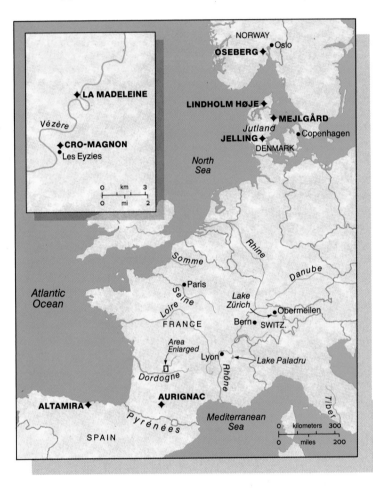

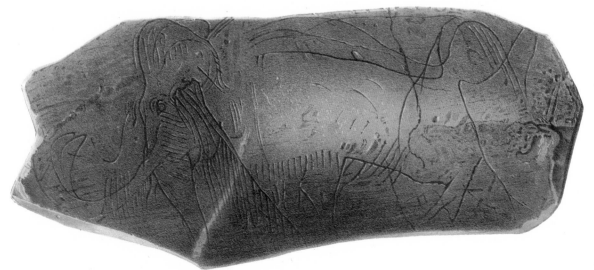

Bison, deer, and wild boar range over the Great Hall at Altamira (opposite), the cavern in northern Spain renowned for its prehistoric art. The lifelike paintings, discovered by a young girl in 1879, date back more than 12,000 years —the first such works to come to light in modern times.

In the 1860s Édouard Lartet dug in caves and rock-shelters in southwestern France (map). There he found proof of Stone Age artistic ability, including this mammoth carved on a piece of mammoth tusk (left).

John Lubbock, a young British banker, visited the Danish sites. He was hard at work on *Prehistoric Times,* one of the first textbooks on the subject. As Keller had done before, Lubbock compared prehistoric societies with living Stone Age peoples. He found similarities between the prehistoric Danes of the shell middens and the Fuegian Indians of South America, "who dwell on the coast, feed principally on shellfish, and have the dog as their only domestic animal."

Prehistoric Times, which appeared in 1865, was a bestseller. Lubbock used sites and artifacts to show how human societies slowly changed from hunter-gatherer cultures to elaborate civilizations. Employing the Three Age System, he delved back to the epoch of the primitive hand axes and the French rock-shelters—the time period called the Old Stone Age, or Paleolithic. Next came the New Stone Age, or Neolithic, characterized by polished stone tools but no metals. During this era the first Swiss lake villages were built and the Danish kitchen middens formed. The Bronze and Iron Ages that followed were much shorter than the Stone Age.

The technological stages of the Three Age System fit nicely with Victorian notions of human progress. The Victorians saw their industrial civilization as the pinnacle of human achievement. In an era of imperial expansion and ardent nationalism, it was easy to think in evolutionary terms and to see in prehistory an inevitable, ordered progress. "The whole analogy of nature," wrote Lubbock, "justified us in concluding that the pleasures of civilised man are greater than those of the savage."

The days of casual excavation were drawing to a close; the Swiss lake sites and the Danish middens had shown what good preservation conditions and careful excavation could yield. The time was ripe for new approaches to archaeological excavation. They came in the hands of a British military man preoccupied with firearms and technological progress.

Capt. Augustus Henry Lane Fox, a tall, moody man with a quick temper, spent much of his military career working with firearms. When he visited the Great Exhibition of 1851 in London, he was profoundly influenced by the symbolic message of material progress, of ever improving technology. He began to collect muskets and primitive weapons from all

Masterpiece of Stone Age art, a bison 12,000 to 15,000 years old curls within a stony recess at Altamira. Paleolithic artists took advantage of the cave's natural contours to add depth to many of their paintings— an attempt to portray with three-dimensional realism the animals they knew. Constant temperature and humidity preserved the vivid polychrome murals for thousands of years. Latter-day admirers, marveling at the ceiling's artistry, have dubbed Altamira the Sistine Chapel of the Ice Age.

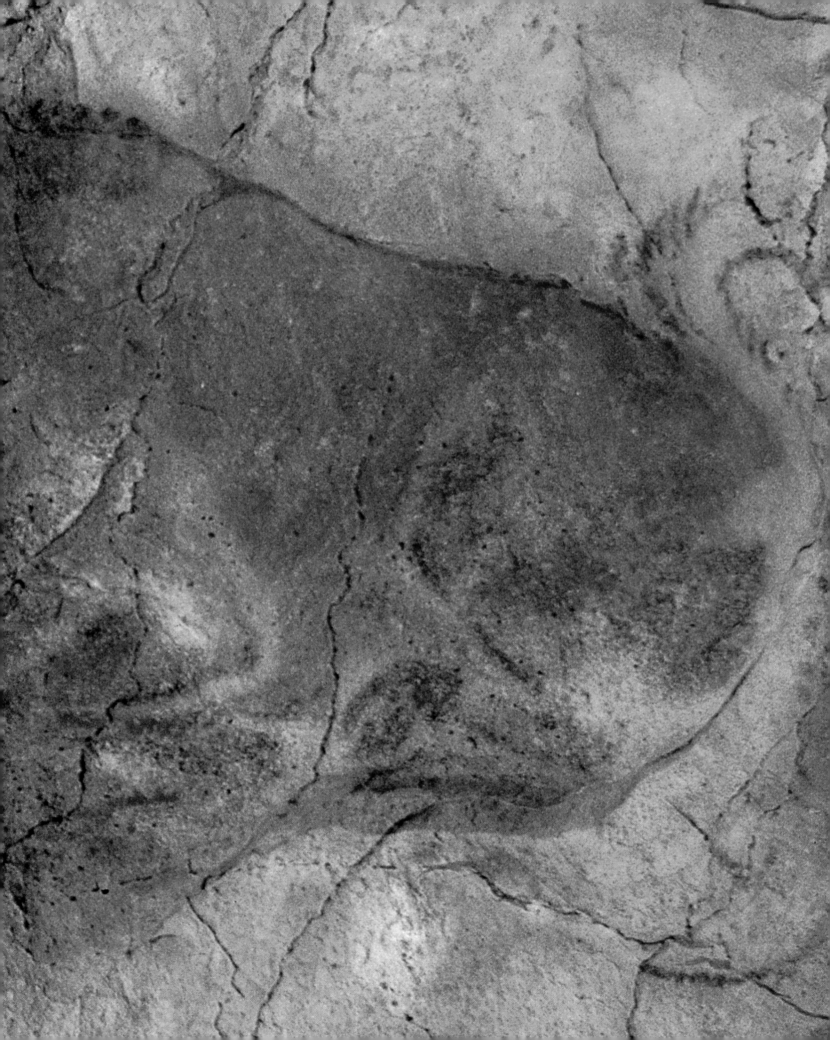

over the world, arranging his artifacts in series that illustrated the gradual development of each form—the material progress made by their designers and manufacturers.

In 1864 Fox surveyed prehistoric earthworks in Ireland and became interested in archaeology. Back in London he read in the *Times* that 20 cartloads of animal bones had been removed from the building site of a wool warehouse. He visited the site almost daily for two months and recovered Roman leatherwork, coins, metal objects, and the bones of deer, horse, ox, and other animals. His interest growing, he visited Canon William Greenwell's barrow excavations in Yorkshire in northern England.

Fox came back to London fired with enthusiasm for excavation and went on military half pay. He started digging at Cissbury hill fort, an Iron Age fortress in southeastern England. (These defensive enclosures encircled hilltops and protected settlements or livestock.) Greenwell joined him. As far as Fox was concerned, the main purpose of the dig was to find flint tools that he could fit into the artifact sequences in his growing collections. He dug 30 pits, noting later "the great number of flint nodules . . . mixed with finished and partly finished implements in great abundance, which had obviously been fabricated out of similar nodules." This indicated to Fox that the site had also been a Neolithic flint mine. But, he concluded, "I left it for others to discover the extent of the pits and the galleries branching from them."

Meanwhile Greenwell cleared another flint mine near Brandon in eastern England, a 39-foot shaft with the antler digging tools of the miners still lying in the fill. Greenwell lectured on the excavation, impressing Fox with his clearly presented evidence. From then on Fox's aims and excavation techniques changed radically.

Fox returned to Cissbury in 1875. Instead of searching for artifacts for his collections, he made excavation a quest for historical information. This came from objects small and large and even from the soils that formed the earthworks. He cut a cross-sectional trench through the fort's rampart and recorded not only the original ground level but also the turf, chalk, and rubble layers of the fortification. The rampart

yielded 25 potsherds—some red, some black. Fox realized that these must predate the building of the fort, so they could reveal the approximate date of construction.

Faithful to his new approach, Fox kept minutely detailed records of his Cissbury excavation, left a cross section of the rampart open for geological experts to study, and commissioned a model of the section for display in his collection. The model reflected his greatest strength as an excavator, perhaps acquired in his days of military surveying—a talent for thinking of a site in three dimensions.

Rising to the rank of lieutenant general in 1882, Fox accepted an appointment the next year to be inspector of ancient monuments. He had recently inherited the 27,700-acre Pitt Rivers estate in southern England, which lay partly within a great tract of medieval hunting country called Cranborne Chase. Much of Cranborne Chase had never been plowed, so any archaeological sites remained undisturbed. Here was the chance of a lifetime. The terms of inheritance stipulated that Fox adopt the family name of Pitt Rivers; he did so and immediately began a campaign of meticulous excavations.

Pitt Rivers organized everything with soldierly precision. Workers were supervised by a trained assistant and two subassistants—one a draftsman and illustrator, the other an expert at making models. The staff lived on a paternalistic estate with free meals and lodging. Though no one had formal qualifications, the general had created one of the first archaeological research teams in the world.

Pitt Rivers started by excavating barrows near the mansion he lived in, then moved on to Winkelbury Camp, an Iron Age hill fort. There he cross-sectioned ramparts and ditches as he had done at Cissbury in 1875. A big change came in 1884, when he turned from familiar earthworks to a completely different challenge: a Roman period site on Woodcutts Common—several acres of low banks, humps, and hollows. Pitt Rivers had his men clear off the surface soil, then dig out the irregularities in the white chalk subsoil and trace the outlines of pits, hearths, and ditches. This seems common sense today, but it was revolutionary in the 1880s.

Pitt Rivers' records abound in lavish detail. He compiled four quarto volumes that consisted mostly of annotated

King and commoner share the thrill of a dig on a mound in Denmark. The king: Frederick VII (seated), whose zeal for archaeology led him to take part in many excavations, including this 1861 dig at Jelling in southern Jutland. The commoner: Jens Jacob Worsaae (standing before the king), who was regarded by successors as "the first professional archaeologist." His work in peat bogs and burial mounds confirmed the theory of a Stone Age followed by Bronze and Iron Ages.

Muscle and shovel uncover Wor Barrow (left), a burial mound in southern England that yielded human skeletons from the Stone Age and Roman times. From a ditch (above) encircling the mound came Bronze Age pottery and more skeletons dating to the Roman era. In 1893-94 Wor Barrow's secrets were unearthed by retired Gen. Augustus Henry Pitt Rivers, "the father of British archaeology," whose military training and attention to detail established standards of thoroughness that still prevail.

illustrations and tables. He described Woodcutts Common as a Roman-British village occupied by farmers who owned some Roman tools, ornaments, and coins. His clerks listed even the most prosaic objects, such as undecorated potsherds and tiny bones. The general measured ancient horse bones, then had modern horses slaughtered to compare their measurements. The ancient horses, he found, were smaller—the size of a modern pony.

In 1893 Pitt Rivers excavated Wor Barrow, a Neolithic earthwork of a type often used for communal burial. His predecessors had simply cut into barrows and taken out skulls and pots. Pitt Rivers removed the entire mound, including 16 skeletons, leaving a line of earthen pillars down the middle to show the original layers. At one end of the mound he found a rectangular outline of trenches in the chalk containing the remains of wooden posts—evidently the uprights of a large building in which six of the corpses had been placed.

In a final investigative tour de force, Pitt Rivers left prehistoric ditches around the barrow open for four years after excavation, then returned and cut new sections through them to see how chalk ditches break down and fill after abandonment. Understanding how fast and in what sequence ditches fill with soil and debris can help excavators judge the relative age of their contents. Archaeologists today still follow the general's interpretations of ditch fillings.

Pitt Rivers had little patience with excavators who dug merely to enrich museums, however noble their motives. His original passion for collecting artifacts had turned into concern for digging for information, for excavating whole sites, and above all, for studying the daily lives of prehistoric people from commonplace clues. His systematic excavations would deeply influence future archaeologists.

Observing that science could be defined as "organized common sense," Pitt Rivers followed this principle throughout his own excavations. Not that he invented scientific excavation by himself. He added his notion of common sense, administrative organization, and a touch of insightful genius to the work of the archaeologists who preceded him.

Pitt Rivers pursued the seemingly trivial with such thoroughness that many people thought him eccentric. It was a long time before other excavators followed his example. But Pitt Rivers was unrepentant in his "eccentricity," just as he was in providing free Sunday concerts on his estate for visitors to the museum housing his collections. He believed that archaeology should be part of everyone's education. The public lacked a sense of history. "They must learn the links between the past and present," he wrote. In this, as in many other archaeological matters, the general was prophetic.

Stone ships set a course for Valhalla, paradise of Viking battle heroes, at a cemetery in Lindholm Høje, Denmark. Long buried in drifting sand, about 700 graves dating from A.D. 500 to 1000 were found in the 1950s—some beneath these stone markers. The Vikings also buried their dead in ships, such as the vessel (opposite, lower) excavated in 1904 at Oseberg, Norway. A wood carving of a massed fleet (opposite, upper) depicts later ships that copied the swift and graceful Viking models.

Greece, 1876: Heinrich and Sophia Schliemann unearth a noblewoman's riches at the ancient citadel of Mycenae.

TOMBS, TEXTS, AND TROPHIES

For weeks the German archaeologist and his young wife had been digging within the crumbled walls of a hilltop fortress in southern Greece. The year was 1876 and the Schliemanns, Heinrich and Sophia, were here in the ruins of ancient Mycenae to search for the graves of King Agamemnon and other legendary heroes of the Trojan War—warriors immortalized by Homer in the *Iliad*. For here, the poet had written, Agamemnon had been stabbed to death by his faithless queen and her lover.

The Schliemanns and their workmen had thus far turned up thousands of pottery fragments, the foundations of a double circle of stone slabs, and several "tombstones" decorated with armed charioteers. Schliemann was ecstatic. Here must lie the remains of Agamemnon—just as Homer had written. Schliemann ordered watch fires lit which, he later wrote, "carry back the mind to the watch kept for Agamemnon's return from Troy."

As Schliemann recounted, he and his wife, working on hands and knees, had picked away soil from a man's head "covered with a massive golden mask." The mask bore the features of a long-dead warrior, including his well-groomed beard. Another mask covered a face still partly fleshed under the gold. "Both eyes were perfectly visible, also the mouth, which . . . was wide open, and showed thirty-two beautiful teeth." Eager to record his discovery before it crumbled to dust, Schliemann summoned an artist to paint a portrait. A local druggist poured a mixture of gum arabic and alcohol over the remains in an attempt to preserve the body so that it could be moved to Athens.

Those were the early days of Mediterranean archaeology, when dreamers like Schliemann, armed with little more than a knowledge of the classics and a copy of Homer, looked for ancient civilizations. Schliemann's digging methods were clumsy and unsophisticated, but so were those of other excavators. Yet their discoveries sparked widespread, sometimes enthralling, interest in archaeology. Even while Schliemann and his crews tore into Mycenae with shovel and pick, a new breed of scholars painstakingly recorded the minutest details of Greek temples, studied the smallest objects as well as the most spectacular artifacts, and, for the first time, illustrated their reports with photographs.

105

The development of Mediterranean archaeology into a science began in 1799, with the discovery by French soldiers in Egypt of one of archaeology's greatest finds—the Rosetta Stone. Of all the Egyptian antiquities brought back to Europe, none stirred more interest and excitement than this enigmatic stone. Its polished face bore texts written in Greek, in a cursive form of hieroglyphic writing called demotic, and in traditional Egyptian hieroglyphs. By translating the easily read Greek, scholars eventually were able to crack the hieroglyphic code of the ancient Egyptians.

A key figure in this breakthrough was Jean-François Champollion, son of an impoverished French bookseller. Champollion was only 11 years old when a meeting with one of Napoléon's scientists imbued him with the desire to unlock the secrets of the Rosetta Stone. By age 17 he had learned a dozen languages, including Coptic, which was spoken by early Christians living in Egypt. In 1808 he achieved his first success, matching 15 of the Rosetta Stone's demotic signs with equivalent Coptic letters. But it would take Champollion 14 more years before he would master hieroglyphic writing. Thus did Champollion, in a remarkable display of scholarly dedication, elevate Egyptology from frustrating guesswork to a potential science.

Not until 1828 did Champollion, by now curator of the Louvre's Egyptian collection, travel to Egypt for the first time. As leader of a museum-sponsored expedition, he journeyed with 15 other young men from temple to temple, reading the inscriptions as no one had in 1,500 years. At Dandara, Champollion and his companions visited the temple under a full moon and wandered through the ruins in the silvery light, "a picture that made us drunk with admiration," as one member of the party recalled.

In 1821, seven years before Champollion's Egyptian journey, a British explorer named John Gardner Wilkinson had arrived in Egypt primarily to study tomb paintings and inscriptions. A loner, he camped on the desert and in tombs while copying hundreds of inscriptions and compiling the first reliable chronology of Egypt's rulers. Wilkinson spent twelve years in Egypt preparing his three-volume work, *The Manners and Customs of the Ancient Egyptians.* He wrote of

kings and battles and also of a cheerful, busy people who cultivated their fields, practiced skilled crafts, and thoroughly enjoyed life—a civilization surprisingly little changed by the passage of thousands of years.

The careful study of Egyptian antiquities begun by Champollion and Wilkinson continued with the work of a German scholar named Karl Richard Lepsius. In 1842 the king of Prussia sent Lepsius to the Nile to survey and record ancient monuments as well as to collect antiquities. Lepsius prepared for his mission with meticulous care, studying lithography, copper engraving, and hieroglyphic writing. When Lepsius returned home three years later with a mountain of notes and 15,000 artifacts and plaster casts, the king subsidized 17 lavish folio volumes of illustrations and text.

Despite the work of Champollion, Wilkinson, and Lepsius, the plundering of Egyptian treasures proceeded on all sides. British troops blasted their way into pyramids. A French adventurer stole the zodiac relief from the temple at Dandara. The relief, carved on a ceiling, represented celestial Egypt and a panoply of its gods and goddesses. The temple itself had been quarried to provide stone for a saltpeter factory.

Egyptian archaeology resembled a battleground in 1850, when a young Frenchman named Auguste Mariette arrived in Cairo. His mission: to collect ancient Coptic manuscripts for the Louvre. But the Coptic patriarch was hostile. His monasteries were closed to foreigners. Several years earlier some Englishmen had plied his monks with drink and had stolen an entire library of rare manuscripts. So Mariette decided to excavate instead.

With very little money, no excavating experience, and no permit, Mariette dug into the necropolis at Saqqâra, near Cairo. Guided only by guesswork and the ancient writings of the Greek geographer Strabo, Mariette and his crew in a few months uncovered several sphinxes and a temple mentioned by Strabo. Digging beneath the stone slabs of a ceremonial avenue, the workers unearthed a cache of bronze statues. Several months later they opened the tombs of the bull god Apis and found mummified bulls in 60-ton granite coffins. Although most of the animals had long been stripped

Spades flying, Egyptian workers clear the sands of two millennia from Saqqâra, a sacred city of the dead near Cairo (opposite). Statues draped in classical folds represent Homer, Plato, and other Greek philosophers and poets, and reflect Egypt's status as a Macedonian outpost in the third century B.C. Excavation of the site, begun by Frenchman Auguste Mariette in 1850, continues to this day—within view of Egypt's oldest stone edifice (left), the Step Pyramid built by King Djoser 4,600 years ago.

of their funerary treasures, a sepulcher from the reign of Pharaoh Ramesses II survived intact, the footprints of the burial party still visible in the sand around the sarcophagus.

By now all of Cairo buzzed with rumors of Mariette's discoveries. Because he had agreed to cede new finds to the Egyptian Museum, Mariette resorted to trickery. By day he loaded the amulets and statuettes found earlier. At night he set up crates close to a trapdoor leading to the bulls' tombs and packed the spectacular artifacts from the supposedly unopened tombs below. After the jewelry and gold had slipped off to the Louvre, Mariette blandly showed disappointed Egyptian officials the empty tombs.

Mariette's energy and ambition soon won him powerful friends, among them Ferdinand de Lesseps, builder of the Suez Canal. De Lesseps' intercession with Egypt's ruler, the pasha, won Mariette an appointment as the first curator of

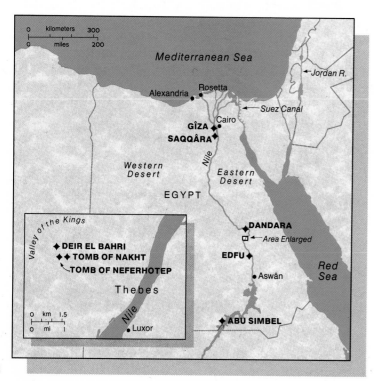

"Though half buried it is more beautiful than if laid open and reminds me of . . . the Forum of Rome." So wrote British artist David Roberts, who portrayed Egypt's Temple of Edfu a decade before Mariette began excavating the site in 1850. One of Egypt's best preserved temples, Edfu was completed in 57 B.C. by Cleopatra's father to honor Horus, the falcon-headed god of the sky. Edfu and other major sites (map) have proved a fertile ground for scholars since the days of Mariette.

the Egyptian Museum, then a dusty, vermin-filled old mosque. The year was 1858, and it marked the beginning of excavations on behalf of the Egyptian government. Mariette set out on a massive sand-shoveling operation, at one point dragooning all the men in several rural villages to excavate sites from Cairo to Aswân simultaneously.

He worked fast. His crews opened tombs with dynamite and battering rams; his overseers urged the pickmen on with whips. Only artifacts mattered, not careful observation and recording. Mariette's workers emptied more than 200 tombs near Cairo, cleared the mortuary temple of Queen Hatshepsut at Thebes, and peremptorily evicted villagers from the roof of the buried temple at Edfu so he could clear the ruin.

Though Mariette's methods were ruthless, his opponents—corrupt officials and unscrupulous dealers—were even more so. One day Mariette learned that the golden sarcophagus and jewelry of Queen Ahhotpe had been found intact at Thebes. The local governor, seeking to ingratiate himself with the pasha, seized the jewels and secretly sent them downriver as a political gift. Incensed, Mariette summoned his steamer and intercepted the governor's craft. Boarding the vessel, Mariette demanded the jewels. When the crew balked, a heated argument ensued. Fists flew. One man nearly toppled over the side, and finally, at gunpoint, the governor's henchmen relinquished the hoard. So pleased was the pasha with the treasure—and Mariette's escapade—that he provided funds for a new museum at Bulâq, in Cairo, to house the queen's possessions.

But the dedicated Frenchman's finest hour came in Paris in 1867, when he set up a display of Egyptian antiquities at the International Exhibition. Queen Ahhotpe's jewelry excited the cupidity of the empress Eugénie, who intimated to the pasha that she would be pleased to receive them as a gift. "There is one more powerful than I at Bulâq," replied the pasha. "You should apply to him." Not even the displeasure of a powerful empress could sway Mariette. The jewelry collection returned to Egypt intact.

Mariette worked tirelessly for 30 years, excavating 37 sites during his career. His museum protected antiquities and kept them in Egypt, slowing the rape of the Nile. When he died of diabetes in 1881, a grieving Egypt buried the man to whom it owed so much at the door of his museum.

Mariette's energy and industry, incredible as it was, paled beside the accomplishments of his successor at the museum, Gaston Maspero, another Frenchman. The author of more than 1,200 articles about ancient Egypt, Maspero brought a new level of scholarship to Egyptology. He set up an extensive network of antiquities inspectors to regulate foreign excavations in Egypt. These agents alerted him to illegal activities, especially in Thebes, which was then a hotbed of tomb robbing, forgery, and intrigue.

Maspero long had heard tales of royal papyri and funerary statuettes turning up in private collections—treasures bearing the names of kings and queens from tombs unknown. Suspecting that Theban antiquities dealers were involved, Maspero sent an agent to Luxor, posing as a wealthy tourist. The agent soon picked up the trail of a family who had long been involved in smuggling illicit antiquities into Thebes, often concealing the loot in bundles of clothing or baskets of vegetables. Two of the brothers were arrested, but neither would divulge the source of the valuables—even when imprisoned and beaten with palm rods.

Three months later one of the brothers recanted. He confessed to smuggling and agreed to lead Maspero's German assistant, Émile Brugsch, to the source of the booty, a crevice in the cliffs across the Nile from Luxor. Apprehensive about entrusting his life to a known tomb robber, Brugsch

111

The terraced temple of Egypt's Queen Hatshepsut lends grace to the russet cliffs of Deir el Bahri (opposite), a cluster of tombs and temples at Thebes. The queen reigned about 3,400 years ago, a prosperous time when Egyptian fleets traded far and wide. Mariette first dug here in 1858, but so haphazardly that it took later archaeologists years to sort out the clues he left heaped in piles of rubble.

Gaston Maspero, Mariette's successor as the director of Egyptian antiquities, here reclines at the mouth of a passageway that in 1881 led to a fabulous discovery—some 40 royal mummies, including the flower-strewn remains of Amunhotep I (upper). The warrior-king helped strengthen Egypt's rule in the Near East and Africa around 1500 B.C.

armed himself with a rifle before descending into the cleft. Fear gave way to awe as the shaft opened into a 200-foot-long tunnel. Pushing a candle ahead as he crawled down the passage, Brugsch barely had room to squeeze past coffins or to avoid crushing the astonishing array of funerary pieces. Like the contents of some ancient attic, alabaster jars, bronze libation vessels, boxes of statuettes, and a funerary tent had been scattered along the tunnel by the burial party.

As Brugsch inched forward, the thin yellow light from his candle fell on coffins and mummies, revealing the names of Egypt's greatest pharaohs and their consorts—Ramesses II, Seti I, Ahmose the Liberator, Thutmosis III. The discovery explained why so many of the royal tombs in the Valley of the Kings nearby were empty. Ancient priests, fearful of rapacious grave robbers, had hidden more than 40 royal mummies in this remote, nearly inaccessible crevice. Here, for 3,000 years, they had escaped detection.

Brugsch immediately conscripted 300 laborers to remove the mummies and their trappings to a government steamer. As the loaded vessel pulled away several days later, the villagers wailed and fired rifles, leaving Brugsch to wonder whether they were saluting their departing pharaohs or

113

Vignettes from life accompany the dead at Thebes. In the tomb of Nakht (left), a royal scribe who died around 1400 B.C., a mural depicts peasants as they winnow a harvest of grain.

At the nearby sepulcher of Neferhotep, a priest of the god Amun, mourners escort the deceased across the Sacred Lake of the Dead (above). John Gardner Wilkinson copied the scene in the early 1800s. The Englishman's drawings provide the only record of many tomb paintings since damaged by time and treasure hunters.

mourning the loss of a very convenient source of income.

Maspero and his colleagues eventually unwrapped some of the mummies and gazed on monarchs whom they had never expected to know as anything more than names. Seti was especially well preserved. Maspero noted that "a calm and gentle smile still played over his mouth."

The destruction in Egypt continued, much of it at the hands of European museum officials. Wallis Budge of the British Museum boasted of outwitting local officials and rival collectors by smuggling out a shipment of nearly 800 skulls in boxes labeled "bone manure." On one occasion, to foil police, tomb robbers were hired to tunnel from Budge's hotel to a dealer's house next door so that Budge could spirit away ancient papyri he had hidden there—a deed for which British Museum trustees commended him for his "energy." He justified his activities by arguing that if one archaeologist

would not buy, then another would. Besides, Budge wrote, "once a mummy has passed into the care of . . . the British Museum, it has a far better chance of being preserved there than it could possibly have in any tomb."

By the 1870s Egyptomania was sweeping Europe. Novels about the pharaohs sold by the thousands; schoolchildren learned about hieroglyphic writing. A British surgeon paid the then colossal sum of 10,000 pounds sterling to ship an obelisk known as Cleopatra's Needle to London.

Thomas Cook and other pioneer travel agencies turned Egypt into a fashionable tourist attraction. One such traveler, popular British novelist Amelia Edwards, arrived in Cairo in November 1873 and rented a sailing boat with five other gentlefolk. She had come to the Nile to be educated and entertained; she left it shocked by the destruction and blatant tomb robbing she witnessed at every turn. Thebes was thick

THE ILLUSTRATED
LONDON NEWS.

No. 1928.—VOL. LXXI.   SATURDAY, OCTOBER 27, 1877.   WITH TWO SUPPLEMENTS | SIXPENCE

Trophies of conquest since Roman times, ancient Egypt's granite obelisks honored the sun gods—and captured the imagination of the Victorian world. Europeans dubbed these two obelisks (opposite) Cleopatra's Needles, though both were erected some 1,500 years before she ruled Egypt around 50 B.C. The toppled column, packed into an iron cylinder (above), reached England in 1878 after a harrowing sea voyage (inset). Its twin today stands in New York's Central Park.

with tourists, haunted everywhere they went by antiquities dealers eager to peddle their ill-gotten or fraudulent wares. These "grave men in long black robes and ample turbans" would linger patiently nearby for days. Everyone bought something, often skillful forgeries. Dealers aged many of their small fakes by passing them through the digestive tracts of turkeys until, as Edwards wrote, they acquired "a degree of venerableness that is really charming."

Most tourists left Egypt and shrugged. Not Amelia Edwards. She embarked on a whirlwind of writing and lecturing about the need to preserve Egypt's past. The narrative born of her trip, *A Thousand Miles up the Nile,* captivated armchair adventurers. She castigated collectors, tomb robbers, the quarriers of monuments, and careless excavators. So strongly did she feel about ancient Egypt that she gave up writing novels altogether and lobbied for serious excavations. Her efforts bore fruit in 1882, when a group of scholars formed the Egypt Exploration Fund to sponsor expeditions in Egypt. The fund became one of the first associations to focus on research and publication, not on the acquisition of artifacts for museums and private collections.

Meanwhile interest in the Holy Land had been growing, touched off some 40 years earlier by the publication of *Biblical Researches in Palestine, Mount Sinai, and Arabia Petraea.* The American authors, theologian Edward Robinson and missionary Eli Smith, had clothed this obscure province of the Turkish Empire with its ancient landscape of biblical sites. The book enjoyed success throughout the Christian world. "Palestine is no more of this work-day world," wrote Mark Twain. "It is sacred to poetry and tradition—it is dream-land." He and thousands of other pilgrims came to see for themselves the birthplace of Christianity. Biblical archaeology was born among these travelers, many of whom suspected some of the sites shown them were fraudulent.

The French arrived in the Holy Land in 1850, in the person of Félicien de Saulcy, described by a contemporary as a "strange combination of a gunnery officer and a scholar." De Saulcy, as chaperon for a group of wayward aristocratic youths, traveled through Palestine identifying biblical sites, then dug into a ruin outside Jerusalem's city walls known as the Tomb of the Kings. Here he found a broken sarcophagus, which he proclaimed to be the coffin of David, slayer of Goliath and King of the Jews. Though his identification later proved erroneous, de Saulcy's discovery did whet French interest in Holy Land exploration.

France's influence in Jerusalem expanded over the years so that, when a civil war broke out in neighboring Lebanon in 1860, French troops were dispatched to quell the hostilities. An archaeological mission, supervised by theologian Ernest Renan, accompanied the invading force. Hundreds of French soldiers dug into Byblos, Tyre, and Sidon, ancient cities founded by the Phoenicians, seafaring traders of the eastern Mediterranean. Though unscientific, these excavations produced the first archaeological evidence of King David's powerful neighbors in the ninth century B.C.

In the autumn of 1864 a small British team of Royal Engineers, under Capt. Charles Wilson, arrived in Jerusalem to

"Rameses' appetite for coffee was prodigious. He consumed I know not how many gallons a day," wrote British novelist Amelia Edwards of her effort to "face-lift" the pharaoh's statue at Abu Simbel (opposite). Traveling along the Nile on a houseboat in the winter of 1873-74, Edwards and her comrades sought to eradicate "ghastly splotches" marring the statue—traces left by an earlier expedition that had made a plaster cast of the head for the British Museum. Appalled at the desecration, the novelist ordered her crew to erect a scaffold and swab the statue's face with strong coffee, restoring its natural sandstone complexion. The task took three afternoons.

Edwards's book, A Thousand Miles up the Nile, appeared three years later and won instant acclaim. It helped fuel a tourist boom that brought thousands of European and American visitors scrambling to view Egyptian monuments, including the daunting slopes of the Great Pyramid of Khufu at Gîza (above).

survey its topography and hydrology. Wilson's work took him mostly below ground, into the honeycomb of cisterns and channels that lay beneath the modern city. Here his men discovered a wealth of archaeological evidence, including a Roman monumental arch that had formed an entrance to Herod's Temple. The temple, rebuilt by King Herod in the first century B.C. on the ruins of an earlier temple, had been demolished by the Romans in A.D. 70. Part of its wall survived and eventually became the Western, or Wailing Wall, one of Judaism's most hallowed sites.

Wilson's discoveries astounded and delighted his countrymen. In 1865 a festive public meeting in London launched the Palestine Exploration Fund, with Queen Victoria serving as official patron. Two years later the fund sent Lt. Charles Warren and another detachment of Royal Engineers to Jerusalem to excavate beneath the Haram esh Sharif, a walled compound containing some of Islam's most sacred shrines. The troops smashed through a blocked passageway alongside the Haram walls with sledgehammers. The commotion so disturbed and outraged worshipers in the mosque above that they showered the diggers with stones. The governor promptly forbade Warren to excavate on public land or closer than 40 feet to the Haram.

Warren and his men were stymied only momentarily. They leased private lots well away from the Haram, sank vertical shafts to bedrock, and tunneled toward the ancient shrine. Warren found that the 80-foot-high walls of the Haram extended 100 feet below the surface. In four months the Royal Engineers sank more than 27 shafts and traced the northern and southern limits of the old city. With the Warren excavations—the first scientific study of the Holy Land— biblical archaeology came of age.

Back in England, scholars labored for years over the Mesopotamian tablets brought back from Nineveh. One scholar, George Smith, closeted himself with the tablets in the British Museum—sorting the fragments, piecing them together, and translating the crabbed texts. In 1872, while working through a pile of tablets that recorded the mythology of ancient Babylon, Smith came across "half of a curious tablet which had evidently contained originally six columns." He casually scanned the columns. Suddenly his interest quickened. The third column referred to a ship grounded on a mountain and to a man named Atrahasis who dispatched a dove to reconnoiter the land. To the astonishment of Smith's colleagues, he suddenly bolted to his feet and began to tear off his clothes as he rushed around the room. Once calmed, Smith sifted through the rest of the pile and found 11 other fragments of the same epic. "I saw at

Herodium, a fortified palace (above) built by King Herod in the first century B.C., guarded ancient Judaea's frontier near Jerusalem—and sheltered Jews rebelling against Roman rule. French traveler Félicien de Saulcy visited the ruins in 1863; modern excavations have revealed the remains of gardens, royal apartments, and a lavish, Roman-style bath.

Tunneling into the rubble of Jerusalem's past (opposite), Lt. Charles Warren of Britain's Royal Engineers helped plot the city's old boundaries in 1867.

once that I had here discovered a portion at least of the Chaldean account of the Deluge," he wrote.

Later that year a dignified—and fully dressed—George Smith lectured about the tablets to the newly formed Society of Biblical Archaeology. The prime minister attended the meeting; the academic and theological establishment turned out. Smith revealed to his enthralled audience the Chaldean version of the Deluge myth, which closely resembled the biblical story of the Flood. Forewarned of a deluge, the prophet Atrahasis loaded a huge boat with his family and "the beasts of the field, the wild creatures of the field, all the craftsmen. . . ." Smith eloquently recounted how the rains fell and then stopped. At length the vessel came to rest on a mountain, and another bird, this time a raven, signaled that the countryside was once again safe for habitation. Unfortunately there remained a tantalizing gap in Smith's version—a

missing fragment at the beginning of the broken clay tablet.

Smith's revelations revived popular interest in Mesopotamia, the dusty lands between the Tigris and Euphrates Rivers. Enthusiastic crowds flocked to see the tablets at the British Museum. Sensing a scoop, the *Daily Telegraph* offered the museum a thousand guineas to finance a new excavation at Nineveh to find the missing lines.

Only six weeks after his lecture, Smith, who had never traveled beyond Europe or excavated a site, was en route to Mesopotamia. And, incredible as it may seem, he did find the missing fragment—within a week after starting work. The *Daily Telegraph* had its scoop. The tablets, now in the British Museum, still bear the label DT for *Daily Telegraph*.

Whatever his limitations as an excavator, Smith now found himself thrust into the limelight as the world's foremost cuneiform translator and the idol of biblical scholars.

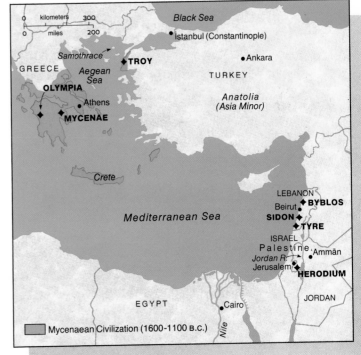

Workmen clear ancient city walls (opposite) during one of Heinrich Schliemann's expeditions to uncover Troy in the late 19th century. Led to classical sites by the writings of Homer, the German merchant-turned-archaeologist amazed the world with his fabulous discoveries in Turkey and Greece. His dig here on a hill called Hissarlik—a Turkish word meaning "fortress"—lasted almost 11 years and established Schliemann as the father of Mediterranean archaeology.

His young wife Sophia, bedecked at left with "Priam's Treasure," often accompanied her husband and became his ablest assistant. Together the Schliemanns recovered golden rings, necklaces, diadems, buttons—nearly 9,000 objects. Schliemann's reckless digging led to error and controversy; the real Troy was identified later at a different level. But his work stirred scholarly interest that subsequently revealed the full reach of the Mycenaeans, warlords of the Aegean (map).

He returned twice to Mesopotamia and recovered more than 3,000 tablets from Nineveh. During his second visit he hired more and more diggers until a small army of nearly 600 men labored on the honeycombed mound. "The mound presented an interesting appearance of bustle and activity," wrote Smith in an understated description of what so much 19th-century archaeology must have been like.

On his way home to England in 1876, Smith contracted dysentery. Even as he lay dying, he worried about his precious cuneiform tablets: In his spare boots he had packed away 35 of them, each about the size of a deck of cards.

At the time of Smith's death, public interest in ancient Greece reached new heights. In the past, wealthy European collectors and diplomats had been content to sketch, collect, and occasionally dig a few trenches to recover temple statuary or fine bronzes. Interested mainly in art and architecture,

Overleaf: Battered by the ages, Mycenae's walls honeycomb a hill situated, as Homer wrote, "in a nook of Argos"—the fertile Greek plain where the city rose to power some 3,000 years ago. It flourished four centuries as a center for far-ranging warrior-merchants, then fell mysteriously into decline. By Homer's time only fading memories of its glories remained. The Schliemanns' 1876 discovery of treasure-laden graves (circular pit at right) kindled popular interest in archaeology.

classical scholars dismissed ancient Greek history as mere myth. Even the most eminent judged as fiction Homer's *Iliad* and *Odyssey*, two epic poems written during the eighth or ninth century B.C. It would take a German entrepreneur-turned-archaeologist to make the point that ancient writings could be a powerful aid in the study of archaeology.

Heinrich Schliemann has been painted, mostly by himself, as a heroic archaeologist, by detractors as an impudent charlatan. This hard-driving, ambitious man excelled at self-aggrandizement and mythmaking. The public loved him. The emperor of Brazil visited his excavations; headlines around the world heralded his discoveries. Modern research condemns Schliemann as a consummate liar with a gift for self-delusion, but unquestionably his archaeological accomplishments were awesome: The problem with Schliemann lies in separating fact from fiction.

A millionaire at the age of 41, Schliemann retired from business as a wholesale merchant and in time turned his considerable energies to archaeology. Though he claimed he had been obsessed since childhood by Homer's epics, Schliemann became interested in the *Iliad* and *Odyssey* only during an 1868 journey to Greece and Asia Minor. There he sought to trace the origins of Homer's stirring tales of the ten-year war between the kingdoms of Mycenae and Troy, brought on by the abduction of the lovely Queen Helen.

Following clues in the *Iliad,* Schliemann traveled to northwestern Turkey. He rode bareback in his business suit across the Trojan plain, examining two mounds as likely sites for ancient Troy: Bunarbashi and Hissarlik. He adopted the archaeological technique favored in Germany—sinking trial trenches down to bedrock. His 1868 soundings at Hissarlik yielded buried stone walls and pottery, which confirmed his belief that this rectangular-topped mound was the more promising site. But to expose its lower levels, he would have to excavate on a large scale.

The following year Schliemann married a 17-year-old Greek girl named Sophia Engastromenos. She was, he said, lovelier than the legendary Helen of Troy. Sophia became his devoted assistant and companion through many years of

124

Seated on boulders strewn before Mycenae's legendary Lion Gate (opposite), Heinrich and Sophia Schliemann savor a respite after working within the city's walls. Other diggers had searched for graves outside the gate, but Schliemann, heeding ancient writings, looked within. A lithograph (right) portrays the half-buried portal before the Schliemanns began their dig in 1876.

The "Treasury of Atreus" (above), a beehive-shaped tomb cleared by the Schliemanns, had long since been looted.

hectic excavation. In the autumn of 1871 the Schliemanns began a full-scale assault on Hissarlik.

Schliemann attacked archaeological problems with single-minded intensity. Convinced that Troy lay at the base of Hissarlik, he had his laborers quarry 33 feet into the mound, ripping out stone walls, destroying house foundations, and shoveling out thousands of potsherds.

When the temperature dropped below freezing, the Schliemanns kept warm in the trenches by day but shivered in their wooden house at night. Pots of water near the fire froze solid. "We had nothing to keep us warm except our enthusiasm for the great task of discovering Troy," Schliemann recalled. Nothing stood in the way—not poor food, bedbugs, or the ever present threat of malaria.

The following year Schliemann returned to the site with an arsenal of digging tools and set to work on an even grander scale. His motto was speed. For two busy seasons an army of more than a hundred workmen sliced into Hissarlik. Down they dug through the centuries, opening a trench more than 230 feet wide and 45 feet deep and hauling 325,000 cubic yards of earth from the mound.

Though critics condemned Schliemann's bulldozer-like methods, he produced results. Unlike many of his peers, Schliemann kept and recorded some of his smaller finds, not just the spectacular pieces. His crews cut through seven ancient cities superimposed one upon the other. The second city from the bottom showed signs of fire and destruction. Schliemann immediately concluded that this must be the Troy that the Greeks had destroyed.

When Schliemann announced the discovery of a golden treasure at the end of the 1873 season, popular acclaim swelled to a crescendo. As he told it, his men were digging 28 feet below the surface when he spotted gold glittering next to a wall. Summoning Sophia, he told her to dismiss the workers. Oblivious to the huge stone blocks teetering above him, Schliemann cut into the earth with a large knife and uncovered the treasure. Sophia quickly bundled it into a red shawl. Her relatives helped smuggle the gold pendants, earrings, bracelets, and rings out of Turkey to Athens—more than 8,700 pieces in all. Schliemann insisted he had found

126

"I do not for a moment hesitate to proclaim that I have found here the sepulchres which . . . tradition attributes . . . to the 'king of men' Agamemnon." So exulted Schliemann of the rubble-choked area (right) that would yield the treasure-filled tombs of Mycenae. Here he and his wife survey the circle of stone slabs where Schliemann "began the great work" of excavation with a crew of 63 laborers—a scene far different from the partly reconstructed site as it looks today (opposite).

the treasure that had once belonged to Priam, King of Troy.

The Turkish government, infuriated by Schliemann's deception, hauled him into court and fined him 10,000 francs for smuggling. Afraid that he might be denied a permit to resume work at Troy, Schliemann donated a sum five times larger than his fine to the Turkish Imperial Museum. Though the Turks finally accepted the offer, his future relations with Constantinople were never easy.

The British were enthusiastic about Schliemann's discoveries, but his German countrymen castigated him for being unscientific. A scrutiny of his notebooks and voluminous correspondence later revealed that Sophia was not even at Troy at the time of the discovery. She had been vacationing in Athens. Almost certainly Schliemann had assembled his treasure from isolated gold pieces found over many months and then had them smuggled from Turkey.

From Berlin to San Francisco the public waited eagerly for news of Schliemann's latest revelation. It came in 1876 from Mycenae in southern Greece, the legendary burial place of King Agamemnon, leader of the Greek armies at Troy. Mycenae had been a familiar landmark for centuries: a ruined, stone-walled city with the famous Lion Gate guarding its entrance. Nearby stood several beehive-shaped "treasuries," actually empty communal tombs. Most 19th-century scholars believed Mycenae's royal tombs lay outside the city walls. Schliemann disagreed. Ancient chroniclers had written that the royal burials lay inside the citadel, and if the ancients thought so, Schliemann reasoned, it must be true.

While the experts shook their heads, Schliemann started digging at his usual furious pace in August 1876. More than 125 men tore soil from the interior of the citadel and hauled it away in carts. Soon they uncovered a double circle of stone slabs set on edge. Quoting the Greek geographer Pausanias, who described a stone circle where the elders met and heroes were buried, Schliemann announced that he had found the sepulchers of Agamemnon and his father, Atreus—even before a single burial had been discovered.

Four months later Schliemann located the first of fifteen or so bodies entombed in five graves. The skeletons were covered with jewels, golden death masks, delicate crowns, 127

engraved ornaments and cups, inlaid weapons—one of the greatest archaeological treasures unearthed to that time. In the flush of discovering the graves with the golden masks, Schliemann telegraphed the king of Greece: "I have gazed on the face of Agamemnon!" Schliemann believed he had found the Homeric king, but archaeologists now date these priceless relics to three or four centuries before the Trojan War, which raged between 1193 and 1184 B.C. The masked bodies defy identification to this day.

Schliemann's astounding discoveries thrust archaeology into the public consciousness on a scale unprecedented. Newspapers ran frequent accounts of his exploits in the field. Troy and Mycenae were on everyone's lips.

While Schliemann was digging at Troy, a quiet revolution in excavation methods had begun among other German archaeologists: In 1873 Alexander Conze, accompanied by two architects and a photographer, started work at Samothrace. The cult center on this rugged Aegean island had attracted worshipers from throughout ancient Greece. From its rocky heights, according to Homer, the sea god Poseidon watched the progress of the Trojan War.

Conze was a systematic and careful worker, more interested in information than in spectacular artifacts. Although unsophisticated by modern standards, his excavations were far more meticulous than those of his predecessors. His architects surveyed the sanctuary's temples and sacrificial pits, plotted a long colonnade, and recovered much valuable information about Greek architecture. The lavish Samothrace report—the first archaeological publication illustrated with photographs—contained architects' reconstructions so detailed that individual stone blocks could be fitted into the overall plans. A greater contrast with Schliemann's

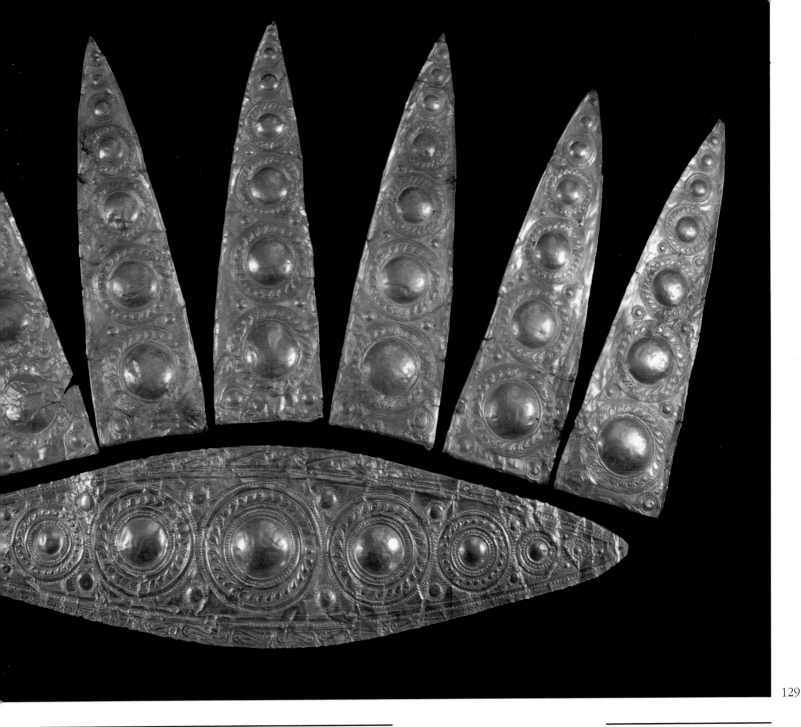

ham-handed excavations would be difficult to envision.

Conze's example was not lost on the German Archaeological Institute, which trained young scholars in classical archaeology as well as in team fieldwork that coordinated the talents of architects, draftsmen, and archaeologists at major sites. The institute began work in 1875 at Olympia, the Greek site of the first Olympic Games. The German government renounced all claims to any finds, except duplicates, and built a museum at Olympia to display the antiquities. The excavations lasted six winters and cost the Germans 600,000 marks, a princely sum at the time. Emperor Wilhelm II personally bore the cost of the last season.

The Olympia excavations set new standards of careful dissection, record keeping, and reconstruction. Classical scholar Ernst Curtius and a team of architects laid bare the sacred precinct and three temples. The diggers uncovered

"I have gazed on the face of Agamemnon!" proclaimed Schliemann when he and his wife opened the fifth grave at Mycenae. Its treasures included this lifelike burial mask with neatly trimmed beard. But Schliemann was mistaken. Some scholars now date the mask to the 16th century B.C.—300 years before the reign of the legendary king Agamemnon. Even so, Schliemann had cause to rejoice. Mycenae's tombs held amazing riches—jewelry, cups, vases, and the diadem above.

the vaulted entrance to the great stadium, carefully noting the position of each artifact and displaced block. Everything was drawn, photographed, and published. Curtius found evidence of Olympia's earliest days, when the ancient Greeks had built their temples of wood and sun-dried bricks. He unearthed votive statues that traced Greek art back to its humble origins. A generation of classical archaeologists learned their skills under the master Curtius.

The lessons of Olympia rubbed off on the flamboyant Schliemann, by now an elder statesman of archaeology. After he returned to Troy, he recruited a scientist trained at Olympia. When archaeologist-architect Wilhelm Dörpfeld came to Troy from Greece in 1882, he introduced the refined methods used at Olympia. His training enabled him to dissect and record the contents of the mound in meticulous detail. Dörpfeld identified Schliemann's sixth city, not the second, as the Troy of Homer's epic verses. But Schliemann had discovered the site of ancient Troy and unearthed the glorious Mycenaean civilization of Bronze Age Greece.

Taken ill while visiting Italy in 1890, Schliemann the tycoon cut so shabby a figure as he lay speechless in a Naples police station near the scene of his collapse that reluctant onlookers debated who would pay to summon a doctor. He died the next day. Diplomats, scholars, and the king of Greece attended the funeral of one of the last of the great archaeological adventurers. More than any of his contemporaries, he had breathed life into the past, just as Homer had.

Schliemann's death marked the end of an era in archaeology. He had conducted an intensely personal crusade, with the writings of Homer in one hand and a pick in the other. A new generation of scholars stood ready to take over where he and other adventurers had left off.

Poised on the threshold of Zeus's temple at Olympia in Greece, a German field team (above) strikes imagined statuary poses in a carefree moment. Led by historian Ernst Curtius, scholars, scientists, and architects in 1875 pooled their talents on a six-year project to uncover the site of the world's first Olympic Games, begun in 776 B.C. Many temple statues were never found, but another prize was—the figures of the Greek god Hermes and baby Dionysus (right), perhaps sculptured by Praxiteles.

131

Height 7′ 1″

Peru, 1911: An artist's imagination captures the thrill of discovery as Hiram Bingham beholds Machu Picchu.

SEEKING THE FIRST AMERICANS

C limbing a precipitous path high in the Andes, American explorer Hiram Bingham burst upon "a maze of beautiful granite houses!... covered with trees and moss and the growth of centuries." He could see "walls of white granite . . . carefully cut and exquisitely fitted together." Describing the scene, Bingham exulted in his discovery of a lost city of the Incas.

But discovery is a matter of viewpoint. Machu Picchu was not lost—only deserted. And the Americas were not a new world discovered by Christopher Columbus in 1492, as posterity claimed. Columbus himself did not think so. To his dying day he believed he had reached islands on the fringe of India, so he named the inhabitants—naked people with "very handsome bodies and very good faces"—Indians.

Most adventurers and explorers who followed Columbus sought gold and showed little interest in the local people, whom the Europeans called lazy, treacherous savages. Then, in 1519, Spanish conquistadores revealed the dazzling world of the Aztecs of central Mexico. A soldier, Bernal Díaz del Castillo, recalled the day he first sighted the Aztec capital of Tenochtitlán, built on an island at the present site of Mexico City: "We were amazed . . . on account of the great tower . . . and buildings rising from the water. . . . And some of our soldiers even asked whether the things that we saw were not a dream?" The astonished Spaniards wandered through the resplendent Indian metropolis and a market in neighboring Tlatelolco that sold everything from fruit to slaves.

Above all the Spaniards wanted gold. "As if they were monkeys they seized upon the gold," reported Friar Bernardino de Sahagún from accounts of an Aztec who survived the conquest. "It was as if their hearts were satisfied, brightened, calmed. For in truth they thirsted mightily for gold; they stuffed themselves with it; they starved for it; they lusted for it like pigs." Two years later, Aztec civilization collapsed under the Spanish attack. Within a few generations most of the gold had been melted down for Europe's royal treasuries.

A handful of Catholic missionaries such as Sahagún delved into Indian history and culture. After arriving in Mexico in 1529, Sahagún learned Nahuatl, the Aztec language. He and other friars gathered teams of Indians for interviews at major missions—chiefly older Aztecs who remembered the

133

days before the conquest. The Indians trusted Sahagún, so, he wrote, "they gave me all the matters we discussed in pictures, for that was the writing they employed in ancient times." Painting by painting, they took him back to the world of their ancestors. The Aztecs, he learned, had settled in the Valley of Mexico a few centuries earlier, then conquered their neighbors. In less than 200 years their capital grew from a hamlet to a city of about 200,000 people. Sahagún described his findings in 12 books. Published in the 19th century, they rank today as an invaluable record of Aztec customs.

Another Spanish missionary, Diego de Landa, admired the buildings of the ancient Maya on Mexico's Yucatán Peninsula. For some 650 years the Maya had ruled the jungle lowlands of Yucatán and the volcanic highlands that swept southward through Guatemala into western Honduras and El Salvador. During this Classic period their civilization flourished around urban centers boasting spacious ceremonial plazas, towering pyramids, and busy markets. The Maya were traders, artisans, and farmers, governed in small city-states by dynasties of rulers competing with each other for power and prestige. Their civilization in the southern lowlands collapsed around A.D. 900.

But the Maya left spectacular monuments. From the scrubby thorn forest rose ornate temples and lofty pyramids—"all of stone very well hewn, although there is no metal in this country with which they could have been worked," wrote Friar Landa in 1566. Landa tortured and imprisoned Indians and was eventually recalled to Spain for trial. As a final gesture before his departure, he destroyed thousands of "idols" and burned dozens of hieroglyphic books because "they contained nothing in which there were not to be seen superstition and lies of the devil." Centuries of Maya records may have perished in the blaze.

Over the next three centuries, people speculated about the origins of the Indians who inhabited the Americas: Were they descended from Noah? Survivors of the legendary sunken continent of Atlantis? Descendants of the Ten Lost Tribes of Israel—exiled, according to the Bible, after their defeat by the Assyrians in the eighth century B.C.? And how had they reached the New World?

134

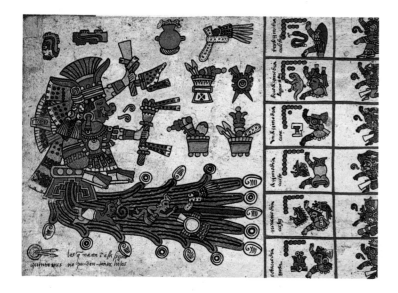

Pieces of a puzzle—paintings, earthen mounds, and objects found in tombs—confront archaeologists reconstructing Indian cultures of the New World. The 18th-century founders of Marietta, Ohio, preserved one of their town's Indian mounds (above), but elsewhere settlers flattened or looted countless earthworks. A stone effigy pipe (right) from the Ohio River Valley reflects the artistry of carvers who lived some 1,600 years ago.

Accurate paintings of Indians, made around 1585 by English colonist John White, include a tattooed woman (left) wearing a garment of Spanish moss. The details give scholars clues about Indian life in what is now the southeastern United States.

Hieroglyphs and portraits of gods fill an Aztec codex (far left), an accordion-folded book with bark pages. Spanish missionaries often burned such art as pagan. But enough survived to reveal a writing system vivid in symbolism: Shield and arrows meant war; tonguelike scrolls, speech.

Length 3¼″

By 1760 in the British colonies to the north, only a sprinkling of missionaries, explorers, and traders had penetrated west of the Allegheny Mountains. With the coming of peace after the French and Indian War, the Midwest opened to land-hungry settlers. As they cleared farmland, they were surprised to discover thousands of man-made mounds as far west as Nebraska. Dreaming of treasure, the settlers dug eagerly into the mounds. They found no gold or silver, only human skeletons, weapons and tools, strange copper and mica ornaments, and stone pipe bowls carved in the shapes of animals. Hundreds of mounds were looted for their alleged treasure or flattened for farmland and town sites.

Settler and scholar alike puzzled over the origin of these mysterious monuments. They did not believe that "savage" Indians could have built such elaborate earthworks. American scholars of the day explained away the mounds as the work of an ancient, long-vanished civilization—probably a superior race from a foreign land. Thus was born the myth of the Mound Builders.

Only a few intellectuals disagreed—among them one of America's first archaeologists, Thomas Jefferson. In 1781 Jefferson began writing *Notes on the State of Virginia,* a treatise on philosophy, geography, natural history, and the ancient and modern inhabitants of his home state. Fascinated by the Mound Builders, he decided to dig for answers.

For his momentous experiment Jefferson chose a low mound of earth and loose stones near Charlottesville in central Virginia. Cautious digging yielded "collections of human bones, at different depths," jumbled as though they had been "emptied promiscuously from a bag or basket." Next Jefferson cut a large trench right through the mound so he "might examine its internal structure." At one end of the cutting, he found four layers of human bones, each covered with earth and stones. Without question he had opened a burial mound. But when had it been built? And why?

Jefferson scrutinized the skeletal remains. He found no bullet or arrow holes in them, so they were not war casualties. He concluded that each layer of bones had been covered with soil until the mound had stood perhaps 12 feet high, acting as a communal grave over a long period of time.

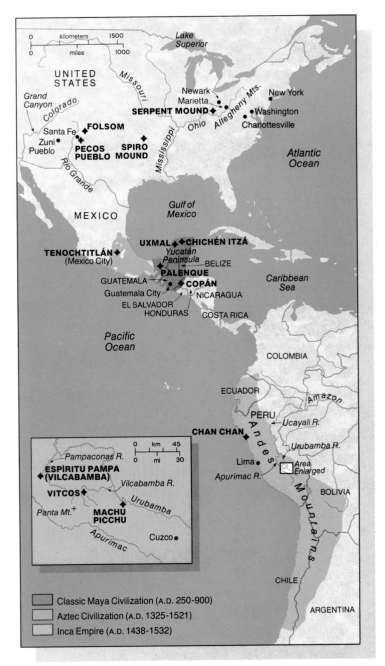

"There seemed to come to me a picture as of a distant time," recalled museum curator Frederic W. Putnam of his vision from atop the Serpent Mound (opposite) in 1883. Fearing that treasure hunters would destroy the quarter-mile-long mound of carefully heaped earth, he raised money to buy it. Now preserved in an Ohio state park, the snake effigy was built by Indians 13 to 30 centuries ago. Another Ohio mound yielded a 2,000-year-old face (right) cut from a sheet of mica.

Height 6"

The original inhabitants of the Americas already had a long history when Columbus, seeking India, misnamed them Indians in 1492. Many varied cultures flourished north and south of the Rio Grande; the map shows three in the south.

The literate Maya studied the heavens and chronicled the exploits of their rulers on stone slabs carved with portraits and hieroglyphs. Then a series of events—perhaps drought, overpopulation, and economic collapse—ended their golden age around A.D. 900.

The Incas ruled a rapidly expanding, 2,500-mile-long Andean realm linked by roads radiating from the imperial capital of Cuzco. Their far-flung empire lasted less than a century, falling easily to a few hundred Spaniards in 1532.

In Mexico the Aztecs built Tenochtitlán, a proud capital of pyramids and palaces. Believing they were children of the sun god, the Aztecs ritually nourished their deity with human blood. But all fell to ruin when Europeans came and changed the map forever.

Jefferson recalled stories of a party of Indians who had visited the mound about 30 years earlier and "staid about it some time, with expressions which were construed to be those of sorrow." Jefferson was certain that he had excavated an Indian burial ground, but almost nobody agreed with this voice of archaeological reason.

Most armchair archaeologists had either a theological or racial bias about the Mound Builders and knew little about Indians. Each amateur mound digger hoped to find the Egyptian hieroglyph or Israelite pot that would finally identify this mysterious race. Among the most eager was Caleb Atwater, an Ohio postmaster. By 1820 he had surveyed dozens of mounds in the Ohio River Valley.

Atwater described some mounds that no longer exist. At Newark, Ohio, he measured an octagonal fort that sprawled across 40 acres. Atwater refused to believe the mounds had

been built by Indians, whose "antiquities . . . are neither numerous nor very interesting." He theorized that shepherds and farmers from India had crossed the Bering Strait, raised the mounds, then moved on to Mexico and South America.

Writers churned out dozens of literary fantasies about the Mound Builders. Between 1833 and 1841 enterprising door-to-door salesmen sold thousands of copies of Josiah Priest's *American Antiquities and Discoveries in the West.* Priest wrote of armies rivaling those of Alexander the Great. The Mound Builders were "white people of great intelligence and skill" who had battled savage enemies all over the region now known as the Midwest.

But in the mid-19th century, serious inquiry also arose out of the intense curiosity about the new lands in the West. In 1845 two acquaintances—editor Ephraim Squier and physician Edwin Davis—decided to examine the mounds in

Length 1⅞″

Diggers bare an Indian burial mound layered with skeletons. This panorama, a fanciful composite of many actual sites, unrolled to illustrate the popular lectures of Montroville Dickeson, a 19th-century collector who claimed he had opened a thousand mounds.

Many collectors prized flint spearpoints. The Folsom point (left) was found in 1927 lying between the ribs of an Ice Age bison in a gully (far left) near Folsom, New Mexico; it proved that hunters lived in America at least 10,000 years ago.

Ohio and adjacent states. Squier, long interested in archaeology, used his leisure time to survey and dig into more than 200 mounds. Davis, a busy physician and the less active partner, provided the funds. Squier cataloged dozens of coarse clay vessels and stone pipes shaped like birds or animals; he identified the shores of Lake Superior as the source of copper for the spears, knives, axes, and adzes in the mounds. But he wore intellectual blinders. He refused to believe that the mounds had been built by Indians—"hunters averse to labor." He wrote that a superior race had raised the earthworks to guard against "the hostile savage hordes."

Squier and Davis's *Ancient Monuments of the Mississippi Valley* appeared in 1848—the first book issued by the newly founded Smithsonian Institution in Washington, D. C. Despite its prejudiced attitudes, this handsome monograph gave credence to the serious study of mounds and remained a definitive work for many years.

In Mexico studies of the past had languished, but two reports kept interest in the Maya alive. The first was the work of Antonio del Río, a Spanish army captain who arrived at Palenque in 1787 to prepare an official report on its Maya ruins. He rounded up 79 Indians to clear the clinging vegetation from the buildings and courtyards. He dug trenches and collected vessels, potsherds, and bas-relief fragments, as Spanish artist Ignacio Armendáriz sketched the stucco figures on the ruins.

Del Río's study would have lain unpublished in official Spanish archives had not a British doctor somehow obtained a copy in Guatemala and sold it to a London bookdealer. It appeared in English translation in 1822—to an indifferent reception. Egypt was all the rage in Europe.

The king of Spain commissioned Guillermo Dupaix, a retired Spanish army officer, to follow up del Río's report with a wider survey of Mexican ruins. Between 1805 and 1807 Dupaix and an artist traveled through the Valley of Mexico, Oaxaca, and the Maya lowlands, recording, describing, and sketching. The climax of Dupaix's travels came at Palenque, where he admired "erect and well proportioned" stone figures that had "a certain expression of dignity." He thought the citizens of legendary Atlantis had built Palenque.

Freed from the jungle's clutch, a Maya pyramid testifies to glories long eclipsed. Around A.D. 730 the Maya erected this stone structure at Copán in Honduras. When American adventurer John Stephens saw the ruins in 1839, "all was mystery, dark, impenetrable mystery." Together with British artist Frederick Catherwood, he endured mosquitoes, deluges, and disease to record ancient Maya monuments. Stephens's books prepared the way for scientific archaeology in Mexico and Central America.

One of the few people to take notice of Dupaix's work was Lord Kingsborough, a wealthy Irishman who believed the Maya and Aztecs were descendants of the Ten Lost Tribes of Israel. He copied every Maya hieroglyph and Mexican picture book he could find and assembled them in nine huge volumes, which he published between 1829 and 1848 under the title *Antiquities of Mexico*. The handsome volumes beggared Kingsborough, who died in debtor's prison.

But Kingsborough's books and the English translation of del Río's obscure report, illustrated with detailed engravings by Frenchman Jean Frédéric Waldeck, prompted two adventurers to go in search of the ancient Maya.

John Lloyd Stephens was a New York lawyer who loved to travel. In 1834, after wandering through Europe, he journeyed on to Constantinople and Moscow before returning to Paris. Next he sailed up the Nile and rode a camel across the

Sinai Peninsula to Petra in Jordan. There Stephens passed through a narrow ravine with "wild fig-trees, oleanders, and ivy . . . growing out of the rocky sides of the cliffs hundreds of feet above. . . ." At the far end rose "the facade of a beautiful temple, hewn out of the rock, with rows of Corinthian columns and ornaments, standing out fresh and clear as if but yesterday from the hands of the sculptor." Enchanted, Stephens became an archaeology buff almost overnight.

While in London in 1836, Stephens met Frederick Catherwood, a British architect and artist who had just returned from a lengthy stay in Egypt and the Holy Land. A man of many careers, Catherwood had repaired mosques in Cairo, drawn ancient Egyptian temples, and even built railroads.

Catherwood soon went to New York to set up an architectural practice. Meanwhile Stephens cashed in on his travels by writing two best-selling books about Arabia and

"Savages never carved these stones," observed Stephens, awed by a massive "broken idol" at Copán (above, left) and by "vast buildings" and "richly ornamented" pyramids at Uxmal (above). At Copán in January 1893, American archaeologist John G. Owens (left) directs porters bearing papier-mâché molds of a "manuscript in stone"—the Great Hieroglyphic Stairway, bound for the United States. Owens, dead from malaria three months later, was buried in the Great Plaza at Copán.

Eastern Europe. Stephens and Catherwood became leading members of New York's literary circle, where they heard talk of mysterious ruins in Mexico and Central America.

Here was the new adventure both men had been waiting for. In October 1839 they left New York for Central America, Stephens armed with a diplomatic appointment he had obtained to ease their way with suspicious local authorities. About five weeks later they arrived at the tiny Honduran village of Copán—"half a dozen miserable huts thatched with corn." The next day a villager led them through dense rain forest to a riverbank. They forded the river and stumbled through the undergrowth and trees covering terraces and pyramids. Their guide hacked a path "among half-buried fragments, to fourteen monuments . . . some in workmanship equal to the finest monuments of the Egyptians. . . ."

Stephens pondered the desolate city. "It lay before us like a shattered bark in the midst of the ocean, her masts gone, her name effaced, her crew perished, and none to tell whence she came. . . ." Around them lay the dark outlines of ruins, shrouded by the brooding forest. "The only sounds that disturbed the quiet of this buried city," remembered Stephens, "were the noise of monkeys moving among the tops of the trees, and the cracking of dry branches broken by their weight. They moved over our heads in long and swift processions, forty or fifty at a time. . . ."

The jungle-wrapped ruins sprawled for miles, a profusion of courts and temples, steps climbing up terraces and pyramids, and engraved stelae—elaborately carved stone monuments. Poor Catherwood suffered agonies trying to copy the unfamiliar hieroglyphs. Hampered by gloomy light and constant rain, up to his ankles in mud, he had to work in gloves because of the mosquitoes.

While Catherwood drew, Stephens looked into the possibility of removing a stela for exhibit in New York. This brought up the thorny question of ownership. Stephens "put on a diplomatic coat, with a profusion of large eagle buttons. . . . a Panama hat, soaked with rain and spotted with mud, a checked shirt, white pantaloons, yellow up to the knees"—and so impressed the owner of the ruins that he was able to buy the site for only $50. The new owners made a

145

Borne to high adventure on an Indian's back, pioneering photographer Claude-Joseph-Désiré Charnay (opposite) is the image of undampened perseverance. To photograph Maya monuments in 1882, the stoic Frenchman, swaying perilously, braved a road that "even the Indians do not trust their animals on."

Stephens's best-selling books inspired Charnay's arduous trek through Mexico with his primitive camera. Charnay coated heavy glass plates with emulsion and set up the bulky instrument (left) in dank jungles, often enduring "dark discouragement and terrible failures" in his attempt to photograph what others had only sketched. But his faith in "photography as a witness" prevailed, helping to launch the camera's long career as an archaeological tool. In 1858 Charnay photographed the Maya city of Chichén Itzá. His photographs, including one of an ornately carved temple (above) in the long-dead city, gave a new dimension to descriptions of Maya ruins.

A Zuni artisan decorates a pot on the roof of a New Mexico pueblo (above). Frank Hamilton Cushing (right), a white man who lived among the Zuni, drew the scene. In 1879 Cushing began nearly five years of a dual life—as an ethnologist studying Indian customs and as a Zuni war chief. Zuni friends, deriding his "mouse-head-shaped hat" and "squeaking foot-packs," urged him to dress in Zuni regalia and named him Te-na-tsa-li, or Medicine Flower, after a sacred plant.

From the Indians, Cushing learned about pottery making. Like most Zuni activities, it had mystic tradition. Women made pots from coils of clay. A potter did not complete the painted "life line" separating the neck of a pot from its "stomach" lest her spirit be trapped inside. During the last stages, wrote Cushing, "no laughing, music, whistling or any other unnecessary noises were indulged in," for fear the sound, entering the vessel, would escape with shattering force when the pot was fired.

complete survey of their purchase in just three days. Catherwood's rough plan of Copán remained the authoritative source for about half a century.

Stephens then rode south as far as Costa Rica and Nicaragua to assess the feasibility of building a shipping canal across the isthmus. Afterward he and Catherwood embarked on an exhausting journey from Guatemala City to the ruins they had read about at Palenque in the Mexican state of Chiapas. Wearing broad-brimmed hats and local dress, the two men climbed tortuous mountain trails on muleback. Descending into the steamy lowlands, they struggled through thick vegetation. Mules could pass, but their riders had to bend double to avoid tree branches. The rains poured down incessantly. Mosquitoes made sleeping impossible.

Stephens and Catherwood reached Palenque in May 1840 and set up camp in the ruined *palacio,* as their Indian guides called the squarish complex of thick-walled rooms grouped around several courtyards. The weary travelers let their supply of turkeys and chickens loose in the courtyard and built simple beds of poles, fastened together with string made from bark and laid on stone supports. Daily downpours and fierce winds prevented the men from lighting candles, so Stephens amused himself by catching fireflies "of extraordinary size and brilliancy." By the light of one he read a newspaper he had brought with him. "It seemed stranger than any incident of my journey," he recalled, "to be reading by the light of beetles, in the ruined palace of Palenque, the sayings and doings of great men at home."

Metal equipment rusted; leather turned green with mildew. Mosquitoes, ticks, and chiggers constantly plagued the men. Stephens described Catherwood as "wan and gaunt; lame, like me, from the bites of insects; his face was swollen, and his left arm hung with rheumatism as if paralyzed."

Despite the hardships, Stephens and Catherwood examined the ruins. Huge trees and dense undergrowth hid structures only a hundred feet away. The men searched for parallels with ancient Egypt but found no striking similarities. Instead of massive columned temples and isolated pyramids, they discovered columnless temples clustered with pyramids around spacious plazas. And Catherwood's drawings revealed sculptures so "different from the works of any other known people" that "they stand alone."

A visit to Uxmal, another urban center, convinced Stephens that the ruins were not of Egyptian origin. Unlike Palenque, Uxmal stood in open ranchland, so he could see the full effect of pyramids and temples decorated with "strange and incomprehensible" designs. The Palace of the Governors, its ornate, 320-foot-long facade rising grandly atop three terraces, did not look like anything from the Nile.

Stephens and Catherwood returned to New York at the end of July 1840. In 1841 Stephens published *Incidents of Travel in Central America, Chiapas, and Yucatan.* Catherwood's accurate drawings, among the finest of all archaeological renderings, enhanced Stephens's bold conclusion that the ruins they had visited were "the creations of the same races who inhabited the country at the time of the Spanish conquest, or some not very distant progenitors."

Even as reviewers were extolling *Incidents,* Stephens and Catherwood sailed for Yucatán again, accompanied by a young doctor and amateur ornithologist named Samuel Cabot. For six weeks they studied Uxmal. Surveying the ruins was made doubly hard by the riotous vegetation that had smothered the buildings since their last visit and by Cabot's penchant for dropping the measuring tape to follow a bird that struck his fancy. While Cabot and Stephens were laid up with malaria, Catherwood made a detailed record of a huge quadrangle. Spanish padres had dubbed it the Nunnery because its cell-like chambers resembled European cloisters.

Eventually malaria drove the trio away. By the time they returned to New York five months later, Stephens was convinced that the Yucatán ruins had been built by ancestors of the modern Maya. "These cities . . . are not the works of people who have passed away," he wrote, " . . . but of the same great *race* which . . . still clings around their ruins."

Stephens corresponded with historian William Prescott. Confined to his Boston study by near-total blindness, Prescott faced extraordinary disadvantages in pursuing his abiding passion: the history of the Spanish conquest. Most of the original documents were buried in Spanish and Mexican archives, so he relied on friends and scholars to obtain and translate manuscripts for him. Into his study streamed a mass of archival material that had been hidden for centuries.

Thousands of these documents provided source material for the *History of the Conquest of Mexico,* which reads almost like an adventurous novel. Prescott set the history of the Spanish conquest against the background of the Aztecs' meteoric rise to power. For the first time, readers could see that America's past held more than mythical Mound Builders and the familiar Indian tribes thought to have come after them. The literary sensation of 1843, Prescott's vivid narrative replaced myth with historical fact and clothed American archaeology with respectability.

Prescott's book appeared as the professional pursuit of ethnology and geology was gaining momentum, especially in the western United States. The men who came to work in this vast natural laboratory were hard-nosed, practical scientists like John Wesley Powell, pioneer explorer of the Grand

Mountain lion and arrowhead join in a fetish that embodies Zuni mysticism. The lion's "heart still lives," wrote Cushing, "even though his person be changed to stone." Flint arrowheads were a gift— the "flesh"—of lightning. Cushing learned that the Zuni believed in the harmonious relationship of all things, from sky to snakes. The Zuni saw animals as close kin to humans and as mediators between people and the gods.

Length 3¾"

American explorer Hiram Bingham poses before his tent at Machu Picchu, the ruined Inca city he stumbled upon deep in the Peruvian Andes in 1911. Sponsored by both the National Geographic Society and Yale University, he led three more expeditions to the stone aerie that had eluded the Spanish conquistadores. He wrote of encounters with insects, vampire bats, bitter cold, mountain sickness, and loneliness. "Taking everything into consideration, I consider myself most fortunate."

Canyon. A self-taught geologist, Powell also studied Indian customs and languages. In 1879 he became the first director of the Smithsonian's Bureau of Ethnology, a government agency set up to study vanishing Indian cultures.

To Powell's fury a group of archaeologists persuaded Congress to divert part of the bureau's funds into Mound Builder research aimed at proving that ancient European civilizations had once flourished in the Midwest. Powell responded by recruiting Cyrus Thomas, an entomologist-turned-archaeologist, to prove that "the prehistoric mound builders and the historic tribes were part of the same fabric of unbroken cultural development."

Fanning out over mound country in 1882, Thomas and his assistants found that popular tales about the mounds had created a fever for collecting artifacts. Landowners were selling them off; collectors traveled around the country digging into mounds and hauling away everything they found.

Trying to stay ahead of the vandals, Thomas's colleagues worked as quickly as possible. Thomas stayed in Washington most of the time, studying the artifacts that poured into the Smithsonian and deploying his excavators from mound to mound. After they had explored more than 2,000 earthworks in 22 states from Florida to North Dakota and collected some 40,000 artifacts, Thomas concluded that the mounds were "to be attributed to the indigenous tribes found inhabiting this region and their ancestors." His 730-page monograph contained exhaustive descriptions of the mounds and of the articles found in them, such as skeletons, pipes, and items of shell and copper. His pioneer work remains a definitive source for today's archaeologists, since most of the mounds he cataloged have been at least partly destroyed.

The destruction of Spiro Mound in eastern Oklahoma is a tragic example. The great conical earthwork excited little interest until 1933, when some pothunters leased it and began to dig holes at random. This method proved too slow, so they hired coal miners to excavate tunnels and then hauled out artifacts in wheelbarrows, trampling priceless textiles in their frantic search. The pothunters sold what they could on the spot, flooding the artifact market with engraved shells, stone effigy pipes, shell beads, and embossed copper plates.

In 1935 Oklahoma passed a law protecting archaeological sites, but pothunters simply ignored it. Archaeologists gained access to Spiro in 1936 and found only a shattered ruin: After finishing their assault, the pothunters set off a powder charge—possibly to thwart rival collectors. Archaeologists spent years tracking down Spiro artifacts.

Convinced by the late 1800s that contemporary Indians were descendants of the first Americans, archaeologists and anthropologists began to work back from the living present to study the past. In 1879 Frank Hamilton Cushing traveled to Zuni Pueblo in New Mexico on a Smithsonian-sponsored expedition, intending to stay only three months. Distrustful Indians almost killed him when he tried to sketch a dance ceremony. Menaced by two Zuni brandishing war clubs, he drew his knife and smiled—a courageous act that startled the pair. They clubbed and knifed a dog to death instead, a scene "too disgusting for description."

Bingham's mules halt the march of archaeology at the banks of the Apurímac River in highland Peru. Bingham, seeking Inca ruins high in the Andes, had trouble with mules in water and on land. At 15,000 feet in a pass near Panta Mountain (left), mules that had never seen snow bolted off the path, tumbled downhill, and fell into drifts up to their ears. Whenever "coaxing and curses" failed, Bingham wrote, "pulling, hauling, and beating were alternately resorted to."

Cushing's cool demeanor and obvious interest in their culture so impressed the Zuni that they let him stay. He remained at the pueblo nearly five years, the first ethnologist to live among Indians for that long. Cushing sat on roofs and sketched Zuni dances, watched the annual routines of planting and harvesting, and spent hours listening to legends and tribal histories. He immersed himself in the intricate and well-regulated life of the Zuni. He learned their language, wore Zuni dress, even scalped a raiding Apache.

After two years Cushing was granted membership in the pueblo's most secret society, the Priesthood of the Bow. To prepare for his initiation, he sat motionless and speechless all day atop a large anthill of stinging ants. During the initiation came "more fasting, more sleeplessness, purifications, vomitings each day, sacrificial pilgrimages, then silent motionless meditation again, filled up, with nightly instructions in the rituals and incantations. . . ." Membership in this war society gave Cushing access to some of the Zuni's most private deliberations. Eventually the Indians made him a war chief—"1st War Chief of Zuñi, U. S. Asst. Ethnologist," as Cushing put it. His widely read *My Adventures in Zuñi* recounted his life in the pueblo and described the customs of a society whose roots stretched far into the past.

Like Cushing, Swiss-born Adolph Bandelier worked "from the known to the unknown, step by step." Bandelier, a bank clerk who studied Spanish colonial history and ethnology in his spare time, arrived at the ruins of Pecos Pueblo, New Mexico, in 1880. "Dirty, ragged, and sunburnt," he surveyed the site in ten days and tracked down people who had lived at Pecos in the 1830s, when it was still inhabited. They told him tribal histories about the founding of the European mission at Pecos and about the Pueblo Revolt of 1680, when

Indians had destroyed the mission church. These oral histories were to become the foundation for the archaeological research conducted at Pecos from 1915 to 1929.

New World archaeology was now moving out of the hands of amateurs into the realm of professional scientists and serious research. But there was still room for daring adventure, especially in remote areas of South America, where fieldwork was in its infancy.

In highland Peru lay the heart of the former empire of the Incas. The first Inca chieftains were petty warlords who lived near the Andean town of Cuzco. In A.D. 1438 a ruler named Pachacuti turned tribal raiding into imperial conquest. His successors followed his lead and carved out a vast empire that stretched from southern Colombia deep into central Chile, straddling both coast and highlands. But in 1532 the Incas, wracked by civil war and disease, were toppled by the Spanish conquistadores in just a few months.

Almost four centuries later a young American historian named Hiram Bingham trekked across the Andes and explored the Inca realm. He thought nothing of riding mules along nearly inaccessible mountain tracks and climbing for hours up steep mountainsides where ancient Inca cities were rumored to lie. In 1910 Bingham described his travels to a group of fellow Yale alumni. The men leaned forward as he talked of the ultimate lure—the legendary Vilcabamba, last refuge of ruler Manco Inca when he fled from the Spanish in 1537. Bingham's enthusiasm prompted his classmates and the university to finance a new expedition in 1911.

Vilcabamba was thought to lie northwest of Cuzco in an unmapped section of the Urubamba River Valley. July 1911 found Bingham and six colleagues, with half a dozen Indian porters and a Peruvian sergeant as escort, threading a foot trail through hot, humid gorges along the banks of the seething river. The party camped beside the Urubamba and heard from a local farmer about Inca ruins high up a steep, jungle-clad mountain on the opposite bank.

The next morning Bingham's colleagues, not expecting the ruins to prove interesting, conveniently found chores to do in camp. Bingham, the farmer, and the sergeant crossed over violent rapids on a bridge so primitive that, Bingham 151

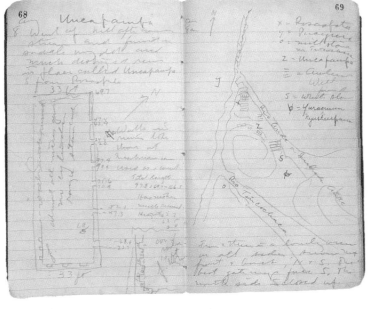

Dense jungle threatens to engulf the carriers on a 1915 expedition to Machu Picchu. Bingham wrote that he walked along this old Inca road with "mingled feelings of keen anticipation and lively curiosity." Near the "white stone" marked with "S" in his notebook (left), he found a temple where Inca priests had thrown kisses to the rising sun. Next to a sketch Bingham added the lengths of two walls: "97.8 + 69.7 = 166.5." Even a Yale professor could slip: The answer misses by a foot.

confessed, he crawled across. They climbed a precipice for an hour and twenty minutes: "A good part of the distance we went on all fours, sometimes holding on by our fingernails." Two thousand feet above the river, the hot, exhausted trio paused at a tiny Indian hut to eat lunch and gulp down gourds of cool water. The farmer stayed there to gossip.

With an Indian boy as guide, Bingham set off again with the sergeant, expecting to find nothing more than a few stone houses. To Bingham's astonishment they came upon stone-faced terraces climbing like giant stairs up the hillside. A twisting path led to some "ruined houses built of the finest quality of Inca stone work." Walls of white granite peeped through bamboo thickets and tangled vines.

The Indian boy led Bingham to a cave lined with cut stone. Above towered a semicircular building that flowed into the natural curve of the rock. The boy urged Bingham and the sergeant to climb even higher. They ascended a granite stairway leading to a plaza with two temples, one containing a huge altar stone, the other three large windows. "The sight held me spellbound," declared Bingham. On this almost inaccessible mountain ridge called Machu Picchu, the Incas had built a noble city, its name lost to time.

153

Machu Picchu's long-hidden glory emerges from beneath its jungle shroud. Indian workers (above) expose temple walls that show the skill of Inca masons. The unmortared stones fit so snugly that, as Bingham wrote, "they might have grown together." A full month of hacking uncovered terraces and rows of granite houses (left). The Incas had designed curving walls with mathematical precision but never made a true arch. And it appears these master masons did not know about the wheel.

Overleaf: *"What could this place be?" wondered Bingham when he first sighted Machu Picchu, a tangled vista of Andean stone and jungle 8,000 feet above sea level. His guess: a lofty redoubt for Inca rulers fleeing from Spanish conquerors. Modern theory describes it as a place of worship for a people who saw gods in sun and mountain.*

Bingham sketched a rough map of the site, then pushed up the nearby Vilcabamba River to Vitcos, Manco Inca's first capital. When Bingham heard rumors of another Inca city, he tramped for days over soggy forest trails deep into the remote Pampaconas Valley. There he found Espíritu Pampa, an overgrown ruin of houses, walls, and watercourses. Which of these three ruins was the lost city of Vilcabamba?

The National Geographic Society and Yale University cosponsored Bingham's further expeditions to Machu Picchu in 1912, 1913, and 1915—the first archaeological projects supported by the Society. Bingham's team cleared and excavated the city and mapped the surrounding region. Convinced that Machu Picchu was Vilcabamba, he held to this theory until his death in 1956.

No one disputed his claim until 1964, when American explorer Gene Savoy retraced Bingham's trek to Espíritu Pampa and found the ruins of shrines, streets, fountains, canals, bridges, and almost 300 houses—a rambling metropolis much larger than Bingham had suspected. Savoy cleared the 12-room palace and recovered crude roof tiles—Inca imitations of Spanish architecture. Spanish chronicles based on firsthand reports from friars and conquistadores placed the city here in the tropical jungle. He was certain from its size and location that he had finally identified Vilcabamba—that Espíritu Pampa, not Machu Picchu, was the last Inca refuge.

But there is never an ultimate discovery; new insights constantly add further dimensions. Five years after Savoy had identified Vilcabamba, American archaeologists Michael Moseley and Carol Mackey, supported by the National Geographic Society and the National Science Foundation, began excavating Chan Chan, the ancient Chimú capital on the Peruvian coast. A huge adobe complex, Chan Chan is dominated by the walled, mazelike palaces of rulers who governed an empire stretching from southern Ecuador to Lima, Peru. Excavation has transformed these ruins into a detailed picture of a powerful civilization that had roads, irrigation, taxes, and laws—some of which the Incas adopted after they conquered the Chimú around A.D. 1470. And future discoveries will answer questions that were not even formulated when archaeologists first dug into Chan Chan's buried past.

156

Height 7″

In a maze of latticelike walls, archaeological detectives outline the dead city of Chan Chan in Peru. From the 10th to the 15th centuries A.D., Chan Chan ruled the 900-mile-long coastal empire of the Chimú. It fell to the Incas around 1470. Young women were buried in large numbers with Chimú kings, whose huge palaces became tombs for ruler and ruled. Desert graves also preserve rare textiles at Chan Chan and the 500-year-old woven doll (left) interred with a mummy farther south.

Mesopotamia, 1899: A basket brigade removes rubble from Nippur, a Sumerian religious center 5,000 years ago.

PUTTING TIME IN ORDER

PUTTING TIME IN ORDER

"**W**hat would our committee at home have said at the sight of this enormous ruin, resembling more a picturesque mountain range than the last impressive remains of human constructions!" Thus did German archaeologist Herman V. Hilprecht express his dismay at the prospect before him in 1888: excavating the sand-drifted Sumerian city of Nippur. But with picks, shovels, and sturdy backs, workers finally unearthed the stark geometry of masonry in the temple area sacred to Enlil, the Sumerian god of wind and storm.

As the 19th century wound down, hordes of diggers were delving into ancient Sumer and the realms of other lost civilizations in the dusty lands around the eastern Mediterranean. Archaeologists vigilantly supervised the laborers who swarmed over their sites; one even watched the work through a telescope while eating breakfast in his hut.

From the seeming chaos of haphazardly dug pits and trenches, a new orderliness gradually emerged. Archaeologists turned to systematic excavation, with its careful study of small artifacts, and to the laborious task of deciphering inscriptions that recorded the news of international politics and military victories many centuries ago. From these clues they pieced together a picture of ancient trade, warfare, and cultural links in the eastern Mediterranean. 159

Excavators in western Turkey pried at the secrets of Greek cities that had flourished there in the second and third centuries B.C. In 1863 the British Museum and the Society of Dilettanti in London sent architect John Wood to excavate the marshy ruins of the ancient Greek city of Ephesus. Ruled around 550 B.C. by the fabulously wealthy Croesus, Ephesus gained renown through the centuries for its devotion to Artemis, Greek goddess of nature and the hunt.

Wood sought the Temple of Artemis, extolled in the second century B.C. as one of the Seven Wonders of the World. Unaware that a German geographer had located the temple 30 years earlier, Wood and his crew scoured the ruins for 6 years before rediscovering it. They spent 5 more years excavating the elegantly carved columns and reliefs that lay 20 feet below the surface. Concentrating his efforts on removing the structure piecemeal to send to his sponsors, Wood never completed a plan of the temple. Decades later a visitor

called the site a "desolate heap of rubbish. . . . It fills a ditch several hundred yards long, a picture of utter neglect. Better to have left it covered than create such damage."

By contrast, a German archaeologist named Alexander Conze had already earned a reputation for meticulous excavations. Karl Humann, a German railway engineer, sent to the Berlin Museum fragments of marble reliefs from Pergamum, the capital of an ancient Greek kingdom in western Turkey. They were identified as pieces of the fabled Great Altar of Pergamum, a templelike masterpiece of the second century B.C. dedicated to Zeus and Athena. In 1877 Conze, head of the museum's department of sculpture, took action.

Conze quietly obtained a digging permit from the Turkish government. In September 1878 he set Humann and a small crew of diggers to work on the citadel at Pergamum—the start of a program that still continues. They dismantled a wall built in medieval times and found it had been made partly of carved marble slabs, each more than six feet long. Surely these had come from the Great Altar. "We have discovered an entire epoch in art," wrote Humann, ". . . the most important remaining work of antiquity." An exaggeration perhaps, but the next year, when Conze himself joined the excavations, he and Humann found the base of the altar and more carved marbles.

Humann invited guests to the unveiling when his workmen freed the marbles. The first slab depicted, in Humann's words, "a huge giant with serpent-like feet . . . and a lion's skin hung over the left arm." The second marble featured "a splendid god, the full chest more powerful and yet more beautiful. . . . The third slab showed a swooning giant sunk on his knees; the left hand grasps, as if in pain, the right shoulder. . . ." A fourth revealed "a giant falling backwards on a rock, the upper part of his thigh has been struck by lightning—I feel thy presence, Zeus!"

To his delight Humann managed to join five slabs to complete a section of the altar's frieze, which portrayed the victory of the Greek gods over the giants. He sat down upon the "splendid god" that was Zeus and wept with joy. Eventually skilled hands reassembled the whole altar in Berlin. The frieze of battling gods and giants encircles the base of the columned monument, ending beneath projecting wings on either side of the altar's wide staircase.

While the Germans dug in western Turkey, archaeologists began to realize that Mesopotamia—the region between the Tigris and Euphrates Rivers—held secrets of ancient civilizations now known to date back as far as the fourth millennium B.C. In 1869 Jules Oppert, a French scholar who studied cuneiform tablets, identified one civilization as the mysterious predecessors of the Assyrians who rose to power in the third millennium B.C. He called this group Sumerians.

These inhabitants of southern Mesopotamia are now credited with the invention of cuneiform script around 3000 B.C. Using a stylus to press wedge-shaped characters into a soft clay tablet that fit in the palm of the hand, Sumerian scribes recorded business transactions and literary compositions. Their successors—the Assyrians and the Babylonians—adopted this system of writing from the Sumerians.

Photographed in a flash of magnesium (opposite), solemn Austrian scholars record for posterity their 1914 visit to a five-story tower on the Greek island of Ándros. Cantilevered stairs spiral up the 2,000-year-old farm fortification.

Hadrian's Temple (above) at Ephesus in western Turkey honored the Roman emperor who ruled from A.D. 117 to 138. A 19th-century British architect named John Wood first excavated Roman and earlier Greek remains in this ancient city.

But few of Oppert's colleagues took his Sumerians seriously. Then in 1877 Ernest de Sarzec was appointed French vice-consul to the sleepy port town of Basra in southeastern Iraq. A man full of energy and drive, de Sarzec took up archaeology as a diversion, his curiosity aroused by mounds strewn with potsherds, inscribed bricks, and broken carvings. He hired some laborers and began digging at Telloh, a four-mile-long cluster of mounds more than a hundred miles northwest of Basra.

On his first ride over the largest mound, de Sarzec had spotted the upper torso of a black dolerite statue of Gudea, one of the most powerful governors of the Sumerian city-state of Lagash. A year later, when his workmen sliced through the 50-foot-high mound, they uncovered the rest of the torso, along with six more statues of Gudea. His clasped hands and calm expression projected an aura of supreme self-confidence. These and other stone images from the end of the third millennium B.C. remain among the most striking masterpieces of Mesopotamian sculpture.

The French government subsidized further excavations at Telloh, and later the Louvre in Paris bought de Sarzec's sensational collections. In addition to the sculptures, his diggers retrieved the most comprehensive archive of cuneiform inscriptions ever found from the earliest periods of Mesopotamian history. His discovery of the Sumerian city-state, home of the world's first known literate society, intensified interest in the excavation of Mesopotamian cities.

In 1888 a group of Philadelphians, hoping that cuneiform tablets and other inscribed artifacts would prove the historical truth of the Old Testament, sent the Reverend John Peters to Nippur, a Sumerian city a hundred miles southeast of Baghdād. Peters, a professor of Hebrew at the University of Pennsylvania, took with him a distinguished Assyrian specialist, Herman V. Hilprecht.

Their first sight of Nippur horrified them. Crumbled brick structures loomed like mountains above a wasteland of swamps and desert. Hilprecht foresaw that more than a half century of effort would be needed to explore the ruins—a remarkably precise prediction. Work continues at the site today, after a hiatus between mid-1900 and 1948.

Cascading down a hillside, the Greek amphitheater (upper) at Pergamum in western Turkey offers a breathtaking view from its 15,000 seats. The last king of Pergamum, who had no heir, bequeathed the rich Greek city to Rome in 133 B.C.

German archaeologists Alexander Conze (left, in doorway) and Karl Humann (at his elbow) pose in 1879 with members of their team, the first to excavate Pergamum. A year earlier they had begun to unearth the city's Great Altar to Zeus and Athena, built in the second century B.C. In a feat that inspired this 19th-century drawing (opposite), workers transported 35 tons of the altar's carved marble slabs to a harbor some 18 miles away for shipment to Germany. The reconstructed altar now stands in its own museum in East Berlin.

Peters' labor force, peaking at about 250, dug through rubble and rock-hard mud brick. Soon quarreling broke out between the Arab workers and Turkish guards. The hostility climaxed in the burning of the excavation camp; in minutes the reed huts were smoldering piles of ashes.

Peters ended the first season with only a sketchy impression of the site, though he recovered more than 2,000 cuneiform tablets and found evidence that Nippur had been occupied from prehistoric times up to the ninth century A.D. Peters returned the next year. He and his men dug into the lofty ziggurat, a terraced pyramid that once formed the base for a temple. On a third expedition, directed by John Haynes, 21,000 inscriptions were found. Yet the excavation was largely haphazard; architectural details were disregarded. A visiting Hungarian engineer drew the only plan of the site.

At the sponsors' request Hilprecht took over direction of the excavations in March of 1900. "Every trench cut henceforth," he wrote, ". . . was cut for the sole purpose of excavating structures systematically and of gathering necessary *data* for the history and topography of ancient Nippur." If sensational artifacts emerged as well, all the better. Hilprecht traced the walls of the city, surveyed buildings, and finished excavating the ziggurat.

Most important of all, the expedition unearthed a cache of tablets that preserved hymns, poems, myths, astronomical observations, legal records, multiplication tables, even the lesson tablets used by pupils learning to write cuneiform. Hilprecht now had more than 30,000 tablets to pore over. Each fragment was usually copied by hand before being deciphered. Work on their decipherment continues today at the University of Pennsylvania Museum, at the Oriental Institute of the University of Chicago, and in Istanbul.

The Nippur tablets transformed the Sumerians from shadowy legend to tangible reality. The world's first known city dwellers, they developed cuneiform writing and used the wheel and the sailboat. Their tablets reveal a contentious and pragmatic people who cherished wealth, power, and personal freedom. The Sumerians apparently lived zestfully but in a state of tension, torn between the demands of their fragile, semiarid environment and those of their gods.

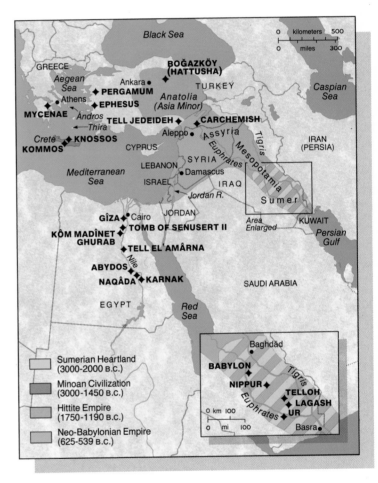

165

The Temple of Enlil (opposite), dedicated 4,000 years ago to the god of wind and storm, emerges again to face the elements in the Sumerian holy city of Nippur. Laborers in 1895 carry baskets filled with debris from the excavations organized by the University of Pennsylvania Museum. The square tower at center was left by archaeologists to mark digging levels. Built upon a ziggurat, or tiered pyramid (left), now covered by sand and rubble, the temple rises above the desert plains of Iraq.

The ancient Sumerians built the world's first known cities, developed the earliest known system of writing, and traded throughout Mesopotamia and beyond (map). Meanwhile the Minoans rose to power in the Mediterranean, building their elaborate city of Knossos on Crete. The aggressive Hittites, pioneers in the smelting of iron, also excelled in sculpture and lawmaking. The Neo-Babylonians briefly restored Babylonian power in western Asia after the old empire's decline around 1595 B.C.

About 2" square

Even such relatively sophisticated excavators as Hilprecht were bedeviled by a fundamental problem: how to identify mud-brick walls. Few trees grew in southern Mesopotamia, so the timber-poor Sumerians made most of their buildings from unfired mud bricks. But a mud-brick structure soon reverts to its natural state—mud or dust or crumbled clay. Excavators sometimes dug through mud-brick walls without realizing it and complained that there was nothing to find. German ingenuity solved the problem.

The Germans did not join actively in Mesopotamian excavations until the late 1880s, when they began experimenting with new techniques for tracing the foundations of mud-brick houses. One of these pioneers, Robert Koldewey, boldly announced in 1897 that he would uncover Nebuchadnezzar's royal city at Babylon. The task seemed almost impossible. The largest city of ancient Mesopotamia, Babylon covered more than 2,100 acres, compared with Nippur's 410. An 11-mile outer defense wall enclosed the city.

Koldewey faced a vast desolation of dusty, pockmarked mounds of crumbled mud bricks. "To those accustomed to Greece and its remains," he observed, "it is a constant surprise to have these mounds pointed out as ruins. Here are no blocks of stone, no columns: even in the excavations there is only brickwork. . . ." With characteristic thoroughness he trained special teams of diggers just to trace miles and miles of mud-brick walls that had slumped into packed mud.

First the diggers scraped the soil with hoes or shovels, looking for changes in soil texture or color between a mud-brick wall and the filling behind it. Then an expert wall technician dug a hole in the filling large enough to squat in. He faced the wall and delicately picked away the soil from the four sides of the chamber, leaving the contents of the room in place for later study. Builders' names inscribed on many bricks distinguished walls erected in different periods.

Koldewey's army of workmen, sometimes 250 strong, burrowed down to the water table and found evidence of human occupation as early as the third millennium B.C. Above lay the city of King Hammurabi, the author of a harsh code of laws. Between 604 and 562 B.C., Nebuchadnezzar rebuilt Babylon, as the Bible says, "by the might of my power, and for the honour of my majesty." Koldewey's crew cleared the Processional Way. Paved with red and white flagstones, it bisected Nebuchadnezzar's capital, from which he ruled the Neo-Babylonian Empire. The street led to the massive Ishtar Gate, faced with glazed-brick figures of dragons and bulls.

Koldewey organized his laborers into teams of twenty men. One pickman loosened the soil, which three shovelers piled into the baskets of sixteen basketmen. They dumped their loads into a railroad car for removal.

Several seasons of digging revealed Nebuchadnezzar's palace. At one corner the excavators discovered a crypt containing fourteen vaulted rooms and an unusual well with three shafts. Koldewey surmised that these were the foundations and irrigation system for the legendary Hanging Gardens of Babylon. A king of Babylon—so the story went—had decked a roof terrace with exotic trees and flowers to console his wife, who longed for the forests of her mountain homeland in what is now northwestern Iran.

Koldewey and his men also excavated the remains of a once colossal ziggurat, which may have soared as high as a 25-story building before being quarried away for bricks. Could this have been the biblical Tower of Babel? Popular belief places it here, though scholars are not sure. But Nebuchadnezzar's father reported, according to an inscription, that a Babylonian god "commanded me [to build] the tower of Babylon . . . to lay its foundation firm on the bosom of the underworld, while its top should stretch heavenwards."

Soon most excavators in Mesopotamia were following Koldewey's painstaking procedures. Though digging techniques lagged behind in Egypt, the Nile also witnessed a revolution in method: Archaeologists were learning that small artifacts—potsherds, tools, coins, and the like—could provide vital information about events of long ago.

Gentle sandblasting removes salt and grime from a clay tablet at Nippur (opposite, upper), revealing clearly the wedge-shaped characters inscribed on it. Excavators must surrender tablets to Iraqi authorities at season's end, so they make latex molds at the site, sandblasting coarse outer deposits when time does not allow lengthy cleaning with toothbrushes and dental picks.

"Bird tracks on wet sand," scoffed one 17th-century European scholar, refusing to believe that cuneiform was a script. Today lexicographers Åke Sjöberg and Erle Leichty (above) of the University of Pennsylvania Museum decipher clay tablets ranging from epic poems to business records. Here Sjöberg examines a wool merchant's account from Ur, written 4,000 years ago.

A clay envelope enclosed a Sumerian IOU for ten shekels of silver (opposite, lower), dating from around 2030 B.C.

In December 1880 a young British surveyor named William Matthew Flinders Petrie arrived in Egypt to measure the pyramids at Gîza. Fascinated with archaeology since childhood, Petrie had already mapped more than 150 prehistoric earthworks in England. He set up camp in an ancient tomb near the pyramids and scandalized tourists (whom he disliked) by wandering through the hot chambers of the Great Pyramid of Khufu in nothing but pink underwear.

Impressed with Petrie's findings, the Egypt Exploration Fund of London sent him back to excavate a site in the lower Nile Delta. Later he branched out on his own, methodically cataloging every object at the exact level found. Thus began four decades of crucial archaeological research in Egypt.

While surveying the pyramids, Petrie had sensed that the commonplace artifacts littering every site held important clues to Egypt's past. Petrie put his interest in the minuscule to good use when he excavated the pyramid of King Senusert II and the tombs of the royal family at El Lâhûn in northern Egypt. Grave robbers had overlooked a gold crown, which Petrie found in a recess of one ransacked tomb. Washing the earth from the recess, Petrie found the royal cobra head that had adorned the front of the crown. "One eye was missing," Petrie wrote. "I washed and searched minutely, preserving the smallest specks of precious stone. Soon a tiny ball of garnet appeared . . . this—no larger than a pin's head—was the missing eye. Yet the gold socket of the eye was missing. I remembered having washed out a bead of gold . . . I found it again, and there was the setting of the eye complete."

The slapdash fieldwork of earlier excavators shocked Petrie. "Nothing seems to be done with any uniform and regular plan," he complained. "Work is begun and left unfinished. . . . It is sickening to see the rate at which everything is being destroyed, and the little regard paid to preservation." To Petrie, archaeology was "weaving a history out of scattered evidence." With infinite care and patience he used potsherds, coins, and inscribed ornaments of known age to date the foundations of temples and other buildings much more precisely than any archaeologist ever had before. He spent his winters in Egypt excavating, his summers in England promptly writing up his discoveries.

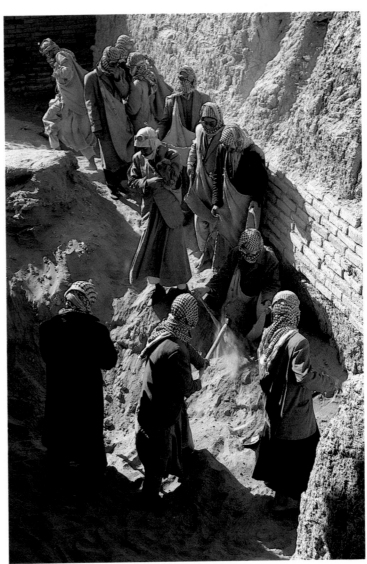

169

Archaeologists and Iraqi villagers (opposite) peer into a 2,000-year-old shaft, part of a fortress built around and over an earlier Sumerian ziggurat at Nippur. Skilled workers (above) clear sand from an ancient wall. Because mudbrick walls crumble to dust, locating them takes an eye for soil stains, changing textures, or flakes of mud-plaster facings. Ceramics experts look for archaeological clues too in the glaze or texture of a potsherd (left), which can tell how skilled the potter was.

Petrie ran his digs on a strict budget and enforced a rigorous life-style at his excavation camps. "He has a cot bed in the tomb of Nefer-maat," a visitor wrote, "...a few miscellaneous books...and two tents, one a kitchen with a petroleum stove." Petrie often lived on boxes of staple foods sent to him from London, and he expected the same of his staff. Digging started at 5:30 in the morning and continued until 6:30 at night, except for a rest during the scorching heat of midday. But at day's end he enjoyed the noisy camaraderie of his workmen. "There is a constant tootling of pipes, singing, clapping, shouting, and general jollity going on," he noted.

Petrie supported his work by selling artifacts to European museums. He paid his workmen not by the cubic foot of earth they removed but by the market value of every object they found. This funneled most items into his possession rather than into the hands of the dealers who haunted the fringes of most Egyptian excavations.

In 1894 Petrie explored a desert cemetery near Naqâda in central Egypt. In a single season his crew worked at top speed to open nearly 3,000 ancient burials. Boys located soft places in the sand; then untrained workmen cleared the shallow graves until skeletons appeared. A team of skilled diggers exposed the burials, which were finally tidied up by Petrie's foreman. The skeletons lay in a doubled-up position in shallow graves furnished with a few pots and beads, sometimes a flint knife or a palette for mixing eye paints.

Then came a breakthrough in dating the prehistoric remains. Petrie noted gradual changes in the shapes of some of the pots and especially the handles. These evolved from functional wavy handles into stylized ridges and then into mere decorations of painted lines.

Petrie used these stylistic changes to group the pots into 50 stages, to which he assigned "sequence dates." He assumed—correctly—that the wavy-handled jars by no means represented the first Egyptian pottery, so he gave this quite early stage the label S.D. 30. His sequence ended with S.D. 80 at the threshold of dynastic times, when the first kings ruled Egypt. Petrie theorized that S.D. 30 corresponded roughly to the year 9000 B.C. (Later experts estimated that this early

170

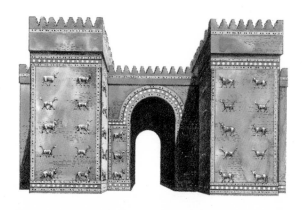

stage ranged between 4000 and 7000 B.C.) Petrie knew that the royal grave of Narmer, the first king of Egypt, dated to around 3100 B.C. By anchoring his sequence-dating chronology at the more recent end, he sought to provide a link between the earliest vessels and historic times. Archaeologists working in the Nile Valley eventually began to use Petrie's timetable to trace the roots of Egyptian civilization.

Between 1880 and 1926 Petrie made more major discoveries than any other archaeologist before or after him. Restless and indefatigable, he excavated 39 sites, trained a generation of Egyptologists, found the tombs of four of the first eight kings, and excavated Tell el 'Amârna, capital of the pharaoh Akhenaten, who reigned about 1350 B.C.

Petrie also furnished the first evidence tying the ancient Egyptians with the Aegean world. At Kôm Madînet Ghurab in northern Egypt, he dug up colorful Mycenaean potsherds decorated with flowers and elaborate patterns—similar to those from mainland Greece and the Aegean islands, where Mycenaean civilization had flowered from 1600 to 1100 B.C. Petrie's findings showed that the Mycenaeans and the Egyptians had traded with each other as early as 1500 B.C.

On a visit to Greece, Petrie confirmed these trade links. Imported Egyptian pottery discovered there was of the same age as his Kôm Madînet Ghurab finds. The ancient Egyptians had not flourished in isolation but had traded with other cultures in the eastern Mediterranean. Petrie's new technique of cross dating—using imported objects of known age to date sites far from the place where the objects were made—is still widely employed by archaeologists.

Knighted late in life, Petrie remained a prickly personality, controversial and defensive, but durable. A self-educated man, he distrusted people who were highly qualified and privileged. He thus was set apart from his near contemporary, Englishman Arthur John Evans, who was born to a life of wealth and high social status.

As a youth Evans fell in love with the Balkans, at that time a boiling pot of European politics. He became a foreign correspondent for a British newspaper, hobnobbing with rebels and landed gentry, tramping over the Yugoslav mountains. But anti-Austrian statements he made on the eve of

171

Once ablaze with brilliantly colored tiles, Babylon fires the imagination even in dusty ruin (upper). Probable site of the biblical Tower of Babel, the Mesopotamian city reached its zenith in the sixth century B.C., when as many as 200,000 people may have lived here. King Nebuchadnezzar built the city's massive Ishtar Gate (foreground) to honor the goddess of love. The painting at far left re-creates the gate's original splendor. Adorned with sacred dragons and bulls, the gate stood at the end of a sunken processional way. Life-size lions of glazed brick (left) stalked the walls along the avenue, "advancing one behind the other" and creating an "impression of peril and horror." So wrote Robert Koldewey, the German archaeologist who worked here from 1899 to 1917. His 200-man crew installed a railway for removing debris, then dug down 80 feet to uncover the Ishtar Gate (center). Koldewey, reported an assistant, "lived for Babylon and thought of Babylon . . . day and night."

172

Yugoslavia's annexation to the Austro-Hungarian Empire landed him in jail for six weeks; on his release he was expelled for good from his beloved Dubrovnik. Evans returned to England and, in 1884, won appointment as keeper of antiquities at Oxford's Ashmolean Museum, where he brought order and new acquisitions to a neglected chaos of valuable collections. An incurable romantic, Evans spent much of his time traveling, leaving his assistant back in Oxford to tell visitors that he was "somewhere in Bohemia."

Evans prowled through Greek bazaars, fascinated by engraved gemstones and stamp seals. Each of the seals—sometimes three- or four-sided, sometimes oval or round—bore symbols similar to those he had seen scratched on Mycenaean jars. In the days before locks and keys, a lump of wet clay was placed over the string securing a document or the lid of a box or jar. The clay was then stamped with a seal.

Evans's myopic eyes could discern at a close distance even the tiniest inscriptions. He bought dozens of gemstones and seals in the Athens marketplace and pored over the symbols. The dealers told him that most of their stock came from Crete. Could that Mediterranean island be the place where European writing had originated?

Evans took his theory to Crete in 1894. A guide led him through olive groves to a hillside traditionally called Knossos, brilliant with purple and white anemones. Evans combed the site in the spring sunshine and found pieces of Mycenaean-style pots lying on the surface. After some five years of negotiating, he bought Knossos for the then considerable price of a thousand pounds sterling. By that time he had found traces of two prehistoric writing systems on Crete; all the evidence indicated that the island had nurtured a great civilization predating the mainland Mycenaeans.

At age 48, with almost no excavating experience, Evans dug into Knossos in March 1900. Within a few weeks his laborers uncovered an elaborate complex of rooms, passages, and foundations. A splendid terraced palace yielded thousands of artifacts—man-high storage jars, hundreds of inscribed clay tablets, gemstones, and painted cups and vases. Lively and colorful frescoes appeared, one portraying a handsome, sinewy male cupbearer.

173

British archaeologist Flinders Petrie shares a moment's rest with his wife, Hilda, during their excavation at the ancient Egyptian city of Abydos in 1900. "The real tranquility and room for quiet thought in this sort of life is refreshing," mused Petrie. He wrote a book about his discoveries almost every year. His wife, also a noted Egyptologist, rendered drawings and supervised the workmen on site.

To help date Egyptian sites, Petrie devised a system of relative chronology—sequence dating—based on gradual changes in pottery styles. Grouping pots into 50 stages, he recorded the evolution of the useful wavy handles on earlier pots (far left) to the decorative stylized ridges on later pots, and then to pots merely painted with wavy lines. Petrie also pioneered cross dating, the technique of dating sites according to "trade pieces"—imported objects—whose age is known.

Overleaf: Frozen in a fresco 35 centuries old, a young Minoan somersaults over a charging bull—a favorite spectacle at Knossos on the Mediterranean island of Crete. Two girls help: One distracts the bull; the other waits to steady the acrobat's landing. This event—either sport or a religious rite—may have inspired the later Greek myth of the half-human, half-bull Minotaur that gored Athenian youths in the labyrinth of King Minos, legendary founder of the Minoan civilization.

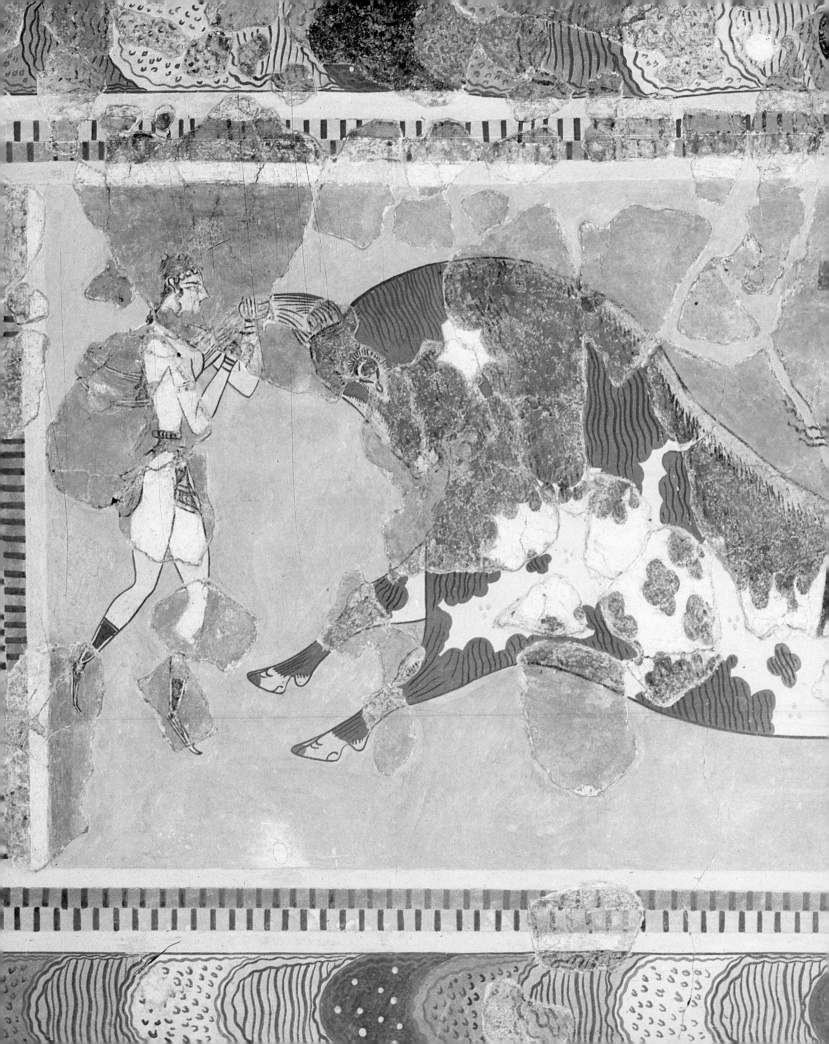

The palace, a vast multistoried structure, surrounded a central courtyard. Paintings of wingless griffins decorated one of the ceremonial rooms where a gypsum throne still sat in place. Evans was jubilant. He believed he had found the palace of the legendary King Minos. Here, according to myth, Minos's lovesick daughter, Ariadne, had helped a young Athenian named Theseus slay the dreaded Minotaur, a half-human, half-bull monster. While Ariadne held one end of a ball of yarn, Theseus unrolled the ball and threaded his way into the depths of the labyrinth where the Minotaur lurked. Theseus killed the monster, then rolled up the yarn to guide his retreat from the labyrinth. The mythical labyrinth could well have been inspired by the mazelike palace itself.

Among the Mycenaean potsherds unearthed in the palace's upper levels, Evans identified some as the same type that Petrie had discovered at Tell el 'Amârna in Egypt. Using

177

From the rubble of one of Europe's earliest cities rises the Palace of Knossos (left). Partial reconstruction evokes the sophisticated Minoan culture, which flourished until 1450 B.C. Once the center of a prosperous city, the palace sprawled across five acres, a maze of ceremonial rooms, residential quarters, kitchens, workshops, and storerooms wrapped around a central courtyard. Colorful frescoes decorated the corridors. An elaborate plumbing system served the palace.

British archaeologist Arthur Evans (above, with notepad) and his pottery specialist, Duncan Mackenzie, oversee local workmen excavating at the palace. Evans's search for the origins of European writing led him to Knossos, which he purchased in 1899. Evans worked here for 35 years, financing the project mostly out of his own pocket.

Petrie's pottery cross-dating techniques, Evans placed the lower levels of the palace as early as 2000 B.C., long before the Mycenaean heyday. Evans hailed the discovery of a civilization he called Minoan, after King Minos.

Evans went beyond discovery. He reconstructed parts of the palace, replacing wooden columns with concrete and painting them in their original deep pink color. From tiny fragments he restored some Minoan frescoes: processions of people, playful dolphins, flowers, mythical animals, and bulls—bulls everywhere. Evans failed in one respect: He never deciphered either the script he called Linear A, or the one he called Linear B, which had taken him to Knossos in the first place. Although more than 90 Minoan settlements and palaces have come to light, Linear A remains a baffling riddle. And not until 1952 did British scholar Michael Ventris decipher the later Cretan script, Linear B, which the mainland Mycenaeans brought to the island around 1450 B.C.

In brilliant monographs Evans unfolded the history of a sophisticated culture. Wealthy merchants and nobles lived on country estates and in elaborate palaces. Minoan merchants sailed to mainland Greece and to ports in the eastern Mediterranean, carrying wine, olive oil, and perfumed unguents, and returned home with tin and copper, amethyst, ivory, silver, gold, and lapis lazuli.

As he stood in the rebuilt palace staircase one moonlit night, Evans's fancy took wing and 35 centuries fell away: "The whole place seemed to awake awhile to life. . . . the Priest-King with his plumed lily crown, great ladies, tightly-girdled, flounced and corseted, long-stoled priests, and, after them, a retinue of elegant but sinewy youths—as if the Cup-Bearer and his fellows had stepped down from the walls—passed and repassed on the flights below."

All had been suddenly destroyed around 1450 B.C.— perhaps by earthquake and fire. Evans thought so. He had experienced an earthquake at Knossos in 1926. He lay still in his bed, almost seasick from the tremors. "A dull sound rose from the ground like the muffled roar of an angry bull," he recalled. Some historians now think the destruction may have coincided with the volcanic eruption of the nearby island of Thíra, which buried the adjacent archipelago in ash.

A gypsum throne unearthed by Evans's crew in 1913 (upper) stands today before a restored fresco of stylized lilies and wingless griffins at the Palace of Knossos (lower). Scholars now theorize that what Evans called the Throne Room was actually a Minoan ritual area rebuilt by the Mycenaeans, who assumed power on Crete after a catastrophe destroyed most of the palace around 1450 B.C. The disaster, perhaps earthquake and fire, brought the entire Minoan civilization to a sudden end.

Evans's team breaks off work (above) to pose with their leader (in white suit and hat) on the Grand Staircase at the Palace of Knossos. "Eight days of dangerous tunnelling brought us beyond the second landing," Evans reported in 1901. His Cretan crew used hand-hewn stone, steel girders, and reinforced concrete to restore the staircase (left). Though critics decry Evans's "concrete Crete," his admirers say his reconstructions brought Minoan history to life and preserved the fragile ruins.

The Knossos excavations filled one gap in the archaeological calendar but left another still blank—the history of the obscure Hittites, an ancient people known chiefly from sparse references in the Old Testament.

As early as the 1830s travelers reported monumental ruins at Boğazköy in central Turkey. Cuneiform tablets in an unknown language were found there in 1893. Intrigued by these mysterious tablets, German archaeologist Hugo Winckler began the first major excavations at Boğazköy in 1906.

Winckler did not relish the scorchingly hot summer days and the cold, windy nights. But with his head and neck covered and his hands gloved against the incessant flies, he patiently studied the hundreds of fragmentary tablets his workers turned up. Within a few days Winckler discovered some tablets written in Babylonian cuneiform. They proved to be correspondence between the king of Egypt and the king of Hatti. "No doubt remained," Winckler wrote, "that we found ourselves on the site of the capital of the Kingdom of the Hittites."

Halfway through the first season, Winckler savored one of those supreme moments of discovery that all too rarely come an archaeologist's way. Under a wall his workers found a well-preserved clay tablet. "One look at it, and all the experiences of my life paled into insignificance," Winckler wrote. He found himself reading a word-for-word copy in Babylonian cuneiform of a peace treaty between Pharaoh Ramesses II and the Hittites, a treaty long known to scholars from a hieroglyphic record on the walls of the Temple of Amun-Re at Karnak in Egypt. Winckler's spirits soared. Eighteen years earlier he had suggested that the treaty might also have been written in cuneiform. Now he held the proof in his hands! The Boğazköy excavations provided the vital archaeological link between Egypt and the biblical lands.

Excavations eventually yielded a hoard of 10,000 tablets that told much of what is known today about the Hittites. A Czech scholar finally deciphered the Hittite language in

180

Height 11⅝"

Minoan sailors may have unloaded cargoes from as far away as Cyprus and Italy at the harbor of Kommos (opposite) on Crete's southern shore. Evans predicted the port's location from clues in Homer's Odyssey and by tracking an ancient road from Knossos on the northern shore.

On arrival in 1924 he found the site, "strewn with Minoan remains." A University of Toronto team began digging here in 1976. Besides Evans's Minoan port they uncovered a Greek sanctuary (foreground) from the fourth century B.C.; beneath a rectangular temple lay remains of the earliest known Greek shrine on Crete.

Though the Minoans built no great temples, a wealth of sacred art proclaims their piety. The painted faience snake handler (left), which Evans reconstructed from fragments (shaded) found at Knossos, may represent a priestess or goddess.

1915. An aggressive people ruled by warrior-kings and skilled in diplomacy, the Hittites rose to military prominence around 1650 B.C. By the late 14th century, they claimed tribute from northern Syria and threatened Egyptian interests in Lebanon. The city of Hattusha at Boğazköy remained their capital until 1190 B.C. The texts peter out, and the Hittites' fate remains a mystery.

While the Germans were excavating Boğazköy, powerful European nations covetously eyed what remained of the Turkish Empire, especially Syria and Iraq. In 1905 the German government appointed a consul to Baghdād and daringly planned a strategic railroad to that city from southern Turkey. The tracks would pass close to ancient Carchemish, a Hittite vassal city that had guarded a key crossing of the Euphrates River on Turkey's border with Syria.

The British Museum had gained excavation rights at Carchemish in 1878, when the local owner bartered a quarter share of the site to the British consul in Aleppo for an embroidered cloak, a pair of blue leather boots, a revolver—and release from prison. But digging did not begin until 1911, with the arrival of archaeologist David Hogarth and two assistants: a cuneiform expert and young T. E. Lawrence, who later achieved fame as Lawrence of Arabia when he led the Arab revolt against the Turks during World War I. The word spread that Hogarth and Lawrence were British agents and that the dig was merely a cover for watching the Germans build the railroad nearby. It was not true, but the British did make use of the archaeologists' survey maps.

Nicknamed the "angel of death" because of his irritable temper before breakfast, Hogarth stayed at Carchemish only two months. In 1912 the British Museum sent a young, hard-driving archaeologist named Leonard Woolley to take over

Eye to eye with the distant past, American archaeologist Robert Braidwood and his assistants (left) carefully unearth an ancient burial at Tell Jedeideh in Turkey. A tarpaulin shades the fragile bones—and the excavators—in this 1930-31 project. Dental picks, brushes, bellows, and a surveyor's transit (below) aid archaeological excavations.

Near Boğazköy (lower), the site of the Hittite capital of Hattusha, scimitar-carrying warriors keep a 3,200-year vigil on a rock wall.

the project. When the local governor refused permission to continue the excavations, Woolley held a revolver to the official's head until he signed the permit.

Woolley's loyal team of 120 Turkish workmen loved his high-handed and arrogant style, his sense of drama. He rewarded spectacular discoveries with bonuses and also with revolver salvos. "The whole thing may sound childish," he wrote, ". . . but in fact it is such things that make the work go well, and when digging at [Carchemish] ceases to be a great game . . . it will be a bad thing."

Woolley and Lawrence lived like princes. Their house featured mosaic floors, a copper bathtub, a large fireplace, and thick sheepskin rugs. Visitors drank coffee from Hittite cups. "If I drop [one]," said Lawrence, "the British Museum will be glad to have the pieces."

But along with the fun was a highly efficient and fruitful

excavation. Woolley brought to light a powerful Hittite city-state that had thrived for almost 200 years. Along a processional way, his workmen dug up reliefs of a triumphant army—foot soldiers, chariots, and horses trampling the beaten foe. Woolley let his mind drift back over the ages: "Very magnificent must Carchemish have been when its sculptures were gay with colour, when the sunlight glistened on its enamelled walls, and its sombre brick was overlaid with panels of cedar and plates of bronze; when the plumed horses rattled their chariots along its streets, and the great lords, with long embroidered robes and girdles of black and gold, passed in and out of the carved gates of its palaces...."

The work at Carchemish illustrated in microcosm the state of archaeology in the decades before World War I: an adventurous academic pastime, at times a somewhat formalized game—but also a serious fledgling science.

184

Workmen at Carchemish in 1912 (right) haul away a stone block, clearing the ruins of this ancient Hittite city on the Euphrates River. British archaeologist Leonard Woolley (above, in hat) found the excavation project "a strange world wherein anything might happen." Woolley and his assistant, young T. E. Lawrence —later famous as Lawrence of Arabia—display a carving of the Hittite three-man war chariot. One warrior drove as his two passengers attacked with arrows and spears.

185

Mexico, 1940: At the ruins of La Venta, excavators uncover a 50-ton monument carved by the Olmec, builders of Mexico's earliest known civilization.

A NEW LOOK AT THE NEW WORLD

They thought it would take two or three hours, no more. Then the huge stone would be free of its earthen tomb. But now Matthew W. Stirling and his team had spent half a day on the job, their picks and shovels biting deep into rocky soil. Mahogany logs braced the sharply listing stone. Here at a jungle site called La Venta, in the Mexican state of Tabasco, the excavators had already unearthed two sculptured stone altars, tantalizing relics of the mysterious Olmec civilization. Now this 1940 expedition, sponsored by the National Geographic Society, was bringing to light another massive Olmec monument.

Not until late on the second day of digging were Stirling and his crew able to uncover the colossal stone stela. It stood fourteen feet high and measured seven feet across. Carved on its underside, two human figures stood face-to-face, each seven feet tall. Frozen in conversation for more than 2,300 years, they represented artistry from Mexico's first known civilization, an influential culture that for 800 years inhabited the steamy Gulf coast lands of Veracruz and Tabasco. Then, about 400 B.C., the Olmec inexplicably vanished.

By the time of Stirling's expedition, archaeology had grown into a science sophisticated enough to provide a fresh look at the New World, from its first inhabitants to its European colonizers. But at the turn of the century, New World archaeology had still been an amateur pursuit.

One such amateur, Leopoldo Batres, began digging into the ruins of Teotihuacán in the 1880s. For more than 600 years this Mexican religious and trading center may have supported a population of 200,000 before sliding into a puzzling decline about A.D. 750. An ex-militiaman, Batres had no qualifications as an archaeologist, but he enjoyed close ties with Mexican dictator Porfirio Díaz. Batres was appointed inspector and protector of Mexico's archaeological monuments, a post that allowed him to dig anywhere in the country. He chose legendary Teotihuacán in the semiarid Valley of Mexico, but realized by 1890 that a thorough excavation of the city would take more funds than the nearly bankrupt government could muster. So for the next few years he looked for easier sites to probe.

Then better times came along. Porfirio Díaz got himself reelected president in 1904, and soon after, Batres proposed a major effort to turn Teotihuacán into a national monument. This, he argued, would enhance Mexico's image and perhaps perpetuate Díaz in office. The idea appealed to the dictator, and he arranged for a sizable appropriation.

Batres set his team of peasants to work unearthing the dominant edifice—the Pyramid of the Sun, 216 feet high, 10 acres at its base. As they labored, clouds of dust rising from the site could be seen from a distance, mingling with white puffs of steam from a locomotive hauling rubble and earth away from the pyramid's base. In 1906 Díaz and his cabinet paid a visit to the dig and pored over plans for clearing and restoring the colossal monument.

Batres's crew spent more than four years stripping thousands of tons of rubble from the pyramid. The men uncovered a square-based structure with a wide staircase from ground to summit. But in his zeal to finish the job in time for the Mexican centennial celebration in 1910, Batres mangled the pyramid, giving it five great stepped terraces instead of the four it originally had.

Though impressed by Batres's discoveries, critics were appalled at his crude and reckless excavation methods. He lost his post in 1910 when Díaz fell from power. A half century later the Mexican government recognized Teotihuacán's potential as a tourist attraction and restored much of its central section on a grand scale. Six hundred men labored on the site, this time supervised by professional archaeologists.

Along the city's main thoroughfares, rebuilt monuments rose in majestic array—the Pyramids of the Sun and the Moon, several temples, two complexes that may have been the city's administrative center, and parts of lavish palace residences. The workers used the surviving stone blocks as guides in reconstructing staircases, walls, and terraces. Today visitors wander through an imposing city of terraced pyramids, columned patios, and avenues that evoke the ancient builders' audacity, self-confidence, and pride.

The urban centers of the Maya also intrigued New World archaeologists. Built in the thorny scrublands of the Yucatán Peninsula and in the jungles of Guatemala, Honduras, and El Salvador, Maya cities had flourished for 650 years until A.D. 900. To one of these sites, Quiriguá in eastern

The colossal Pyramid of the Moon (upper), its tiered platforms linked by a 150-foot staircase, looms over more than a hundred temples and shrines in ancient Teotihuacán. America's first metropolis, Teotihuacán held sway over much of Mexico from A.D. 100 to 750. Aztecs visited the awe-inspiring city six centuries after its mysterious fall. Amazed, they called it Place of the Gods and, ascribing to it their own myths, said the moon and sun had been born in its massive pyramids.

A visitor in 1910 found the Pyramid of the Moon (left), and much of the rest of Teotihuacán, "covered yet with its mantle of grass." Although partly excavated early in the century, the city was not mapped in detail until American archaeologist René Millon arrived in the 1960s. His crew charted eight square miles of temples, apartments, and workshops dominated by the Pyramids of the Sun (opposite) and Moon. The Mexicans have restored much of the city's center.

Guatemala, came Alfred P. Maudslay in 1881. Maudslay, a British gentleman-scholar, was at once a diplomat and a self-trained archaeologist—one of the earliest to work in Guatemala. On his first visit to Quiriguá, he saw only "moss-grown stumps of dead trees covered over with a tangle of creepers and parasitic plants." But when he pulled off the vines and brushed away the moss, he gazed in astonishment—the "stumps" were stelae, elaborately carved stone monuments. Over the next 13 years Maudslay cleared the tangled undergrowth from dozens of sites.

Maudslay did not have an easy time. He paid his own way, traveling all too often with "bad mules, sulky muleteers, and half-drunken Indians." About Palenque, once a vibrant Maya city in southern Mexico, Maudslay wrote: "The great forest around us hung heavy with wet, the roof above us was dripping water like a slow and heavy rainfall, and the walls were glistening and running with moisture." Of Quiriguá he wrote: "At one time the flood-water covered all but a few feet of ground on which our palm-leaf shanty had been built; everything in camp turned green with mould and mildew, snakes and scorpions became very troublesome, and mosquitos were a continual torment. Worst of all . . . twelve of

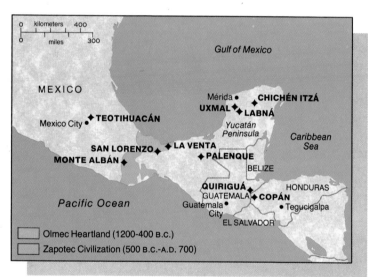

Monte Albán, ceremonial center of the Zapotec, crowns a flattened mountaintop in Mexico's Valley of Oaxaca. From this prominence an elite of priests and princes ruled from A.D. 100 to 900. Their center grew into a great cultural metropolis, rivaling Teotihuacán and the Maya cities to the east (map).

From a plaza nearly the size of four football fields rise Monte Albán's low masonry pyramids. Stepped platforms at either end hide tombs and hold aloft palaces and temples.

In one tomb excavated in 1932, Mexican archaeologist Alfonso Caso came upon a hoard of silver and gold—earrings, pendants, rings, and other ornaments—along with carvings in turquoise, jade, and obsidian. The cache, one of the New World's richest, was left by the Mixtec who, long after the Zapotec fled, turned the city into a vast burial site.

The Olmec, who vanished from the Gulf coast around 400 B.C., also left fine jade carvings as well as colossal heads sculptured in basalt.

192

Beneath a canopy of palm fronds, crew members on Alfred P. Maudslay's 1883 expedition to Quiriguá, Guatemala, cast in plaster the Great Turtle (above), a Maya carving. A similar stone shaped like a tortoise (right) may commemorate the death of Sky Xul, who ruled here in the eighth century A.D. Maudslay, a British explorer and self-taught archaeologist, published meticulous reports with maps, plans, drawings, and photographs—the first serious study of Maya ruins.

the Indians were down with fever at the same time, and all the sound ones ran away to their homes."

Throughout it all, Maudslay diligently recorded his findings. He photographed the monuments and put artists to work drawing them. He made plaster and paper casts of the important carved surfaces, convinced these were more useful for serious study than drawings or photographs. At Copán alone his crew mixed more than four tons of plaster to make 1,400 casts. His documentation was so precise that, even today, scholars rely on his voluminous publications.

Another Maya devotee was tough, self-reliant Edward H. Thompson, who later worked with Maudslay. His childhood hobby of collecting Indian arrowheads sparked a lifelong interest in archaeology. An article that Thompson wrote about the legendary lost continent of Atlantis brought him to the attention of backers in the American Antiquarian Society and Harvard's Peabody Museum. Strings were pulled, and Thompson won appointment as United States consul for the Mexican states of Yucatán and Campeche. His sponsors gave him the freedom to study any Maya sites that struck his fancy.

In 1885 Thompson traveled to Yucatán and began wandering the peninsula, sandwiching archaeological research between his consular duties in Mérida. Seeking out remote, unpilfered sites, he sketched, photographed, and made plaster impressions of Maya monuments. Forty men labored with a train of mules for more than a year, bringing in materials and then hauling out plaster molds from Labná and Uxmal—10,000 square feet of architectural impressions for display at the Chicago World's Fair of 1893.

At the fair Thompson met a wealthy Chicagoan named Allison V. Armour who, soon after, came to Yucatán and toured its ruins. Intrigued by Thompson's research, Armour helped buy the vast property on which the two-square-mile Maya city of Chichén Itzá lay. With income from cattle, crops, and timber, Thompson hoped to fund his scientific ventures. Meanwhile he rebuilt a 17th-century ranch house on the property to live in with his wife and children.

Chichén Itzá's Sacred Cenote fascinated Thompson. A large natural well with vertical walls falling to turbid water, it had been infamous since the Spanish conquest of the 16th century. Wrote a Spanish bishop: "Into this well they have had . . . the custom of throwing men alive as a sacrifice to the gods, in times of drought. . . . They also threw into it . . . precious stones and things which they prized."

Thompson found 35 feet of water in the well. In 1904 he erected a derrick and a crude dredge. Nothing but mud and silt came up from the cenote at first, then aromatic balls of incense, temple vases, and gold pendants. When dredging produced no more objects, Thompson and two crew members dressed in diving suits "of waterproof canvas with big copper helmets weighing more than thirty pounds . . . and lead necklaces nearly half as heavy as the helmets and canvas shoes with thick wrought-iron soles." Thompson was the first to plunge to the cenote's bottom. "I felt . . . a strange thrill when I realized that I was the only living being who had ever reached this place alive and expected to leave it again still living." Thompson delved into the cenote until 1911

Setting up shop inside the Nunnery, named for its cell-like rooms, Maudslay works on a drawing at the Maya city of Chichén Itzá on Mexico's Yucatán Peninsula. An aura of "ghostly grandeur" about the ruined city soon struck Maudslay as oppressive. From 1881 to 1894 he made seven expeditions at his own expense to various Maya sites. "I am only an amateur, travelling for pleasure," he once said. Maudslay's Archaeology, a five-volume set, still serves as a basic reference on the Maya.

and recovered nearly 30,000 sacrificial offerings—copper bells and disks, turquoise masks, jade jewelry, gold earrings, bits of fabric, dart throwers, arrowheads, and the bones of adults and children, some of them deformed.

Thompson prevailed on visiting scholars to take parcels back to the Peabody Museum until most of the objects found safe haven there. He said nothing publicly until 1923, when he boldly announced in the *New York Times* the spectacular results of his work. Shocked, the Mexicans charged Thompson with looting and later demanded that the Peabody Museum return the artifacts. The Mexican government took over Thompson's property, and he returned to the United States. In 1959 and 1976 the museum sent back to Mexico many objects in its collection in exchange for a group of ancient Mexican and Spanish colonial pieces.

Just as the Thompson scandal broke, the Carnegie Institution of Washington, D. C., unveiled plans for a major excavation at Chichén Itzá, with Harvard-trained archaeologist Sylvanus G. Morley as leader. Only Morley's diplomacy enabled the project to go forward. Carnegie agreed to relinquish all claims to artifacts and to reconstruct Chichén Itzá's crumbling pyramids and temples. The bulk of the effort went into excavating and rebuilding, but Carnegie also restored outstanding artifacts. One of them, a nine-and-a-half-inch mosaic disk of shells, turquoise, and pyrite, is now a highlight of Mexico City's National Museum of Anthropology. Carnegie's efforts were the first aimed at conserving Mexican archaeological treasures for public enjoyment.

Morley presided over the work at Chichén Itzá with an easy grace. His excavation camps gained a reputation for the gourmet dishes served up by his Chinese cook. Morley gave concerts with phonograph records in the ancient Maya ball court, which proved to have superb acoustics. When he heard that conductor Leopold Stokowski was experimenting with outdoor acoustics, Morley invited him to Chichén Itzá. Stokowski prowled the ball court for several days, playing records. But he never learned its acoustical secret.

In 1940 the Carnegie Institution closed down its Chichén Itzá project, having set a precedent for conscientious excavation that persists in Mexico to this day.

Height 2¾"

194

"The well into which they threw . . . beautiful things," wrote a 16th-century Spanish bishop of the Sacred Cenote at Chichén Itzá (opposite). To the gods the Maya offered hundreds of objects, including a jade carving of a warrior (above), gold masks, and fragrant balls of incense. Men, women, and children were also sacrificed.

In 1904 United States consul Edward H. Thompson began to dredge the sacred well. Of the many objects he brought up, some were later stolen; the rest he sent to Harvard.

Turn-of-the-century excavations in the southwestern United States were anything but conscientious. Pothunters overran archaeological sites in search of salable objects. Richard Wetherill, a rancher and trader, made artifact collecting a lucrative sideline. Wetherill explored the deep canyons of southwestern Colorado and found many of the Mesa Verde cliff dwellings, one of them a cluster of more than 225 rooms. Here, 700 years ago, lived the Anasazi, the forerunners of today's Pueblo Indians.

At first Wetherill—the Indians called *him* Anasazi—sold whatever pottery and other artifacts he accumulated. One of his collections was exhibited at the 1893 world's fair. But eventually he excavated and collected primarily for an exploration outfit that turned the objects over to the American Museum of Natural History in New York City.

After Mesa Verde, Wetherill eventually moved on to Pueblo Bonito in northwestern New Mexico, the largest and

A compressed-air dredge, far more sophisticated than the one Thompson used, vacuums up treasures from the Sacred Cenote (above). With help from the National Geographic, this 1961 project recovered more than 4,000 artifacts and the skull of a young woman.

Some six decades earlier, Thompson had donned heavy gear like that at right and plunged 35 feet to the well's bottom. The crew bid "a last farewell, never expecting to see me again," he wrote. A later dive left him slightly deaf.

most complex Anasazi ruin. He homesteaded the site and cleared almost 200 of the pueblo's 650 rooms at a cost of $25,000, a huge sum in those days. Wetherill and his brothers erected a trading post against the north wall of Pueblo Bonito. Nearby Wetherill built a house that grew with his family.

In 1906 the federal government, alarmed about vandalism at archaeological sites, passed a law that gave them some protection. The following year Wetherill was forced to relinquish to the Department of the Interior his title to Pueblo Bonito and two other ruins.

In 1915 Harvard-educated Alfred V. Kidder went to Pecos, New Mexico, where a pueblo with more than 700 rooms had flourished as late as the 1700s. He found the pueblo structures "fallen so completely into ruin that they appear to be nothing but vast heaps of tumbled stones. Closer examination, however, discloses the tops of walls, and here and there the protruding ends of wooden beams. The mounds are overgrown with grass and cactus. In rainy seasons the wild verbena carpets the ruins with brilliant purple."

Kidder's workmen cut trenches into rubbish heaps at the edge of the site and collected potsherds from each level of occupation, thus revealing a stratigraphic sequence. Kidder's findings confirmed and amplified the pottery sequence developed for the nearby Galisteo Basin a few years earlier by Nels C. Nelson of the American Museum of Natural History. Nelson had been the first archaeologist to devise a chronology in the Southwest based on stratigraphy.

Kidder also searched for burials in which the mortuary pottery would date the skeletons. At first he offered his laborers a bonus of 25 cents a skeleton. They found so many in the first few days that he reduced the payment to 10 cents, then abandoned the reward. "It was obvious," wrote Kidder, "that we were digging in the greatest rubbish heap and cemetery that had ever been found in the Pueblo region...." After only three seasons of work, Kidder could compare material from almost 700 graves with the potsherds from the trash heaps. After ten seasons he was able to describe six superimposed settlements and eight major cultural stages.

In his later work at Pecos, Kidder flew with Charles Lindbergh to take aerial photographs on survey flights in

Dirt flies as diggers slice into a small temple entombed within the base of the Temple of the Warriors, one of Chichén Itzá's grandest structures (opposite). Once the workers had cleared the underlying chambers, they used steel beams and concrete columns to support the 37-foot-high temple above it. The Carnegie Institution financed this dig in the 1920s, part of its 20-year excavation and restoration of the Maya city.

Sylvanus G. Morley (left), a bon vivant and exuberant Maya scholar ("my Mayas," he called them), headed the project. One building among the many his staff repaired may have been an observatory (above). Spaniards had named it El Caracol—"the snail"— for its interior spiral passage. Openings in its tower appear to align with the setting sun during spring and autumn equinoxes. Gifted astronomers and mathematicians, the Maya perfected a calendar that guided them in selecting dates for such vital occasions as planting and harvesting.

the Pecos area. Lindbergh remembered "hunting for marks of early civilization. . . . From the air we could see dimly but definitely the square or rectangular lines on the earth that marked where walls had stood. . . ."

Kidder sketched a sweeping outline of Pueblo Indian prehistory. For the earliest inhabitants, he postulated "a more or less nomadic people, thinly scattered over the country, ignorant of agriculture and of pottery-making." Kidder concluded that these nomads were succeeded some 4,000 years ago by the Basket Makers, the earliest farmers in the Southwest. They wove baskets but made no pottery. Later inhabitants built permanent homes, became skilled cultivators of corn, beans, and squash, and eventually developed pottery and pueblo architecture. Kidder lamented that "so many hopeful experiments in life and in living were cut short by the devastating blight of the white man's arrival."

But an element was missing from Kidder's sequence: absolute, rather than purely relative, dates. Kidder could only deduce from undated archaeological evidence that prehistoric peoples had been living in the Southwest since long before the time of Christ. He took a keen interest in the research of Andrew E. Douglass, a University of Arizona astronomer studying the relationship between climatic changes and the annual growth rings in weather-sensitive trees. Douglass had noticed that the rings were thinner in dry years than in wet ones. In the early 1900s he took thin cores from living pine trees and found he could study climatic changes for the past 500 years. To carry the scale further into the past, he bored into beams from ancient pueblos. By overlapping the oldest (inner) rings of living trees with the newest (outer) rings of certain beams, he could cross-match the growth record and the climate sequence backward even further.

But Douglass failed to find a link between the tree chronologies from recent centuries and those from all Southwest prehistoric sites. There appeared to be a gap in the 13th century, so Douglass searched for a connection. In exchange for yards of purple velvet and the promise to cap every hole he drilled with a turquoise to keep spirits from entering or exiting, he prevailed on the Hopi Indians of northern Arizona to let him core the time-worn beams of their pueblos. But still no luck. The beams dated only to about A.D. 1260.

Finally in 1929, on one of his expeditions supported by the National Geographic Society, Douglass discovered the bridge across the missing years. At a ruin in eastern Arizona, his crew found a charred log with rings that could be cross-matched to fill the 13th-century hiatus. The "lost" interval had actually been represented in previous beam sections, but the evidence had been too fragmentary to close the gap convincingly. Douglass's new tree-ring time scale showed that the Anasazi had occupied Pueblo Bonito from the 10th to the early 12th centuries A.D. For the first time archaeologists had a precise, though limited, way of dating the past.

Dendrochronology gave archaeologists a time scale for prehistory in the Southwest, but it could not tell them when the first Americans had crossed the Bering Strait from Asia. Twenty-one years earlier, on a fall day in 1908, a New Mexico

"The colossal head to end all colossal heads" gets a face wash at San Lorenzo under Marion Stirling's watchful eye (opposite). Her husband, Matthew W. Stirling (above, in foreground), studied the 2,300-year-old Olmec head in 1946 on the last of eight expeditions he led to southern Mexico. The Stirling party overcame the jungle, intense heat, and swarms of ticks to reach Olmec ruins.

The bars and dots on a stela (right) that Stirling dug up in 1939 date the slab to 31 B.C.

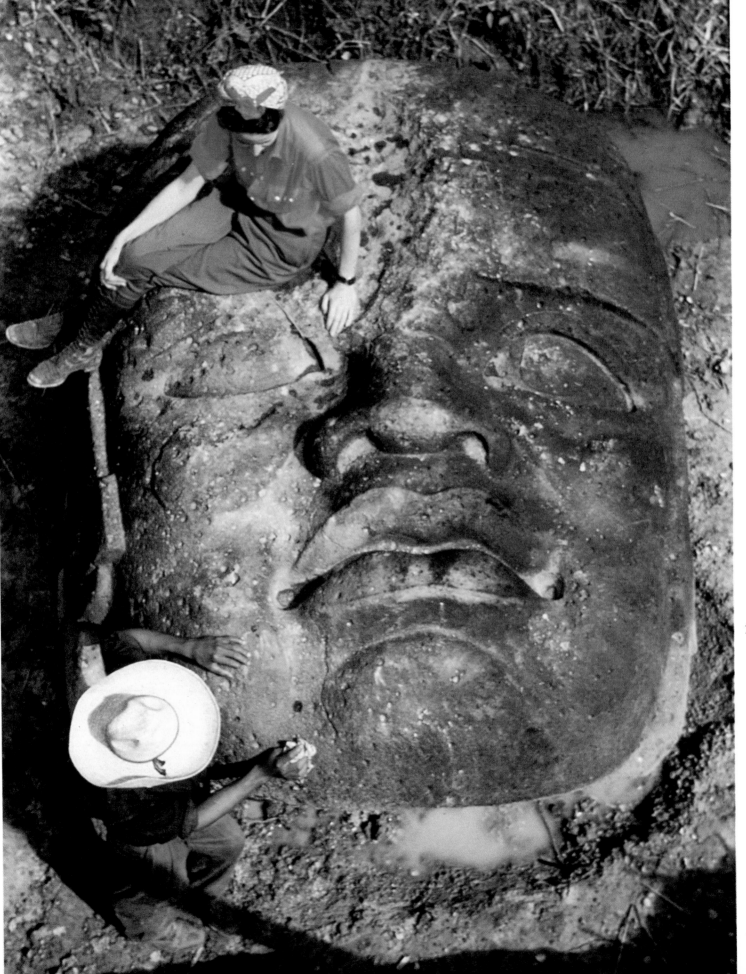

199

cowboy named George McJunkin was riding along the edge of a gully near the town of Folsom. He had ridden such gullies many times before, but on this day he spotted something white projecting from the wall of the ravine. Curious, he pried at the object with a pair of clippers. To his surprise a large bone came loose in his hand. Others followed; they did not look like any cattle or bison bones he had ever seen.

Over the next years McJunkin interested two amateur naturalists in his mysterious bone pit, but it was not until some fossil bones were unearthed in Texas in the early 1920s that one of the naturalists thought to contact Jesse D. Figgins of the Colorado Museum of Natural History about McJunkin's find. Figgins visited the Folsom site in 1926. He realized that the bones were probably those of a species of bison believed extinct since the end of the Ice Age. Four months later an excavator found a finely crafted projectile

point near a spinal bone. Figgins had no doubt that if the point had killed the bison, then prehistoric peoples must have lived in North America at the time of Ice Age animals.

The next year Figgins found still more bones and weapons at the site. This time he left some in the ground and invited several skeptical colleagues to verify his discovery. When the Smithsonian's Frank H. H. Roberts, Jr., arrived, he found a fellow archaeologist brushing the soil away from a projectile point "still embedded in the *matrix between two of the ribs of the animal skeleton.*" Roberts endorsed Figgins's theory: People had lived in the Americas as early as the end of the Ice Age, about 10,000 years ago. The Folsom discoveries virtually doubled the time frame of American archaeology.

As discoveries in the Southwest brought fresh knowledge of early humans in America, events along the James River in southeastern Virginia began to tell the story of much

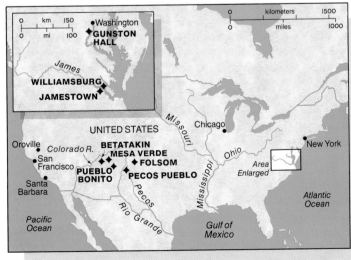

Tourists walk along the rim of a kiva, or sunken chamber, at Pueblo Bonito (above) in New Mexico's Chaco Canyon. These round pits served as social and ceremonial centers. About A.D. 900 the Anasazi, forerunners of the Pueblo Indians, began building 650-room Pueblo Bonito, the largest of their multistoried dwellings. They deserted it 250 years later.

In the early 1920s Neil M. Judd led a National Geographic expedition to the pueblo. He and his workers removed "several trainloads of building stone, adobe, plaster, and wind-blown sand" from the sprawling ruin they found (opposite, upper). A flash flood, one of many desert pitfalls, mired the expedition's car in 1921 (opposite, lower).

Overleaf: Sheltered by an overhanging mesa, the 13th-century citadel of Betatakin clings to the side of an Arizona cave. Drought may have forced the Anasazi to abandon their red sandstone home after only two generations. Judd restored Betatakin in 1917.

more recent arrivals. In 1607 a company of 104 men had disembarked at Jamestown and established the first permanent English settlement in the New World. From a small palisaded fort, the tiny community became the center of a growing colony along the James River and the first capital of Virginia.

Almost three centuries later, three Virginia ladies, members of the Association for the Preservation of Virginia Antiquities (APVA), went to work to improve what was a "picture of desolation" at Jamestown. Mary and Annie Galt and Mary Garrett fenced part of the property against livestock, planted trees, flowers, and grass, and began to excavate the foundations of Jamestown's mid-17th century church. "I dug with my own hands quite deep inside of the south wall . . . and discovered the little inner wall composed of large bricks and cobblestones," Mary Galt wrote. What she found were the remains of an earlier church built in 1617.

The women opened many graves, piecing together fragments of tombstones they uncovered in the debris. The brass tacks the colonists had used to write out names and dates on coffin tops survived, but most of the names had broken apart as the coffins disintegrated. That hardly deterred Mary Galt. In one grave "broken lettering had dropped down among the ribs. As usual, I got into the grave and traced over the letters. Among the disconnected tacks were some connected together to make us pretty sure of the name B. Harrison."

To curb erosion along the shore of Jamestown, the association persuaded the Army Corps of Engineers to build a seawall in 1900 and 1901. In doing so, Col. Samuel H. Yonge and his crew exposed brick foundations, prompting Yonge to take up archaeology as an avocation. He excavated the remains of a 240-foot-long row of attached houses comprising the colonial governor's mansion, the State House, and the Ludwell House, where several families lived. This complex had burned in 1698, spurring the legislature's move inland to a new town, Middle Plantation, which the colonists renamed Williamsburg in honor of King William III. In the cellar of the Ludwell House, Yonge dug up artifacts that helped tell the story of colonial life in Jamestown: "a pipe, scissors, steel sewing-thimble, copper candle stick, ladies' riding stirrup, and an old bottle, all of quaint and antique shapes. . . ."

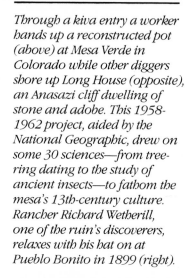

Through a kiva entry a worker hands up a reconstructed pot (above) at Mesa Verde in Colorado while other diggers shore up Long House (opposite), an Anasazi cliff dwelling of stone and adobe. This 1958-1962 project, aided by the National Geographic, drew on some 30 sciences—from tree-ring dating to the study of ancient insects—to fathom the mesa's 13th-century culture. Rancher Richard Wetherill, one of the ruin's discoverers, relaxes with his hat on at Pueblo Bonito in 1899 (right).

Only the 18th-century steeple of Bruton Parish Church recalls Williamsburg's days as a colonial capital in this 1890 photograph. A walk down Duke of Gloucester Street in 1926 helped persuade John D. Rockefeller, Jr., to restore the historic Virginia town. Since then his foundation has torn down many modern buildings, reconstructed almost 500 colonial structures, and restored 88—at a cost of more than $100,000,000. The 1782 Frenchman's Map (right) helps guide the project.

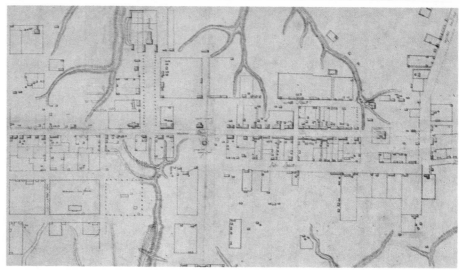

Colonel Yonge and the women of the APVA helped lay the groundwork for historical archaeology in America, the study of sites dating from after the arrival of Europeans. In 1934 the National Park Service joined the APVA in administering Jamestown and later carried on excavations under the leadership of J. C. Harrington, a trained archaeologist. Harrington consolidated and expanded the earlier work and produced a well-rounded picture of agriculture, industry, commerce, and everyday life in 17th-century Jamestown.

America's colonial epoch reached full flower at Williamsburg after the Virginia capital's move there in 1699. During the 1920s W.A.R. Goodwin, a professor at the College of William and Mary, had a dream: To restore the genteelly decaying town, which had known a glorious past as a center of revolutionary zeal in 18th-century America.

Earlier, Goodwin and his eight-year-old daughter Evelyn had excavated under the floor of Williamsburg's Bruton Parish Church, where he was rector. They were seeking coffins of unrecorded parishioners. "So we dug up the old wooden floor," Evelyn recalled, "and dug down to the coffins...." Where strips of leather "had protected the wood it was still intact, and with infinite care we brushed the dirt away and found the inscriptions.... I need no picture to bring back the musty smell of the earth, the strange 'odor of sanctity,' and the feeling of awe that it stirred in me as a little girl."

Goodwin persuaded John D. Rockefeller, Jr., to save what was left of colonial Williamsburg as a shrine to the birth of American democracy. Rockefeller had supported digs in Egypt and had just offered the Egyptians $5,400,000 for a new museum to house the Tutankhamun treasures. When the Egyptians declined, Rockefeller turned to projects closer to home. For more than a year he quietly bought up land in Williamsburg, then announced plans to restore the old town by removing unsightly modern structures and restoring and reconstructing colonial buildings.

In its commanding site at the east end of Duke of Gloucester Street, Williamsburg's Capitol had witnessed democracy firsthand. Patrick Henry's words thundered in its House of Burgesses, George Washington spoke in its chambers, and Revolutionary troops assembled in its courtyard. The building burned to the ground in 1747, was rebuilt four years later, then abandoned before burning again in 1832. Only the foundations remained. Rockefeller's architects, trying to re-create the original floor plan of the Capitol, found traces of the west wing. But precise pictorial evidence provided the greatest help. A researcher working in 1929 in the Bodleian Library at Oxford, England, turned up a mid-1700s copper engraving for a book never printed. The Bodleian Plate showed perspective views of Williamsburg's Capitol, Governor's Palace, and college buildings.

The Governor's Palace, built in 1720, had been home to Thomas Jefferson and Patrick Henry. It served as a military hospital in 1781 before burning down. The rebuilders found that much of the structure's interior had collapsed into the cellar. They could not simply clear the foundation; the debris was too important. The excavators recovered fragments of delftware fireplace tiles, marble mantelpieces, black-walnut

Crab claws and gunflints—excavators uncover these and other signs of daily life in the foundations of a blacksmith shop and kitchen chimney behind Williamsburg's James Anderson House. As public armorer of colonial Virginia, Anderson made and repaired weapons and equipment for the Continental Army. The foundation layout helped a team of archaeologists, archivists, and architectural historians plan the forge's reconstruction. Carpenters did the work using 18th-century tools and building methods for the first time at 20th-century Colonial Williamsburg.

Attention to artifacts, as well as to deeds, inventories, books, letters, wills, and court records, helped Williamsburg's developers rebuild the town with remarkable accuracy. The project stands as a landmark in the restoration of America's historic sites.

paneling, and the black-and-white marble floor of the Great Hall—all of which helped guide the reconstruction.

Excavation of the palace gardens yielded a forgotten cemetery containing 158 skeletons. Nothing but uniform buttons remained to date the bodies to the Revolutionary War. Amputated limbs proved the cemetery had been filled during the palace's few months as a military hospital.

By combining the written record with evidence from buildings and artifacts to reconstruct a historical site, the Williamsburg project extended the lessons learned at Jamestown. The undertaking, which so far has cost more than $100,000,000, today attracts droves of visitors. In the historic area encompassing some 550 restored and reconstructed buildings, interpreters reenact the life of British Virginia.

Early in the 20th century a number of anthropologists recorded the customs of vanishing Indians who remembered the centuries-old ways of their ancestors. One such opportunity arose in August 1911 near Oroville, California. The slaughterhouse watchdogs would not stop barking that warm, misty morning. So the butchers, grumbling, climbed from their beds to investigate. They found the dogs sniffing at a shivering, naked man huddled in the corner of the cattle

Rebuilt to its 18th-century grandeur, the Governor's Palace in Williamsburg (right) rests on original foundations, shown above in 1930. Home of seven royal governors and the commonwealth's first two, the mansion burned down in 1781. Fragments of black-walnut paneling, marble slabs, and other materials that had fallen into the cellar aided in the reconstruction. Excavators found cellar doorways and passages but few of the thousands of wine bottles inventoried in 1770.

corral. Thinking they had caught a wild man, the butchers called the sheriff, who soon realized that his prisoner was an exhausted, terrified Indian who spoke not a word of English. He detained the Indian in the county jail while deciding what to do with him. No one, not even other Indians, could understand the captive. He became an instant celebrity. Reporters and sightseers besieged the jail.

The news reached anthropologists Alfred L. Kroeber and Thomas Waterman at the University of California in Berkeley. Experts on California Indians, they knew at once that the sheriff's "guest" could well be the last of the Yana Indians, a tribe devastated a generation earlier by vigilantes. A few Yanas had survived into the 20th century by hiding in the wilderness, hunting small game and gathering acorns. Waterman met the prisoner and wrote Kroeber: "This man is undoubtedly wild. He has pieces of deer thong in place of

ornaments in the lobes of his ears and a wooden plug in the septum of his nose. He recognizes most of my Yana words."

The anthropologists took custody of the Indian and gave him a room at the university's anthropology museum in San Francisco. They learned he had been alone since 1908, when a surveying party raided the camp where he lived with his mother, sister, and an old man. His mother died soon after; the others disappeared. Exhausted by starvation, he had strayed into the 20th-century world that August morning. Waterman named their guest Ishi, the Yana word for "man."

For nearly five years Ishi was a star attraction at the museum. Kroeber and Waterman studied him as he made weapons and tools from obsidian, sinew, and wood. Fascinated visitors watched him produce Stone Age artifacts, chipping flakes of obsidian from lumps of volcanic rock and fashioning them into arrowheads, which he would often give away.

In May 1914 Kroeber, Waterman, and two companions took Ishi by train and pack mule back to his home country in the northern California foothills. There they learned more about Ishi's close relationship with the environment. In his old hunting grounds they watched him stalk deer with infinite patience, squatting silently for hours as the animals fed.

When Ishi died of tuberculosis in 1916, his friends at the museum mourned him greatly. One admirer wrote: "His were the qualities of character that last forever. He was kind; he had courage and self-restraint, and though all had been taken from him, there was no bitterness in his heart." The research of Kroeber and Waterman into a vanishing Indian culture is an invaluable resource for today's anthropologists, archaeologists, and historians.

John Peabody Harrington, a Californian who grew up in the 1890s, also left a record of Indian ways. As a boy he lived in the land of the Chumash, fishermen and gatherers who had once prospered along the Santa Barbara Channel in an environment so plentiful that a Spanish missionary remarked, "for them, the entire day is one continuous meal." By the early 1900s the Chumash had been nearly wiped out by disease and poverty brought on by compulsory resettlement into missions and other injustices at the hands of both Spanish and American settlers.

Harrington studied anthropology, linguistics, Latin, and Greek at Stanford University. Each summer he learned Indian languages in the field. In 1915 the Smithsonian Institution hired him as an ethnologist, and he spent the rest of his life among Indians. He scrutinized their daily lives and probed their memories for minute details of their earlier ways, jotting down answers to his questions on anything handy—scraps of paper, matchbox covers, old envelopes. Harrington worried about elderly Indians' dying before he could complete interviews with them. During a 50-year career he amassed more than 800,000 pages of field notes. Later, it would take a full-time archivist years to organize them.

Harrington suffered chronically from dysentery and other ailments, but his most serious affliction was paranoia. He became so secretive about his work that he pretended to be in one place when really in another. His notes in English,

High-tech detective work reveals details of the original design and decoration of Gunston Hall (left), the 1759 Virginia home of colonial statesman George Mason. In the mansion's ornate parlor (opposite), an architectural historian on a scaffold searches for traces of the original wallpaper with a high-intensity light. Ultraviolet black light (above) discloses the outline of a ribbon-and-bellflower molding that once decorated the room.

Such new techniques fuel growing interest in accurate restoration. Historians once depended on descriptions and drawings to tell them how a building looked. Now they can read the building itself for clues.

Anthropologists also work back from the present to study the past. Interviews with old-timers, observations in the field, and historical records help them reconstruct vanishing lifeways.

German, Spanish, and even Indian languages listed hundreds of his sources' names in code.

In 1961 John Harrington died, almost forgotten. Few researchers made use of his notes until 1974, when Travis Hudson of the Santa Barbara Museum of Natural History became interested in Chumash canoes. Hudson found that Harrington's record included more than 3,000 pages about canoes.

To test Harrington's reliability, Hudson had a Chumash canoe built from driftwood, using modern power tools but the traditional Indian techniques. A crew of Chumash descendants paddled the canoe, as their ancestors had done, along the Santa Barbara Channel. Swift and seaworthy, the canoe could easily carry four or five people and several hundred pounds of cargo.

John Harrington provided unique insights into the rich symbolism of Indian life. Anthropologists are still studying his voluminous notes, delving into Chumash astronomy, folklore, and tribal histories. Harrington's documentation shows just how incomplete a picture of prehistoric life in the Americas comes from the archaeologist's spade. Fortunately the legacy left by the anthropologists of the pre-World War II years fills in many of the blanks.

Chumash descendants paddle a 1976 reconstruction of an ancient plank canoe along the California coast. The craft's design followed notes left among ethnologist John P. Harrington's voluminous papers on the Indian tribe. Its culture was all but extinct in 1914, when he posed (above, in the center) with a similar canoe he had helped build.

When not interviewing or writing notes, the obsessive Harrington steeped himself in Chumash ways, even learning to hurl a throwing-stick (left).

Egypt, 1925: Howard Carter unveils the second of Tutankhamun's three nested coffins in the Valley of the Kings.

SCIENTISTS IN THE FIELD

SCIENTISTS IN THE FIELD

S lowly, carefully, Howard Carter peeled the gossamer shroud from the last of the king's three coffins. The refined countenance of the Egyptian pharaoh Tutankhamun stared up at him in a gaze sculptured more than 3,000 years ago. It was a wondrous face, a mask of solid gold. Beneath it lay the mummy.

The face of the pharaoh had haunted Carter for years. And after that unforgettable moment in November 1922, when the candle in his trembling hand first shed light upon the gold in the tomb, Carter had dreamed of uncovering Tutankhamun's mummy. At first sight he could not know whether the king's sarcophagus lay within the tomb and, if it did, whether the coffin had been emptied by robbers long ago.

A careless excavator might have torn down the walls of the burial chamber and ripped into its multiple shrines and coffins to find the mummy. But Carter waited. He was one of a new breed of archaeologists—men and women of the early 20th century whose perseverance yielded remarkable finds in Egypt, the Near East, Europe, and India. Their perceptions were scholarly, their records organized, their field methods slow and meticulous. From Carter's first glimpse of the golden chaos in Tutankhamun's tomb to the moment when he gazed at the face of the centuries-dead king, more than three years of painstaking work had elapsed.

215

But there were others more impetuous than Carter. Ten years before the discovery of Tutankhamun's tomb, Ludwig Borchardt of the German Oriental Society was at work at Tell el 'Amârna, the Nile-side capital of Pharaoh Akhenaten. On December 6, 1912, a worker led Borchardt to a narrow chamber filled with debris. Moments later Borchardt lifted a bust of Queen Nefertiti, Akhenaten's wife, from the rubble.

The portrait was radiant, mesmerizing, and Borchardt had to have it, though his permit allowed him to export only duplicates or inferior pieces of art. Somehow, perhaps with the aid of a corrupt official, he smuggled Nefertiti out of Egypt. The first news the Egyptians had of the discovery came when the bust went on display in Berlin in 1923.

Furious, the Egyptians demanded Nefertiti's immediate return. Borchardt refused. The Egyptians insisted that unless they had the statue, no German archaeologist would ever work on the Nile again. It was years before the Germans returned to Egypt, though Nefertiti never did. She remains to this day in a West Berlin museum.

In those first decades of the 20th century, every Egyptologist sought the permit granted by the Egyptian government to work in the desolate Valley of the Kings at Thebes. Here lay the tombs of some of Egypt's greatest pharaohs. Most of the sepulchers had been found empty—ransacked centuries earlier by treasure hunters. In 1914, when American magnate Theodore Davis relinquished the coveted permit to George Edward Stanhope Molyneux Herbert, the fifth Earl of Carnarvon, he departed with the words: "I fear that the Valley of the Tombs is now exhausted." Howard Carter, a British draftsman-turned-archaeologist, thought not. He believed that one tomb remained to be found in the Valley of the Kings—the tomb of Tutankhamun.

Tutankhamun had ascended Egypt's throne in 1361 B.C., at the age of nine. An ambitious advisor named Ay guided the young pharaoh in affairs of state. When Tutankhamun was not yet twenty, he died and Ay succeeded him. The cause of Tutankhamun's untimely death—accident, illness, or murder—has remained a mystery. It seemed that the circumstances of his burial would remain so too—until Carter reached the Valley of the Kings.

Carter, in Lord Carnarvon's employ, set out to find the missing tomb in 1917. He faced a brutal task. The valley was mantled with vast piles of rock and sand dumped helter-skelter by earlier excavators. Near the entrance to the tomb of Ramesses VI, Carter and his diggers came upon an ancient cluster of workmen's huts built on masses of flint boulders. In other parts of the valley, such boulders had signaled a nearby tomb entrance. "Our natural impulse was to enlarge our clearing in this direction, but by doing this we should have cut off all access to [Ramesses VI's] tomb . . . above, to visitors one of the most popular in the whole Valley." So Carter struck out in a different direction. Six futile seasons and more than 200,000 tons of sand and rubble later, he returned to the entrance to Ramesses' tomb. Four days after starting work on November 4, 1922, Carter's workmen unearthed a stairway cut in the rock. Tutankhamun's tomb lay only a few feet from where they had started work in 1917.

216

Deep in the barren hills at Thebes, Egyptian pharaohs once lay in secret graves. No pyramids marked their tombs; piles of boulders blocked small, inconspicuous entrances. But still their treasures fell prey to thieves who ransacked the Valley of the Kings thousands of years ago. Tutankhamun's tomb, though robbed twice, was spared total devastation, perhaps because the entrance (lower right) was buried underneath rubble left from the construction of Ramesses VI's tomb above it.

For nearly three weeks Carter waited for Carnarvon to join him from England. On November 24 workmen cleared the stairway. At the bottom they found a rock-hewn doorway blocked with boulders and coated with mud plaster. Undisturbed in the plaster were ancient impressions left by the seals of the royal necropolis guards. Carter and Carnarvon burrowed through the doorway and down a rubble-choked passage, and on November 26 reached a second door. Beyond it the two men would find their missing king, his seals proclaiming his royal name: Tutankhamun.

When Carter pried a few stones from the doorway and thrust a candle inside, hot, stale desert air sighed out through the hole; the flame wavered in the draft.

"Can you see anything?" Carnarvon whispered.

Carter could barely speak. "Yes," he breathed, "wonderful things."

Carter and Carnarvon dismantled the second door and stepped into a glorious disarray of exquisitely carved and bejeweled furniture, alabaster vases, bowls crafted of gold and silver. Chests and coffers stood everywhere. On one chest an inscription proclaimed, "Sandals of His Majesty. Life, Health, Strength!" Another announced, "His Majesty's wardrobe when a child." And beyond the glittering chaos, two gold-kilted sentry statues flanked a sealed portal—the door to the burial chamber. "It was the day of days," Carter wrote, "the most wonderful I have ever lived through."

Altogether, Tutankhamun's tomb consisted of a burial chamber and three rooms filled with the king's belongings. Within the burial chamber, four shrines, one nested within another, left only a few feet of space for the men to move. Each shrine held still more magnificent objects. Inside the fourth shrine were three mummy-shaped coffins—the last molded from more than 2,000 pounds of solid gold. And finally the mummy, bedecked with 143 gold and jeweled ornaments, and nearly burned away by unguents applied too lavishly 33 centuries earlier.

Carter spent ten years clearing Tutankhamun's tomb. He cataloged the contents of every room. With photographer Harry Burton from New York's Metropolitan Museum of Art, he recorded every object in its place. Carter purchased tons

Under the watchful gaze of Howard Carter (opposite), a painted wood bust of Pharaoh Tutankhamun sees daylight for the first time in more than 3,000 years. Gangs of tourists waited each day for such processions. "Great was the excitement, always," wrote Carter, "when word was passed up that something was to be brought out of the tomb. Books and knitting were thrown aside, and the whole battery of cameras was cleared for action...."

No picture, though, could equal the opulence that Carter beheld in the tomb (right), first in the antechamber (1), then in an annex (2). In the burial chamber (3), four shrines enclosed the sarcophagus; within it lay three coffins and the king's mummy. Four urns in a storeroom (4) contained Tutankhamun's viscera.

Today the mummy reclines in the burial chamber (upper), the only king remaining in the valley. Paintings on the walls show the mummified pharaoh ritually reanimated by his successor, Ay.

of packing materials as well as gallons of chemicals for cleaning and restoration work. Each object was crated, loaded onto railroad cars, and pushed five and a half miles to the Nile. In heat that reached 120°F, a few lengths of railroad track—all that were available—were lifted and relaid, lifted and relaid as each load of artifacts inched toward the river. The site remained under heavy guard day and night; still, throngs of tourists gathered to gaze at the golden procession that emerged daily from the tomb. Swarms of journalists clamored for new reports; the high and the mighty arrived demanding conducted tours.

The Tutankhamun excavation took its toll on both Carter and Carnarvon. By the time he had finished, Carter was an old man in ill health, too worn out to publish a scientific record of the priceless artifacts. Carnarvon lived less than a year after the discovery of the tomb; when he died in 1923—

of pneumonia brought on by an infected mosquito bite—all the electric lights in Cairo blacked out for a brief, unexplained moment. On that same night his dog in England reportedly dropped dead. Carnarvon's death unleashed a furor over the "curse of the pharaohs," immortalized in a 1932 movie called *The Mummy,* starring Boris Karloff as a hyperactive mummy. But, as one archaeologist remarked, "If there was a curse, there would be no living Egyptologists today."

The Tutankhamun discoveries whipped up a mania for everything ancient Egyptian. European art and fashions copied the pharaoh's splendid trappings. Egypt was blessed with a burgeoning tourist trade. Tourists still flock to the Egyptian Museum in Cairo to gaze at Tutankhamun's wealth.

The fragile condition of most of the treasures alerted archaeologists to the insidious decay that had long been eating away at the tombs and temples along the Nile. In 1924 at the

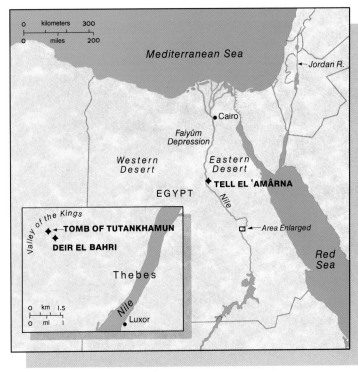

Length with rudder 62½"

From the limestone dust of Herbert E. Winlock's 1922 excavations at Deir el Bahri (above, left) emerged a large mortuary temple built around 2050 B.C. for Egypt's King Mentuhotep. In the nearby tomb of Meketre, Winlock had peered through a crack in the wall into "a little world of 4,000 years ago" (upper)— wooden models of the wealthy dignitary and a bevy of his servants engaged in everyday activities, such as sailing on the Nile (left). The models ensured smooth sailing in the afterlife.

University of Chicago, Egyptologist James Henry Breasted founded the Oriental Institute, which began to survey and record the inscriptions on Egypt's ancient monuments. The institute continues the work to this day—a race against salty groundwater, tourists, and the winds and sands of time.

Egypt's monuments and royal tombs did not answer a question that Breasted and other archaeologists had been asking for decades: Where had civilization first developed? Some scholars thought the answer lay in ancient Egypt. But Breasted proposed a Fertile Crescent bounded by three river valleys—the Nile, the Jordan, and the Tigris-Euphrates—where, he believed, humans had first raised crops, built houses, gathered in villages, and used a written language. His idea gained currency in 1925, when British archaeologist Gertrude Caton-Thompson excavated a small prehistoric farming community in Egypt's Faiyûm Depression. Here she found basket-lined storage pits containing carbonized wheat and barley grains more than 6,000 years old.

Traces of an equally old civilization had been discovered in Mesopotamia near the Euphrates River. Excavations here at Ur would yield evidence of human occupation 5,000 years before Christ and prove the Sumerians to be the first literate, urbanized people yet found in the world.

In 1854 Henry Creswicke Rawlinson, a British Army officer and student of ancient writings, had examined inscriptions from a great mound that rose more than 60 feet above the plain. He immediately identified the site as the biblical Ur of the Chaldees, cited in the Book of Genesis as the home of the Hebrew patriarch Abraham.

Fortunately for British archaeologist Leonard Woolley—and for posterity—Ur suffered neither rampant looting nor careless excavation during the 68 years that passed before Woolley reached the site. When he did arrive in 1922, he had the financial support of the University of Pennsylvania Museum and the British Museum. Less common now were wealthy individuals who sponsored expeditions to enlarge private collections; more frequently, backing came from learned institutions. The focus of archaeology was changing: "Our object was to get history, not to fill museum cases with miscellaneous curios," wrote Woolley.

222

"We must aver we find many persons still living who look more decayed!" exclaimed Egyptologist Kurt Lange over well-preserved mummies like that of Seti I (right), who ruled between 1313 and 1292 B.C. Seti's was one of some forty royal mummies exhumed from a mass grave at Deir el Bahri in 1881.

British anatomist Grafton Elliot Smith made the first comprehensive examination of these mummies in 1912. He preferred to X-ray the delicate mummies so as not to damage them, but the equipment was hard to come by. Undaunted, Elliot Smith once propped up a mummy in a hired carriage and headed for the only X-ray equipment in Egypt—at a sanatorium near Cairo.

Today all of Egypt's royal mummies have been X-rayed. Seven exposures create a composite portrait of Seti I (opposite). Ancient grave robbers broke off his head but missed a funerary ornament on his left arm, hidden under yards of linen wrappings and a protective coating of resin.

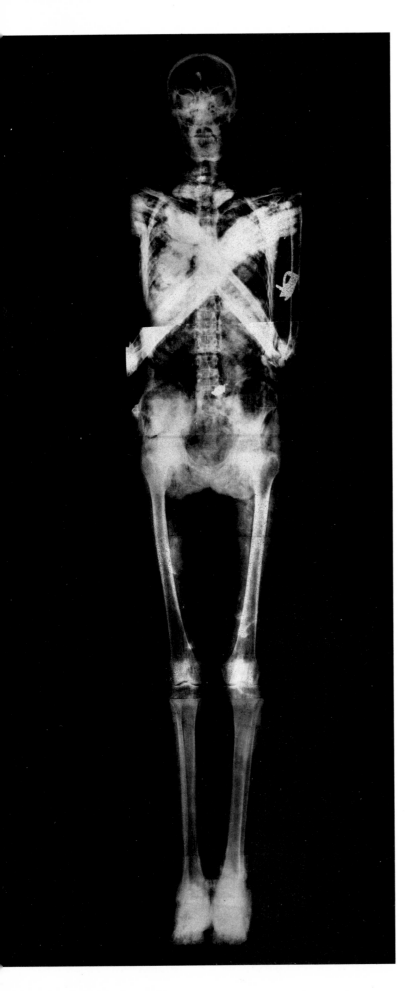

The son of a clergyman, Woolley had considered joining the clergy himself before turning his considerable energy and enthusiasm to archaeology. He was at his best when guiding visitors through Ur's mud- and baked-brick houses with their central courtyards and plastered, whitewashed interior walls. Wrote his friend Max Mallowan, an archaeologist who spent six seasons at Ur: "Woolley's observations missed nothing and his imagination grasped everything. 'This is the Headmaster's house, take care of the bottom step, it is much too high to be practicable. There was once a wooden step in front of it, but this has long ago perished. You see, the owner had to have the maximum possible rise before the turn of the stairs which ran over the lavatory behind you; in that way he was able to avoid bumping his head.' "

Woolley was an equally imaginative manager, supervising hundreds of men with unusual flair. When he suspected that workmen were pilfering gold beads from the site, he announced that for every gold bead found, he would pay a baksheesh—about three times what the local goldsmiths were offering. "The announcement," he recalled, "was greeted with astonishment and very obvious chagrin. This was a Saturday; on the Monday the trench-diggers produced a surprising harvest of gold beads—all of which had on the Sunday been bought back from the goldsmiths."

The old foreman, Hamoudi, played no small part in maintaining order and efficiency. Woolley remembered him fondly, "perched like a great eagle on the side of a cliff, exhorting and encouraging the men, prevailing over them by a mixture of threats, invective and sarcasm." When Hamoudi's own efforts failed one blisteringly hot afternoon, he hired a singing boatman to serenade the shovelers.

As an excavator, Woolley was patient and precise. When a trench dug in 1922 yielded evidence of a cemetery containing great riches, Woolley postponed further work there for four years until he had trained his workers in the delicate art of digging. "The delay was fortunate," he wrote, "for the excavation . . . was not only of immense importance but one of the most difficult that I have ever undertaken. . . ."

Woolley had discovered the Royal Cemetery, which held more than 2,000 commoners' graves and 16 royal 223

Overleaf: *"Indeed, the whole design of the building is a masterpiece," wrote British archaeologist Leonard Woolley of Ur's ziggurat. Built by the Sumerian ruler Ur-Nammu around 2100 B.C. to honor the moon god, Nanna, this Mesopotamian "mountain of god" once rose in three tiers to an estimated seventy feet. The ziggurat, now restored up to the second tier with ancient bricks, was topped by a small shrine where priests daily washed, fed, and clothed a gilt statue of the deity.*

tombs. The metalworkers of Ur had fashioned containers of silver and copper, helmets of beaten gold, and headdresses of gold, carnelian, and lapis lazuli. The city's architects had designed sepulchers with arches, domes, and columns. Ur's engineers knew of the wheel and used it on chariots, wagons, and potters' equipment buried in the royal tombs.

The task of unearthing the treasure was immense. "The Antiquities Room was filled to the brim," wrote Mallowan; "there was gold scattered under our beds. . . ." Yet Woolley worked slowly and carefully. He taught his diggers to recognize subtle changes in the soil. "Generally the first sign that a workman had of a grave as he dug down into the mixed soil of the cemetery was a paper-thin wavy line of white powder, the edge of the reed matting that lined the original shaft, or else a few small holes set in a line and running down vertically into the earth, holes left by the decay of the wooden staves which strengthened the sides of a wooden or wickerwork coffin." Wood, Woolley found, loses all its substance in the ground but "retains its appearance and its texture and can with care be exposed in such condition that a photograph of it looks like the real thing whereas it is but a film which a touch of the finger or even a breath obliterates more easily

"One has to look out for . . . little things," recalled Woolley of the meticulous care he demanded from his diggers at Ur (opposite). At the first sign of a grave or artifact, the shoveler summoned Woolley or an assistant. One of the ablest was Woolley's wife, Katharine. She was also domineering and temperamental, so most other women stayed away from the site.

Above, the Woolleys inspect baked-clay pipes that rid Sumerian homes of waste water and also served as

conduits for pottery drinking vessels and models of boats that Sumerians tossed down their drains. The motive? Woolley speculated that they sought the blessing of Enki, lord of the sweet water ocean under the earth.

A lyre (right) lay beneath the bones of a gold-crowned harpist in Ur's Royal Cemetery. For its sounding box, now restored, Sumerian artisans had crafted a bitumen-and-shell mosaic topped with the gold head of a bull, his eyes and beard of lapis lazuli.

Height 5'

227

than it dislodges the plumage from the wing of a butterfly."

Woolley devised methods for reconstructing partially disintegrated objects. By pouring plaster of Paris into cavities in the soil left by decayed wooden parts—of a harp or a lyre, for example—he formed a new skeleton for the preserved, inorganic fittings to adhere to.

When Woolley unearthed several skulls covered with ornaments, he wanted to preserve them just as they were in the ground. "The wreaths and chains and necklaces restrung and arranged in a glass case may look very well, but it is more interesting to see them as they were actually found," he wrote. So Woolley cleaned away loose dirt with small brushes and knives, then poured boiling paraffin over each skull to form a lump of wax, earth, bone, and gold. He pressed waxed cloth over each lump to strengthen it, then cut the entire skull out of the ground, mounted it on a plaster base, and cleaned off the superfluous wax.

The Royal Cemetery yielded more than an array of Sumerian artifacts. It revealed the macabre details of 16 mass suicides—one to accompany each royal burial. "The sight of the Royal Cemetery when we were in full cry was amazing," recalled Mallowan. "One of the royal tombs, which contained no less than 74 bodies buried alive at the bottom of the deep royal shaft, appeared, when exposed, to be a golden carpet ornamented with the beech leaf head-dresses of the ladies of the court, and overlaid by gold and silver harps and lyres which had played the funeral dirge to the end."

How were so many people persuaded to die in the graves of Sumerian royalty? In other ancient civilizations, too, servants and other subjects accompanied rulers into the afterlife. Nothing that remains of Sumerian literature has solved the mystery of the Royal Cemetery, but Woolley was able to tell the grisly tale of each burial.

For most the procedure was the same. First, a team of grave-diggers tunneled 30 feet into the earth, carving a 30-by-45-foot rectangular shaft with steeply sloping walls. At the bottom they built a stone tomb chamber. Pallbearers then carried the royal body down the passageway and sealed it, with three or four personal servants in attendance, into the tomb. The servants, perhaps, were killed or drugged before 229

"An ill-considered excavation is liable to develop into a chaos...," cautioned British archaeologist Mortimer Wheeler. To combat confusion, he devised a grid system of "accumulative squares" for large excavations (above, left), and in 1934 used it at Maiden Castle (left), a prehistoric hill fort in southern England. At a Roman temple within the site's maze of protective ramparts, Wheeler (opposite, in pullover) found a votive bronze bull (right) fashioned during the fourth century A.D.

Height 3⅝"

the door was shut. Then came a great procession of members of the dead ruler's court: soldiers, male servants, musicians with harps and lyres, and women decked out in brightly colored garments and elaborate headdresses. Chariots drawn by oxen and attended by grooms rolled down the slope, followed by a guard of soldiers. All carried small cups made of clay, metal, or stone and, after a funeral service, drank a deadly potion. They lay down to die in their assigned places, and someone came to kill the animals, whose bodies fell on top of their grooms.

After excavating the Royal Cemetery, Woolley focused on his search for the origins of Sumerian civilization. In a small mound near Ur, he had found an early settlement of reed houses. Could their occupants have been the first farmers to settle in southern Mesopotamia?

Clues would come from Ur itself. In 1930 Woolley's

Local people named it Mohenjo Daro, "mound of the dead," and believed that the hill of sand (above) on the vast Indus River floodplain in Pakistan was an ancient burial ground. In 1950 Wheeler excavated the baked-brick walls (right) of the 4,000-year-old city of 40,000 people—"the oldest example yet known of systematic town planning." He discovered an orderly grid of streets, apartment houses supplied by indoor wells, and a sewer system that reached nearly every home in the city.

crew opened a 60-by-75-foot trench that cut down 64 feet into the floor of the excavated cemetery. They dug through eight levels of houses and many feet of potters' workshops, then through 11 feet of river silt. Below the silt lay three levels of mud-brick and reed houses identical to those from the small mound nearby. The "bottom" of Mesopotamia was a stiff, green clay that had once been a marsh.

Woolley had the evidence he wanted. He could trace the development of Sumerian civilization from a tiny village to the great cities of the third millennium B.C. In the 11 feet of silt, he also found proof of a vast flood. Cuneiform records mentioned a flood of similar magnitude—one that had destroyed hundreds of small communities—so Woolley concluded that this flood and Noah's were one and the same. "Here," wrote Mallowan, "was a discovery after Woolley's heart; a plausible authentication of the Old Testament record, for the excitement of the Bible-reading public...." Woolley's alluvial deposit turned out to have been left by a flood much earlier than Noah's biblical Flood, but Woolley's uncanny blend of field and interpretative skills guided a new generation of archaeologists. They began to place the results of their work into a broad historical context.

Another British archaeologist, Mortimer Wheeler, built on the examples of Howard Carter and Leonard Woolley. For Wheeler, archaeology was above all an instrument for reconstructing human history. "Archaeology," he wrote, "is a science that must be lived, must be 'seasoned with humanity.' Dead archaeology is the driest dust that blows." To his interpretative skills Wheeler added the lessons he had learned from the detailed, late 19th-century records of Gen. Augustus Henry Pitt Rivers, a master of meticulous excavation. Wheeler described archaeology as a science of "controlled discovery," where the planning and execution of an excavation were as important as the results.

Wheeler started his career as an inspector of ancient monuments, then served as an artillery major during World War I. He emerged from the war eager to hone his excavating skills. The Romans had occupied Britain between A.D. 43 and 410, and Wheeler was anxious to investigate sites where their legacy lingered. After accepting an appointment as the

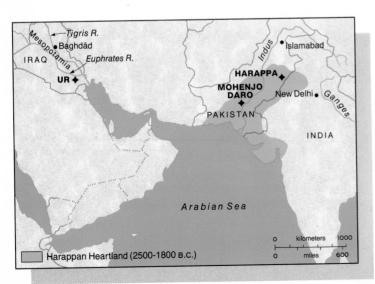

Scientists coax a camera-equipped dirigible over the ruins of Mohenjo Daro, seeking pictorial clues to the mysterious origin of Harappan civilization. Wheeler called this society "the sudden offspring of opportunity and genius," for it seems to have sprouted full blown from the fertile soil of the Indus Valley around 2500 B.C. Uncertain are the origins of a people who spread over an area almost as large as ancient Mesopotamia and Egypt combined (map). They made wheeled chariots and carts, crafted weapons of copper and bronze and ornaments of gold, farmed and traded, and wrote in a script yet to be deciphered.

Beneath Mohenjo Daro the water table rises, fed by canal and irrigation projects. The water leaches salts from the soil; the salts then crystallize on the ruins, eventually reducing the ancient bricks to powder. Workers (above) replace ruined bricks with new ones and insert concrete slabs near ground level to protect the walls from the salty water.

A wealth of Harappan wit and wisdom was crafted into objects of clay and stone. A terra-cotta pig strikes a pose (right); toy wagons are among the earliest known models of wheeled vehicles (below, right). The Harappans sculptured busts of their gods or priest-kings (opposite) and made seals of steatite (below). They carved animals on the seals, perhaps to invoke protection against harm or illness. Engraved inscriptions may have named the owners or labeled merchandise.

keeper of archaeology at the National Museum of Wales, he began his first major excavation in 1921 at Segontium, a Roman fort in northwestern Wales.

Wheeler worked for two seasons at Segontium. He cleared the fort's principal buildings and found jewelry, hundreds of coins, a statuette, and an altar inscribed to Minerva, the Roman goddess of wisdom. But Wheeler's most important accomplishment was refining the use of stratigraphy. His drawings of the excavation clearly illustrated the successive layers of earth he cut through. He numbered, named, and filled each section with symbolic representations of soil and stone types. Wheeler did not hesitate to include a definitive interpretation of each layer; this last practice drew criticism from some of Wheeler's contemporaries, who felt he often jumped to premature conclusions.

A dig between 1930 and 1933 at Verulamium tested Wheeler's skills. The excavation of the Roman town sprawled across five miles of countryside in southern England. Wheeler was surprised to find no traces of any Iron Age settlement beneath the Roman fortifications of the second century A.D.

Looking for signs of an earlier settlement, he followed a string of clues through tangles of ditches, banks, and earthworks—and even through local pubs. "A rumour reached us one evening that workmen digging a sewer . . . had found a shovel full of silver coins. The workmen were 'foreigners' to the district, it was the end of the day and no time was to be lost. We spread ourselves quickly through the innumerable public-houses of the vicinity and, with an immense expenditure of pints and patience, recovered 'in confidence' forty of the coins. . . ." Wheeler traced the coins to nearby Wheathampstead. There he uncovered an Iron Age settlement where, he theorized, the Celtic king Cassivellaunus had made his last, unsuccessful stand against Julius Caesar in 54 B.C.

By the end of the Verulamium dig, Wheeler had left a lasting imprint on the archaeology of

Height 3¾"

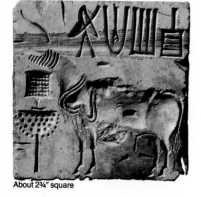

About 2¾" square

Length of cart 12½"; height of bust 6½"

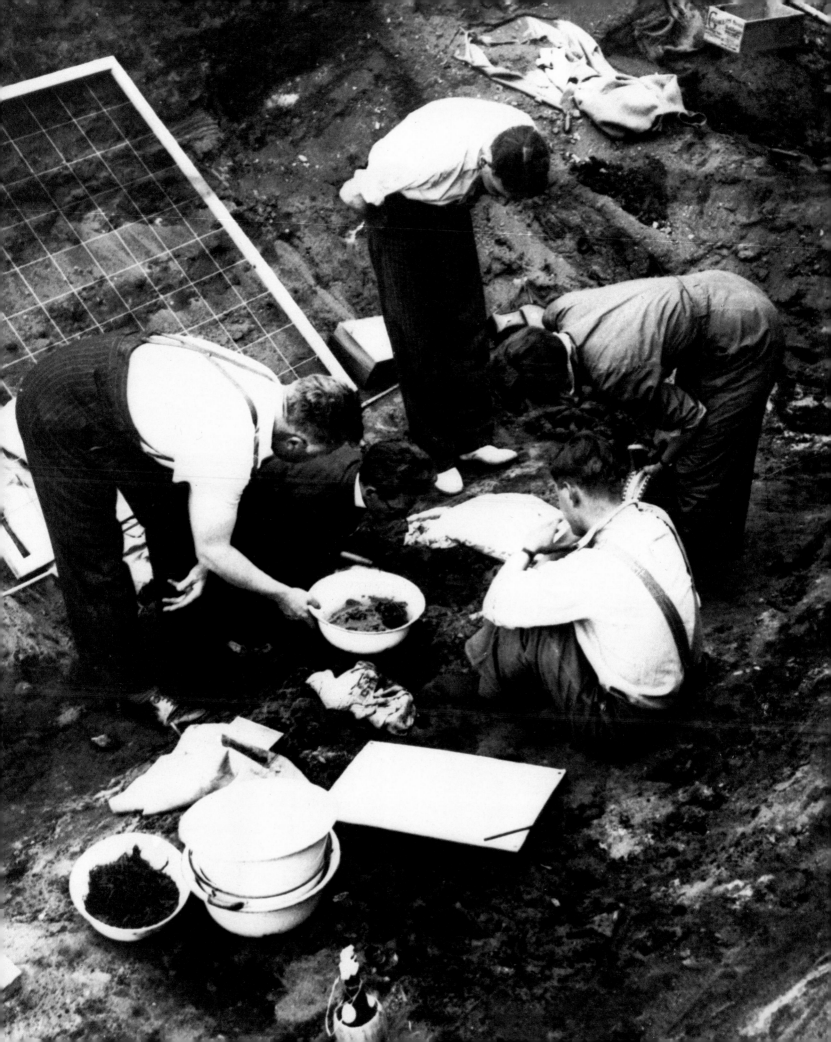

Roman Britain. But he had grown tired of the Romans. In 1934 he grabbed the chance to investigate prehistoric Maiden Castle. The earthen fortifications of what Wheeler called this "monstrous artifact" straddle a low ridge in the fertile chalk country of southwestern England. Steep ramparts and precipitous ditches enclose some 45 acres.

Wheeler and his wife Tessa tackled the site with panache. They raised money not only from learned institutions such as the Society of Antiquaries but from the public as well. They held carefully orchestrated press days each week, and hundreds of people visited the dig on summer weekends.

About a hundred assistants, students, and volunteers dug under Wheeler's guidance at Maiden Castle. It was here that Wheeler perfected the grid system—a digging technique well suited to excavating large as well as small areas. The workers would dig a square with sides at least ten feet long; this provided four sections that were easy to see and to photograph. New squares radiated out from any of the first four sides, and so on in any chosen direction. Stretches of uncut ground remained between the squares to support a digger and a wheelbarrow.

For four seasons, until 1937, Wheeler dug through the layers of history at Maiden Castle. He found evidence of an enclosure and a burial mound built by Stone Age farmers in 3000 B.C. During the fourth century B.C., Celts fortified the hilltop. Two centuries later, sling-warfare experts arrived and devised a maze of overlapping ramparts at each end of the compound. Maiden Castle grew into a small fortified town.

At the eastern entrance Wheeler's diggers discovered 38 human skeletons. Wheeler realized they had found the place where the Celts had buried their dead when Maiden Castle fell to the Romans in A.D. 44.

Wheeler reconstructed the bloody day. First came a barrage of Roman catapult artillery upon the eastern entrance; then the infantry, protected by their tall shields, charged from rampart to rampart, mercilessly cutting down the defenders. Wheeler found signs of several burned huts just outside the entrance; the Romans had torched the huts, then advanced under cover of the dense smoke. A massacre ensued; the dead were buried in the night near the ashes of the burned huts. Many of the skeletons of men, women, and children that Wheeler found bore signs of savage wounds.

At Maiden Castle and throughout his career, Wheeler encouraged students to join his digs. Dozens of fledgling archaeologists—some destined to become eminent scholars—surrounded him always. They remember Wheeler as flamboyant, energetic, innovative, and authoritarian and arrogant to the point of offensiveness. Descending on a trench, he would seize a trowel, supervise the taking of a photograph, bully an unfortunate digger into nervous anxiety.

Though the students found Wheeler difficult and demanding, they always learned. And the lessons stayed with them wherever they excavated—in Britain, Africa, India, and Australia. They modified his techniques to suit local needs and thereby created a quiet revolution in field methods.

Emerging from World War II a brigadier general, Wheeler went next to India. In 1944 he became the director

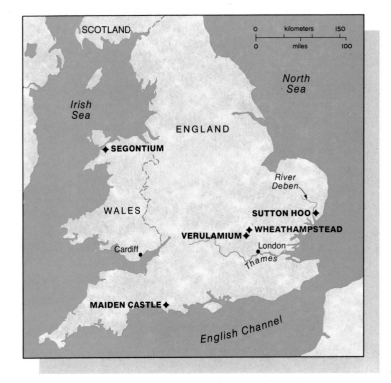

237

From the sand of an Anglo-Saxon burial ground at Sutton Hoo, a team of skilled excavators led by Charles W. Phillips extracted the richest archaeological treasure found anywhere in England. In 1939, equipped with trowels, tablespoons, and portable grids, they scraped away the highest mound at the site (opposite). Beneath the nine-foot-high barrow, the diggers discovered the remains of a wooden ship and the dazzling funerary array of a monarch who had ruled in the seventh century A.D. Though his body was never recovered, and in fact may never even have been buried here, the king's accoutrements gave evidence of a cosmopolitan civilization that imported luxuries from hundreds of miles away—a copper bowl from Egypt, silver bowls from Constantinople, gold coins from France.

general of the Archaeological Survey of India, then the largest organization of its kind in the world—and one of the most disorganized and ineffective. Wheeler swooped into the survey headquarters with a characteristic flourish: "I stepped over the recumbent forms . . . past office windows revealing little clusters of idle clerks and hangers-on, to the office. . . . As I opened my door I turned and looked back. The sleepers had not stirred, and only a wavering murmur like the distant drone of bees indicated the presence of drowsy human organisms within. I emitted a bull-like roar, and the place leapt to anxious life."

For three years Wheeler trimmed, reorganized, and revitalized the survey. In the process he trained a new generation of Indian archaeologists in up-to-date European methods. His students still direct excavations.

Much of Wheeler's work in India centered on the Indus Valley, where a Bronze Age civilization comparable to those in Egypt and Mesopotamia had thrived in the third millennium B.C. John Marshall, Wheeler's predecessor at the survey, had excavated at the two major Indus cities, Harappa and Mohenjo Daro. Finding no evidence of fortifications at either site, Marshall concluded that the Indus, or Harappan, civilization was more peaceful than Egyptian and Mesopotamian societies, which were ruled by ambitious kings.

Wheeler arrived at Harappa by cart on a warm May evening in 1944. The next day he saw several mounds and suspected that the yellow mud encasing the highest, almost 60 feet tall, could only be the eroded remains of a massive mudbrick wall. A morning's excavation revealed that the wall, 40 feet wide at the base, had fortified a citadel that dominated

the city. At Mohenjo Daro, 400 miles south on the Indus River, Wheeler found a similar fortified citadel. Whether the Indus people were warlike or not, they had built fortifications to defend their cities against attack.

Further excavation at the two cities revealed granaries like those in Egypt and Sumer, indicating that the Indus civilization was based on agriculture. Mohenjo Daro turned out to be a carefully planned city divided into 400-by-200-yard blocks; along the streets stood rows of drab, standardized houses, most with drains linked to an elaborate public sewer system. There were merchants' and artisans' quarters, too, and dozens of humble laborers' abodes. Hundreds of stone seals bore the emblems of long-forgotten Indian gods and the elements of a script not yet deciphered. The discovery of similarly inscribed seals in Mesopotamia indicated that the

Every iron nail that had joined the ship's wooden ribs and planks remained, packed in place by the damp sand of Sutton Hoo (opposite). But more than 1,300 years after the ship was dragged here and buried in a custom-dug trench, nothing remained of the wood except a film of discoloration and an 89-foot imprint (composite, below) so vivid that scientists discerned signs of wear and repair, and thus determined that the vessel had been seaworthy—not just a replica built to be buried.

Many artifacts in the ship's burial chamber area were so badly corroded that earlier

239

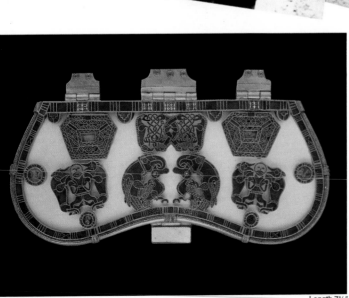

Length 7½"

excavators might have thrown them away as rubbish. But using drawings, photographs, and notes from the project, archaeologists restored many treasures. They discovered a gold-framed purse lid (left) decorated with garnets and glass; its pouch had rotted away, but not the 37 gold coins it contained. These helped fix the date of the burial.

seals may have been used to label merchandise traded between the two civilizations.

Before Wheeler began his search for the origins of human history in northwestern India, British archaeologists in 1939 had discovered a link to the past in eastern England. From a mound on the Sutton Hoo estate overlooking the Deben River emerged the remains of an 89-foot-long rowing ship. The vessel, containing the burial chamber and regalia of an Anglo-Saxon king, had been dragged half a mile from the river some 1,300 years earlier, hauled a hundred feet up an embankment, and buried in a trench under more than a thousand tons of turf cut from the surrounding heath.

A local archaeologist discovered the burial, then immediately turned the dig over to Charles W. Phillips, a don at Cambridge University. The importance of the find was clear, for the period of Anglo-Saxon settlement in Britain—after

the Romans and before the Norman Conquest of A.D. 1066—is poorly documented. From the Sutton Hoo excavations, archaeologists would learn that the kingdom of East Anglia in eastern England had been quite well established, and its kings wealthy and powerful.

Phillips and a team of experts soon realized that nothing more than the impression of the ship's planking was left in the sand of the burial trench, along with rows of iron nails that had once held the ship together. Before refilling the trench, they recovered from the burial chamber remnants of iron-bound wooden buckets, cauldrons, spears, and a battle ax. There were also silver-tipped drinking horns, a dismantled lyre inside an Egyptian bronze bowl, and 37 gold coins. The Sutton Hoo treasure spent World War II stashed in an unused London subway tunnel along with the Elgin Marbles and other treasures from the British Museum.

The British Museum reexcavated the Sutton Hoo trench between 1965 and 1971, adding to classic Wheeler-like techniques a full repertory of the most modern methods. Excavators made a plaster cast of the ship's impression and by soil analysis hypothesized that the mound had been built on a plowed field. Coin experts have recently improved on the earlier estimation of a burial date between A.D. 600 and 650, narrowing the date to between 620 and 630. Almost certainly the Sutton Hoo ship burial was that of the Anglo-Saxon king Raedwald, who died around 625.

Archaeology has come a long way since the days of Howard Carter, Leonard Woolley, and Mortimer Wheeler. Today's archaeologists draw on an impressive array of scientific aids to perform almost incredible feats of historical reconstruction. With new tools and skills, they weave human history around artifacts from the buried past.

Work continues today at another Sutton Hoo mound (above), first opened before World War II. Metal detectors (opposite) find objects as small as buttons. Now, with modern equipment such as ground-penetrating radar, archaeologists can map the subsurface features of the site. With ultraviolet light they can detect the fragile remains of bodies; with chemicals they consolidate them into sand figures and may even be able to detect the age and sex of the remains.

England, 1954: Londoners queue up to see the Roman temple ruins discovered beneath their city.

WHEN, WHERE–AND WHY

"Archaeologists of all parts of the world momentarily have turned their attention from Egypt to England," reported the *Evening Star* of Washington, D. C., in October of 1954. Not only archaeologists, but also thousands of curious Londoners came to see the ruins of a small Roman temple, discovered under a bombed-out site where construction of a high-rise office building would soon begin. More than 15,000 people filed past the temple on the first day of public exhibition.

At the end of World War II, acres of London, Rotterdam, Hamburg, and other European cities lay in ruins. Whole blocks of London had been razed. But this grim desolation did create a unique opportunity for archaeologists. The newly formed Roman and Mediaeval London Excavation Council probed deep under the rubble, searching for Londinium, the riverside town founded by the Romans around A.D. 43. There the Romans had built a temple to the god Mithras, chief deity of a cult popular with Roman soldiers.

Discovery of the temple stirred the imagination and pride of the war-weary British. The shrine was about to be destroyed by pile drivers when the government bowed to public opinion and prevailed upon the contractors to move it to a nearby courtyard, where it continues to attract visitors.

World War II ushered in a new era for archaeology. With the surge of technical advances made during the war years and afterward—from aerial photography to sophisticated metal detectors—technology began to assume a major role. And as the war-torn world struggled to put itself back together, interest arose in human ecology—the interrelationship of humans with each other and with the natural world. Archaeologists began to ask new and challenging questions: How had humans lived during prehistoric times? When and why had people first cultivated the soil and begun to live in permanent settlements?

Questions such as these demanded new approaches that relied on the teamwork of specialists, from zoologists and botanists to geologists and chemists. Research teams worked together and studied not only the terrain, ruins, and artifacts at a site but also animal bone fragments, tiny seeds, even fossil plant pollen. This closely focused research would add depth to modern images of life in prehistoric times.

Not that the era lacked spectacular discoveries. In 1940 four boys were exploring a wooded area near the town of Montignac in southwestern France. They came upon a small hole in the ground. Curious, the boys enlarged the hole with their knives, then crawled inside, down a narrow passage, and into a dark underground chamber. When they raised their oil lamp to look around, the boys were astounded to see brilliantly colored animals painted on the white limestone walls and ceiling. Cattle, bison, stags, and horses danced in a great frieze.

The boys reported the discovery to their former schoolmaster, who was somewhat skeptical. But his telephone call brought the Abbé Henri Breuil, doyen of prehistoric art, who declared the Lascaux cave paintings to be authentic.

News of the discovery attracted sightseers as well as dozens of archaeologists and journalists. Those willing to negotiate the hazardous entrance were admitted in small, carefully watched groups. The French government and the landowner constructed a safer entrance with doors to protect the paintings. After World War II thousands of tourists journeyed to Lascaux to marvel at this prehistoric art.

Another world-famous discovery came in 1950, when two peat diggers uncovered a corpse in Tollund fen, Denmark. The police looked at the corpse and then asked archaeologist P. V. Glob at the nearby University of Århus to examine it. Naked except for a leather cap and belt, the 2,200-year-old Tollund man lay on his right side, as if asleep, his legs bent. His face bore a serene expression. But there was a leather rope twisted around his neck. Tollund man had been executed, probably a religious sacrifice.

The Tollund investigation involved archaeologists, anatomists, and botanists, who analyzed everything from the man's cap to his last meal. The skin was intact over most of the upper body. The well-preserved head still retained its cropped hair and beard stubble. Tollund man had been about 30 years old. His stomach and intestines contained the remains of his final meal: a gruel of barley, linseed, and wild seeds. In 1954 two British archaeologists sampled a modern version of the gruel. They judged it barely palatable, even when washed down with good Danish brandy.

244

Magic power for hunters or symbols of life? Scholars still debate the purpose of Stone Age cave paintings discovered throughout western Europe. Handprints and horses (above and right) decorate Pech-Merle cave in France. Cattle, deer, and other beasts cover a ceiling in nearby Lascaux cave (opposite). The artists used charcoal or powdered minerals for their work.

Closed to the public in 1963 to conserve its paintings, Lascaux cave now has a twin, a duplicate built nearby.

Like the Danes, British archaeologists enlisted a variety of specialists to study another waterlogged site, a small Stone Age campsite at Star Carr in northeastern England. During the summers from 1949 to 1951, Grahame Clark and his colleagues and students uncovered a rough birchwood platform lying under a field that had been a lakeside reed swamp 9,500 years ago. They also found rolls of bark, a wooden canoe paddle, and dozens of spearpoints made of antler, all well preserved by the peat that had formed over the site.

Clark was not content merely to study the artifacts and count the animal bones from Star Carr; he attempted to reconstruct the ecology of the campsite as well. By analyzing pollen samples, botanists learned that a birch forest had bordered the site. From deer and elk antlers, zoologists deduced that Stone Age hunters had camped at Star Carr during the winter and early spring.

The date for the site came from distant Chicago. In the 1940s Willard Libby, a nuclear chemist at the University of Chicago, developed radiocarbon dating, a new method for calculating the age of ancient bones, charcoal, and other organic substances. Libby experimented first with objects whose ages were already known, such as sequoia trees from California and wooden boats from ancient Egypt. He refined the method until test readings were accurate to within 5 to 10 percent of the known age.

Here was the dating method that archaeologists all over the world had been waiting for—an absolute method that revealed the actual number of years rather than the relative age provided by methods such as stratigraphy and pollen analysis. Libby won a Nobel Prize for his work. His Chicago laboratory was soon inundated with samples: charcoal from early American Indian campfires, dung from the extinct giant sloth, ancient Egyptian coffins, birchwood from Star Carr.

A dramatic test of radiocarbon dating came in 1951, when Libby dated a fragment of linen wrapping from a Dead Sea Scroll. He fixed the date at A.D. 33, with a margin of error of plus or minus 200 years. This reading confirmed the dates estimated by scholars who had examined not only the scrolls but also coins, pottery, and other objects left by the people who hid the scrolls. It also finally persuaded skeptics that the scrolls were indeed authentic.

With trowel and surveying pole, archaeologist P.V. Glob investigates Denmark's Tollund peat bog in 1950. The abundance of tannic acid and absence of oxygen in peat bogs preserve organic material, including corpses. The 2,200-year-old Tollund man (opposite, upper) was unearthed here by peat cutters. Botanists analyzed pollen deposits in the peat, layer by layer, to date the burial. Hundreds of ancient corpses have been recovered from northern Europe's peat bogs.

Like Tollund man and Lascaux cave, the Dead Sea Scrolls were discovered accidentally. According to one account, in 1947 a Bedouin youth was idly searching for a lost goat at Qumrān, Jordan, near the Dead Sea. He came upon a cave and tossed a stone inside. It broke a jar and the strange noise scared him away. But he returned with a friend and found many jars, full of scrolls wrapped in linen cloth. The boys gathered them up and took them back to their camp. Eventually some of the scrolls were sold to a monastery in Jerusalem and the rest to a professor at the Hebrew University in that city. To the delight of biblical scholars, the scrolls included a copy of most of the Book of Isaiah.

Now the scramble was on. Bedouin and archaeologists alike eagerly explored more caves. So far, thousands of manuscript fragments have been found, including portions of every Old Testament book except Esther.

The rope twisted tightly around his neck belies the serene facial expression of Tollund man (above), who was probably a sacrificial victim in an Iron Age religious rite. He willingly "took the noose," wrote Glob, "knowing . . . that by his death he ensured the life of his people for the coming year."

The deeply slashed throat of Grauballe man (left), who was found in 1952 in another Danish bog, also indicates a sacrificial death. Radiocarbon dating and pollen analysis placed the event at about 20 centuries ago—and finally persuaded local Danes that the man was not a recent murder victim.

Corpses deteriorate rapidly when exposed to the air. To preserve Grauballe man, archaeologists completed the natural tanning process that began in the peat bog.

A seasonal campsite for about four families of 9,500 years ago, Star Carr in England hosts visitors again in 1949. British archaeologist Grahame Clark and his team members dig trenches (upper) to learn about the site's Stone Age visitors. Along with flint axes and arrowheads were tools and weapons made of organic material—bone, antler, and wood—well preserved in the swampy site. Clark used a vacuum tank (lower) to saturate the fragile antlers and bones with a preservative.

Who were the people who made and then hid these scrolls? In the 1950s archaeologists from Jordan, France, the United States, and other countries excavated the Qumrān caves and nearby Khirbat Qumrān, the ruins of an ancient Jewish community. Diggers uncovered a large stone community center with a kitchen and assembly rooms. In a big room equipped with tables, benches, and inkwells, scribes had produced many of the scrolls found in the caves. A cemetery yielded the graves of more than a thousand people, buried without jewelry or any other adornment. The Manual of Discipline for the sect confirmed that these Jews had led an austere life: "The order of the community; to seek God . . . to do what is good and upright before him."

Qumrān had been occupied at least twice by this sect—once for about 70 years until an earthquake in 31 B.C. drove them away, and again until A.D. 68, when the Jews fled from Roman persecution. It was then that the Qumrān community hid its precious scrolls in the caves, intending to recover them once peace had returned.

As specialists unraveled the mystery of the Qumrān sect, archaeologists from the University of Chicago began piecing together the story of a much older community. In 1948 Robert and Linda Braidwood dug shallow test pits into an ancient hilltop mound in northeastern Iraq. They were searching for prehistoric farming villages, hoping to learn when and where and why humans first began to raise crops. The Jarmo mound, more than 5 acres in area and at least 25 feet high, looked promising. The Braidwoods returned to Jarmo in 1950 to resume excavation. Their team of specialists included a botanist, a geologist, and a zoologist. From the village of Ash Sharqāt the Braidwoods recruited skilled excavators who had earlier been trained by German archaeologists. Local Kurds made up the rest of the labor force.

In the deepest part of the mound, the excavation crew found evidence that the villagers had not only hunted animals and gathered wild vegetable foods but also farmed the land and kept domesticated animals. Botanist Hans Helbaek examined the grains—and impressions of grains in house walls and oven floors—at Jarmo and identified them as wheat and barley. Radiocarbon dates revealed that people were farming at Jarmo at least as early as 6750 B.C., almost 3,000 years earlier than archaeologists had believed.

But why had people begun farming? Geologist Herbert E. Wright, Jr., went to Lake Zeribar in Iran to look for clues. There he drove long tubes deep into the lake floor to pull up mud samples. Layer by layer, the amounts and types of pollen in the sediment revealed climatic conditions over thousands of years. Wright suggested that, as the Ice Age ended, the warming of the climate in this region enabled people to leave their caves and live in the open. It also brought changes in vegetation. The climatic conditions after about 11,000 years ago—rainy winters and dry summers—were the conditions favorable for wild barley and wheat to migrate into the region. Thus the stage was set. Gradually, after centuries of gathering these wild grains, the people of Jarmo and other sites in the area learned to domesticate them.

Intensive studies such as those at Jarmo made every

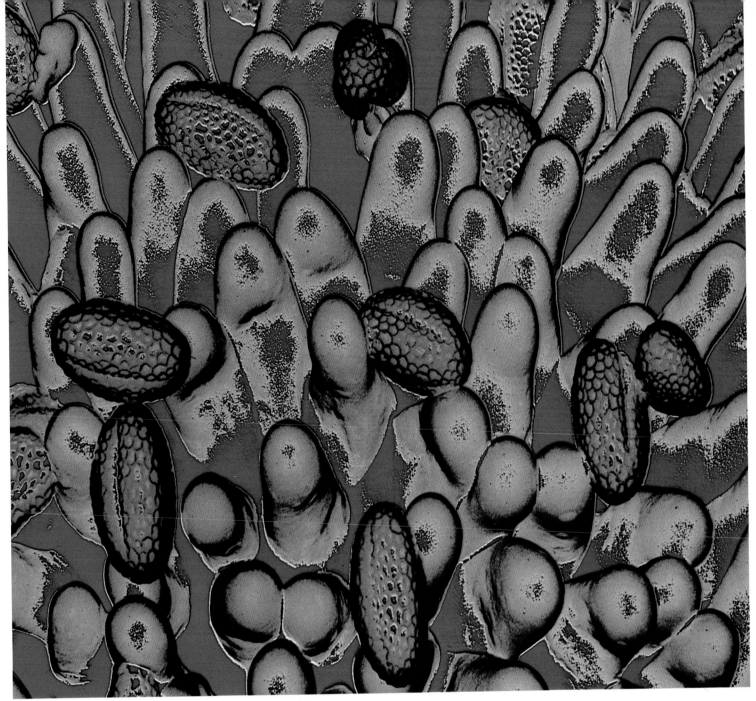

textbook on prehistory obsolete. British archaeologist Kathleen Kenyon's work at Jericho in the Jordan Valley contributed even greater surprises. The huge Jericho mound, on the outskirts of modern Jericho, was well known as the site of the biblical siege in which Israelite priests blew their trumpets and the people "shouted with a great shout, that the wall fell down flat." Excavators who had probed the mound were interested chiefly in biblical history. Then, in the 1930s, British archaeologist John Garstang dug more deeply and discovered, at the lowest level of the mound, evidence that people had been living at Jericho more than 8,000 years ago.

World War II delayed further investigation. Finally, in 1951, Kathleen Kenyon began to organize her expedition.

Kenyon and her crew dug a trench through the mound and studied each level of occupation. The work continued for three months each year, from 1952 until 1958. At 7 a.m.

Magnified about 1,800 times, pollen grains on the stigma of sweet alyssum reveal their identity to experts. Analysis of the amounts and kinds of pollen deposited in the soil over thousands of years provides a history of changes in climate and vegetation, as well as a relative time frame for the artifacts found in each layer. Scandinavian botanists pioneered this science early in the 20th century as they studied archaeological sites in peat bogs, where fossil pollen is best preserved.

DATING THE PAST

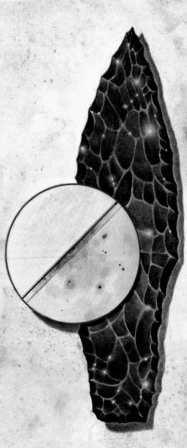

Carbon 14. *All living things absorb radioactive carbon 14. This assimilation ends when a plant or an animal dies. Its stock of carbon 14 then disintegrates gradually, at a known rate. In about 5,730 years, half the carbon 14 is left; in 17,190 years, about an eighth lingers. By measuring the amount of carbon 14 remaining in an ancient organic object and comparing that with a modern standard, experts can gauge how long ago the organism died. Rope from a sandal, bones from a tomb, even charcoal from a campfire can be dated back 50,000 years. Older objects retain too little carbon 14 to measure accurately.*

Obsidian Hydration. *Rapidly cooling lava often forms outcrops of a natural glass called obsidian. Ancient people frequently used this material to make scrapers and spearpoints. Obsidian absorbs water, which forms a very thin hydration layer over its surface. When an ancient toolmaker broke off a piece of obsidian for a spearpoint, a new layer began to form on the cut surface. Scientists today can measure the thickness of the hydration layer on an excavated spearpoint and learn when the spearpoint was made. They have determined the layer's growth rate for various climatic conditions and types of obsidian.*

Documentary Evidence. *If an artifact, such as this stoneware jug, matches one in a painting of known date and origin, the archaeologist has a clue to when and where the object was made and even how it was used. The jug shown above, pieced together from fragments found at a colonial American settlement, matches one in a Dutch painting of 1656. Other dated documents —letters, inventories, wills, diaries, and the like—that describe, for example, a new bracelet or a broken sword, aid in dating and identifying objects. Thus archaeological sleuths find clues in libraries and art galleries as well as in trenches and laboratories.*

Dendrochronology. *In many trees a dark ring marks the end of each year's growth. Scientists can learn a tree's age by counting the rings in a cross section of the trunk. Since growth rings are wider in wet years and narrower in dry, tree rings provide a history of climate changes. Archaeologists can also match the ring pattern in a living tree with successively older trees and logs, establishing a chronology that now, in one area of the southwestern United States, reaches back 2,300 years. Thus the tree-ring pattern in a post from an ancient dwelling may reveal the post's age—and a clue to the age of the dwelling.*

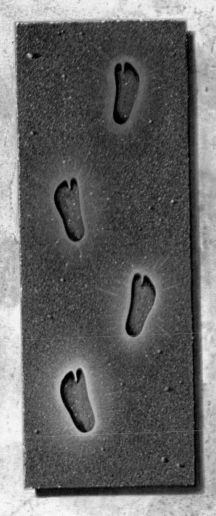

Potassium-Argon. *The isotope potassium 40 decays at a known rate into two other isotopes: calcium 40 and argon 40. As volcanic rock is formed, its heat drives out the existing argon 40. Scientists today can measure the ratio of potassium-40 atoms and argon-40 atoms in a sample of volcanic rock and learn when it was formed. Thus they can determine the age of fossils by dating the rock in which the fossils are embedded, such as the 3.6-million-year-old hominid footprints made in volcanic ash in East Africa. Unlike carbon 14, potassium 40 decays so slowly that this method can date rock that is billions of years old.*

Postholes. *The space once occupied by a wooden post may tell an archaeologist more than just the location and shape of a building or fence. A coin, button, or other datable object found in the backfill—soil, rocks, and rubbish added to support the post—can reveal the earliest date the post could have been installed. Artifacts in the posthole itself indicate the earliest date when the post had rotted away or been removed, since the objects probably fell into the hole after the post was gone. This method also helps in dating other sites: An iron nail found in a grave thought to be from the Bronze Age loudly proclaims that it is not.*

Archaeomagnetism. *The location of the north magnetic pole slowly changes over time. After clay containing a magnetic compound, such as iron oxide (rust), is heated to high temperatures, these particles realign with the earth's magnetic field. Thus the clay floor of a kiln or fire pit, or even a clay tablet in a burned palace library, may hold particles that point to where the north magnetic pole was at the time they were heated. Because scientists have been able to chart the pole's wanderings over the past several thousand years, these clay "fossil compasses" can be dated by matching them with the pole's past locations.*

Thermoluminescence. *The clay that is used in making pottery stores energy from natural radioactivity. Heating such clay to 930°F or more releases this stored energy in the form of light. All of this thermoluminescence is released when a potter first fires a clay pot or figurine; the clay then begins storing energy again, at a rate determined in the laboratory for each sample. Scientists can heat a sherd of ancient pottery and learn its age by measuring the amount of thermoluminescence it releases. This method is also used to date the soil of some buried sites, since soil begins storing energy after it is no longer exposed to the sun.*

the workmen assembled for instructions, then labored until 4:30 in the afternoon. The archaeologists' day lasted much longer. Staff members would lay out the day's pottery finds so that Kenyon could look them over and discard any potsherds not worth keeping. The work of sorting and classifying sometimes went on into the night. Kenyon occasionally broke this strenuous routine with an evening of canasta or a sing-along. But she was a stern and conscientious taskmaster who drove herself harder than anyone else.

The Kenyon excavations probed steadily down through several Bronze Age cities, then uncovered a much deeper settlement dating to 7000 B.C. To Kenyon's surprise this village covered at least eight acres, far more than villages such as Jarmo. The inhabitants had lived in mud-brick houses with stone foundations and plastered floors. Kenyon's excavations were so careful that she could identify thin, white films

on the plastered floors, the remains of rush mats. One mat showed the track of an ant that had eaten its way across it.

When the workers uncovered part of a human skull in a trench wall, Kenyon told them to leave it there. One of her strictest rules was that an archaeologist "never goes burrowing about an ancient site just to remove things." At the end of the season, Kenyon finally ordered that the skull be removed. As the work began, the site supervisor reported that the skull seemed to be plastered with clay. But no one was prepared for the dramatic and poignant clay portrait that covered the face of the skull. Its features were delicately modeled, the eyes inset with shells.

More skulls were visible behind the first one. The excavation camp had already been dismantled for the season, so Kenyon and her helpers spent an uncomfortable week sitting on the floor and eating makeshift meals while they

Submerged for centuries, the village of Biskupin in Poland reappeared in 1933. A local schoolmaster, on an outing with his class, noticed evenly spaced wooden posts—ancient pilings—poking out of a lake. About 2,300 years earlier, poor harvests and numerous invasions finally forced the thousand residents to abandon their thriving village, built on an island in the lake. The site then gradually disappeared under rising lake water until modern river dredging again lowered the water level.

Excavation began in 1934, uncovering orderly log streets (left) in a carefully planned village about six acres in area, surrounded by defensive walls and an embankment of logs. The muddy site yielded beads, weapons, pottery, and tools, such as the stone mortar and pestle shown above. The well-preserved remains guided archaeologists reconstructing much of the village, including a row of houses joined by a common roof (above, left). Biskupin thrives again—as a center for prehistoric studies.

carefully uncovered six more skulls. "They lay in a tumbled heap, one skull crushed firmly on top of another, with stones and very hard earth all round," Kenyon wrote.

The following season Kenyon's team recovered two more skulls from the same house, as well as about thirty skeletons from under the floor of a lower dwelling. The heads had been removed from many of these bodies. Kenyon believed that she had found evidence of an ancestor cult in which the modeled skulls of cherished forebears were revered by later generations.

Kenyon also discovered a massive—and puzzling—wall built of boulders from a streambed half a mile away. Then she found an earlier wall, a stout tower complete with an interior staircase, and a ditch nearly 30 feet across and 9 feet deep cut into the bedrock. Why had ancient Jericho needed such defenses? Jericho was a famous oasis with a reliable spring and fertile soil. Kenyon deduced that there must have been constant competition for its priceless natural resources.

The massive walls and tower protected a town of about a thousand inhabitants, who lived in beehive-shaped houses and farmed the land. Radiocarbon tests dated this settlement at about 8000 B.C., an astoundingly early date for agriculture.

Then came evidence of the very first building at Jericho —a rectangular stone structure that may have been a shelter or shrine. Tiny flint tools and a bone harpoon head told of a band of hunter-gatherers who had camped by the bubbling oasis spring around 9000 B.C.

New archaeological techniques such as those used at Jericho and Jarmo made wholesale digging less important. New excavations were often smaller and more specialized, requiring meticulous collection and scrutiny of tiny objects and close collaboration among experts in many fields.

Former students of the pioneer excavators directed many of these new projects. Kathleen Kenyon had studied with Gertrude Caton-Thompson and Mortimer Wheeler. Max Mallowan, one of Leonard Woolley's assistants, came to Nimrud on the Tigris River exactly a century after another Englishman, Austen Henry Layard, had tunneled into the site.

A quiet and efficient scholar, Mallowan had worked with the Woolleys at Ur from 1925 to 1931 (and married a famous visitor to the dig, mystery writer Agatha Christie). In 1932 Mallowan branched out on his own, excavating several important sites in northern Mesopotamia. In 1949 he obtained a permit to dig at Nimrud—the first archaeologist to work there in 70 years.

Nimrud was a major military headquarters in the ninth century B.C., when Assyrian troops began their conquest of much of the Near East. Layard's army of 130 workmen had uncovered bas-reliefs sculptured in stone but made no attempt to excavate mud-brick structures. Mallowan believed that Nimrud contained rich archives of cuneiform tablets that his illustrious predecessor had ignored, as well as many more Assyrian ivory ornaments than the few that Layard had brought back to London in the 1840s.

Mallowan worked under humbler conditions than did Layard, with never more than 70 diggers and a dozen expert helpers. Mallowan's crew soon unearthed a series of private

Carvings decorate alabaster urns in an Etruscan tomb (above) reconstructed at the Archaeological Museum in Florence, Italy. The Etruscan civilization flourished in Italy from the eighth to the first century B.C. The Etruscans built elaborate tombs and stocked them with supplies and luxuries for the afterlife. The terra-cotta couple at left, whose hands originally held banquet foods, reclined atop one coffin. Clustered in huge cemeteries, the tombs were dug in hillsides or soft rock or, like these near the town of Cerveteri (opposite, lower), constructed of boulders and then covered with earth.

In 1955 Carlo Lerici, a retired civil engineer, began to apply his technological skills to archaeology. By using aerial photography, electronic detectors, and a drill equipped with a periscope and camera (opposite, upper), Lerici and his colleagues could find and investigate Etruscan tombs without disturbing them. The Lerici Foundation has located about 1,300 tombs.

dwellings, a trove of information about the lives of Nimrud's wealthier citizens. From business records and storerooms of merchandise discovered in one house, Mallowan learned that a wealthy merchant named Shamash-shar-usur had owned the dwelling. He advanced funds against harvests, supplied birds for the royal sanctuary, and enjoyed a long career that lasted about 50 years.

Private houses such as this fascinated Christie, who was a conscientious assistant at her husband's dig. "I like to find a little dog buried under the threshold, inscribed on which are the words: 'Don't stop to think, Bite him!' Such a good motto for a guard-dog; you can see it being written on the clay, and someone laughing."

In the domestic wing of the king's palace, Mallowan unearthed many ivory ornaments and the grave of a princess. The administrative quarters contained brick boxes—ancient

Careful brushing clears the dust from an eight-foot-long scroll of thin copper (above), found broken into two pieces, part of the Dead Sea Scrolls hidden in caves at Qumrān, Jordan. Most of the scrolls were made of leather. This lone copper scroll perplexed experts, who spent four years seeking a way to unroll the metal without damaging it; finally they cut it into strips. The scroll proved to be a record of the Qumrān sect's buried treasure, but no trace of the riches has been found.

News of the Qumrān cache sent both archaeologists and Bedouin scurrying to search other caves in the rugged Judaean wilderness (left), an ancient haven for rebels and refugees. Discoveries include letters and other documents left by the followers of Jewish hero Simon Bar Kokhba, who led an unsuccessful revolt against the Romans in A.D. 132.

filing cabinets—and piles of cuneiform tablets, the provincial records of a king who had reigned in the eighth century B.C. The archives lay mantled in the ash that fell on them when invaders burned the palace in the seventh century B.C.

Outside the main entrance to the throne room, Mallowan's crew cleared away layers of collapsed brick walls. There they uncovered an inscribed sandstone slab just over four feet high, erected by King Ashurnasirpal II in 879 B.C. to commemorate the completion of his new palace and the rebuilding of the town. The inscription described the beauties of his palace, the canal that carried water to the town's gardens, and the great feast he held for a total of 69,574 guests: 16,000 residents, 1,500 royal officials, 5,000 diplomats from all across the Assyrian Empire, and "47,074 workmen and women summoned from all the districts of my land." For ten days the king "feasted, wined, bathed, anointed, and honored them and then sent them back to their lands in peace and joy." The guests devoured 16,000 sheep, 10,000 skins of wine, and lavish quantities of dates and nuts.

Mallowan worked at Nimrud for ten seasons. In 1952 his excavators cleared a series of wells in the administrative wing of the palace. From one well they recovered what Mallowan called "a king's ransom" of Assyrian ivory ornaments, including two small ivory plaques depicting a black man being mauled by a lioness in a papyrus thicket, a carved head of a maiden with flowing black hair, and ornaments that had once adorned royal horses. Christie spent several weeks carefully drying out the soft ivories, covering them with damp towels until the ivory adjusted to the drier environment above ground. "For me there will never be any fascination like the work of human hands," she wrote.

Archaeologists in the New World were also using the team approach to take a new look at the past. American archaeologist Richard S. MacNeish enlisted a variety of specialists to help in his study of early agriculture in the Americas.

MacNeish knew that ancient peoples had lived in dry caves and that such caves would preserve the corncobs and other plant remnants and artifacts their occupants left behind. In 1949 MacNeish began searching caves in northern Mexico, then moved south, and in 1960 centered his work in

Fifty feet down and 10,000 years back, a trench dug in Jordan's Jericho mound in the 1950s uncovers the world's oldest known walled town. The excavation, directed by British archaeologist Kathleen Kenyon, revealed layers added to the town wall over several centuries of occupation. The second man from the top in this photograph stands on the massive tower Kenyon's crew unearthed. The man at the bottom stands in a moat cut into the rock by Jericho's earliest permanent residents.

the scrub- and cactus-covered basin encircling the town of Tehuacán. There he found the kinds of sites he was looking for: caves that had been occupied for thousands of years following the end of the Ice Age.

MacNeish looked in vain at dozens of caves that he had heard about. Finally there was only one left on his list. With two Mexican helpers he arrived there "after a long, hot walk along the edge of the mountains, through thick stands of cactus and mesquite." The cave rewarded their effort. In particular, MacNeish wrote, "the quantity of vegetal material that lay beneath the goat dung covering the floor showed that this was a site to be tested."

The three men dug into the middle of the cave floor, sifting dirt through mesh screens and finding older and older layers of human occupation. Then, among the artifacts of a prehistoric people, the diggers unearthed three corncobs about an inch long, early ancestors of modern corn. Radiocarbon testing proved them to be the oldest that had ever been found, dating back to about 5000 B.C.

Archaeologists, botanists, ethnologists, and other specialists studied the Tehuacán area and the artifacts excavated from 12 sites, including a total of 138 levels of human occupation. These studies produced a story of development that began about 10,000 B.C., when the people here still depended chiefly on animals for food but were beginning to collect seeds and plants. Just as in the prehistoric Near East, people adjusted to the gradually warming climate and changing vegetation by turning more and more to plant foods, accumulating knowledge that eventually led to the beginnings of agriculture. Their life-style changed from the wanderings of hunter-gatherers to the settled village life of farmers.

This region also attracted archaeologists studying more recent human history: the magnificent civilization of the Maya, which flourished between A.D. 250 and 900. Their descendants still farm the scrub forests of the Yucatán Peninsula, the jungle lowlands and volcanic heights of Guatemala, and the mountains of the Mexican state of Chiapas.

Knowledge of both the ancient and modern Maya advanced rapidly after World War II. The United Fruit Company decided to produce a documentary film called *The Maya*

Kenyon and her assistant at Jericho, Douglas Tushingham, examine traces of a white-plastered earthen embankment built in the middle Bronze Age.

Respected for her methods as well as her achievements, Kenyon refined the now standard stratigraphical techniques developed by her teacher, Mortimer Wheeler. "Maintaining a straight, vertical edge . . . so that layers marking successive settlements may be recorded accurately, is a cardinal rule," Kenyon wrote. This strict policy, she admitted,

delayed an astonishing find. Embedded in a trench wall were 9,000-year-old skulls (left) with features modeled in clay and painted with lifelike tints. Kenyon regarded this ancient "portrait gallery" as evidence of spiritual sensitivity among Stone Age people.

Through the Ages. In 1946 photographer Giles Healey began to work in a remote part of southeastern Mexico. A sensitive and patient man, Healey won the confidence of the isolated Lacandon Maya. One day a Maya friend showed him an astonishing sight—frescoes painted on the walls of three rooms inside a temple overgrown with vegetation. One scene depicted a battle or raid in progress, with figures in crested helmets tumbling over one another. In a second scene Maya lords wearing feathered headdresses gathered for a ceremony. A band of musicians played trumpets, drums, rattles, and turtle shells, which they beat with deer antlers. A third mural portrayed a richly adorned ruler or priest standing in judgment over some captives. Their fingernails had been torn out, and a severed human head lay on a bed of leaves nearby.

Stained by fungus and bat droppings, dimmed by calcium deposits, marred by encroaching tree roots, the Bonampak murals were nonetheless a remarkable addition to the world's art treasures and a valuable source of information about the people who had painted them.

Scholars had regarded the ancient Maya as simple peasants who joined together to build elaborate ceremonial centers, such as Tikal and Palenque. But postwar research by

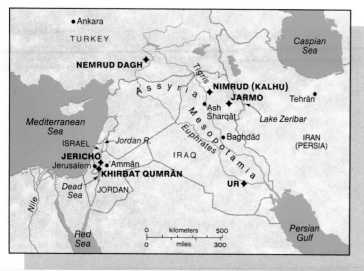

From the colossal pyramids of early Egyptian rulers to the remote caves in Jordan where a Jewish sect hid its precious scrolls, Mediterranean sites (map) hold special interest for biblical scholars as well as for archaeologists. At Jericho (right), photographed in 1971, excavations made by Kenyon and others pierce the mound formed by successive ancient settlements. The same copious spring that has attracted visitors and settlers for more than 11,000 years still supplies water to modern Jericho.

American, Guatemalan, and Mexican scholars began to reveal the unsuspected sophistication of Maya society.

In 1949 archaeologist Alberto Ruz Lhuillier and a crew of workers started to clear the Temple of the Inscriptions at Palenque in Mexico. Jungle growth cloaked the nine-tiered stone pyramid and the temple on top of it. In the temple's flagstone floor Ruz discovered a hidden entrance to the pyramid, a staircase that the ancient Maya had blocked with dirt and rubble. Exploring the staircase turned out to be a frustratingly slow task. "So difficult was the work—the breaking up of the rubble packing and the lifting out of the stones with ropes and pulleys," Ruz wrote, "that in the first season's labor, we got only 23 steps down—about eight steps a month."

The workmen gradually descended 46 steps to a landing and then 25 more steps to a horizontal passage that was sealed by a wall of rubble. During the 1952 season they broke through, only to find the corridor blocked by still another wall. In front of it lay pearls, jade ornaments, and pottery—clearly an offering, but to whom? The second wall was 12 feet thick. "For a full week we toiled to break it down," Ruz wrote. "The men were almost buried in the damp lime which burned and cracked their hands, to a point almost beyond endurance." In the corridor beyond was a masonry box that contained the skeletons of six young people who had apparently been sacrificed.

A huge, triangular stone slab covered the entrance to the final room, "an enormous empty room," wrote Ruz, "that appeared to be graven in ice." The chamber measured about 13 by 29 feet, with a vaulted ceiling 23 feet high. Stalactites hung like curtains; stalagmites rose from the floor like gigantic dripping candles. Bas-relief figures marched across the walls. On the floor, almost filling the room, lay a limestone slab decorated with hieroglyphs and reliefs.

Eventually Ruz and his assistants laboriously raised the five-ton slab. It covered a sarcophagus, the first ever found in a Maya pyramid. Inside lay the bones of a venerable Maya leader, accompanied by lavish jade ornaments, pearls, and a jade mosaic mask. "I was gazing," Ruz later wrote, "at the death face of him for whom all this stupendous work . . . had been built." Archaeologists had believed that Maya pyramids were only temple foundations; now they knew that these pyramids could be royal tombs as well.

A long inscription adorned the sarcophagus lid, but scholars could not interpret it. Maya hieroglyphs were still a mystery. Most scholars assumed that the inscriptions dealt only with the measurement of time. A major breakthrough came in 1960. Tatiana Proskouriakoff, a Maya specialist at Harvard University, noticed that inscriptions from Piedras Negras in Guatemala began with a seated figure in a niche at the top of a ladder; footprints indicated that the person had just climbed onto his seat. This scene, she discovered, was always included on the first monument erected at each Maya temple. She also found dates that seemed to record the birth of an important person who later ascended the throne. By linking hieroglyphs with scenes in sculpture, Proskouriakoff showed that much Maya writing was concerned not just with calendars but with the histories of ruling families.

262

Layers of latex paint topped by strips of gauze produce a mirror image of inscriptions for archaeologists working at Nemrud Dagh. On this Turkish peak 2,000 years ago, King Antiochus I of the Greco-Persian kingdom of Commagene built a temple to honor "all the gods." The head of the Greek god Heracles (opposite) fell from its huge statue during an earthquake. Led by American archaeologist Theresa Goell (above), a 1963-64 survey of the site was aided by the National Geographic Society.

263

Other scholars built on Proskouriakoff's research, deciphering Maya hieroglyphs that revealed a panoply of rulers vying for political and economic power. The man whom Alberto Ruz had found buried under the Temple of the Inscriptions was named Pacal, which means Shield. He is thought to have been born on March 26, A.D. 603. He ruled Palenque from July 29, 615, until his death on August 31, 683, at the age of 80. Fortunately for modern scholars, Pacal had commissioned a series of texts that recorded the history and death dates of his predecessors.

While epigraphers toiled over Maya inscriptions, archaeologists reexamined Maya sites long assumed to have been ceremonial centers for villagers living in small, dispersed settlements. In 1956 the University of Pennsylvania Museum and the government of Guatemala embarked on an ambitious study of Tikal, one of the largest Maya sites. Dense vegetation mantled the remote ruins. Only the summits of the pyramids poked above the forest canopy as signposts to the ancient city that lay below. The archaeologists arrived in DC-3s, landing on an airstrip hacked out of the rain forest. In the early seasons they camped in palm-thatched huts and drank water from an ancient Maya reservoir.

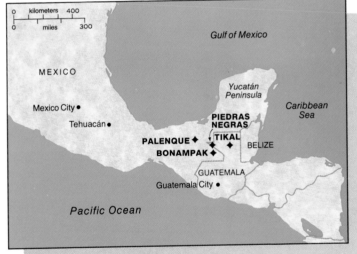

265

Liberated from the voracious Guatemalan jungle, fabled Tikal, one of the largest Maya centers, attracts scholars in many fields of study. More than a hundred specialists have helped investigate the ruins in a project begun by the University of Pennsylvania Museum and the Guatemalan government in 1956.

Other Maya sites in Mexico and Central America (map) have also increased knowledge of this sophisticated culture, which flourished between A.D. 250 and 900.

Over a period of 14 years, more than a hundred specialists—from architects to hydrologists—worked at Tikal. First, local workmen cleared the Great Plaza, which proved to be the center of a city that covered more than 50 square miles. Then the surveyors fanned out with cameras and compasses. They mapped 6 square miles of temple-pyramids, intricately carved stone monuments, underground chambers cut into the bedrock, wide causeways, and thousands of low house mounds. A 35-foot-wide trench was dug across a 2-acre religious complex, uncovering evidence of human settlement dating back to 600 B.C. and traces of temples from as early as 300 B.C. Hundreds of smaller trenches revealed ball courts, a marketplace, and residential compounds.

Guatemalan engineers cut seven-mile-long pathways through the forest in four directions. Archaeologists penetrated about 275 yards into the jungle on each side of these trails. The Tikal map that emerged from these limited surveys showed densely populated suburbs spreading for several miles from the center. Tikal had grown rapidly from the small village established on a well-drained limestone hill some six centuries before Christ. By the eighth century A.D., about 40,000 people lived in the metropolis.

What made Tikal such an important center? One major reason was probably its strategic location. Tikal lay on a portage route between river systems linking the Caribbean Sea and the Gulf of Mexico. Tikal's powerful rulers may have controlled far-flung trade networks between the Guatemalan highlands, the Gulf of Mexico, and the Pacific coast.

The Guatemalan government followed up the Tikal excavations with a comprehensive restoration program. Thousands of visitors came to Tikal National Park every year, until political turmoil discouraged tourism. But here was one of the first sites where a shrewd investment in archaeology paid off handsomely in tourist dollars. Since the 1960s many other governments have followed a similar strategy.

The Tikal Project provided new insights into ancient Maya agriculture. Archaeologists had seen the modern Maya burn the overgrowth to clear forest gardens, and they assumed that the ancient Maya had done the same. But the house mounds at Tikal were only 500 yards from each other,

Constructed in the eighth century A.D., Temple I at Tikal awaits restoration in 1960 after workers cleared away the rubble and dense vegetation that covered it. Rising steeply in nine tiers, a number sacred to the Maya, this limestone temple-pyramid towers some 155 feet above the city's Great Plaza—and a royal sepulcher. Archaeologists believe that the temple was originally painted red. A lintel carving inspired its modern name: Temple of the Giant Jaguar. In front of the pyramid stand stone slabs,

some carved with hieroglyphs recording major events in the lives of Tikal's rulers.

The archaeologists at right excavate beneath the slightly smaller Temple II, searching in vain for a burial chamber. The map above shows how Tikal's sprawling ceremonial hub probably looked about 1,200 years ago, with its plazas and causeways, reservoirs, royal residential complexes, and numerous temple-pyramids. Scholars still ponder the reasons for the city's sudden decline and abandonment.

too close together for the residents to have survived by this simple slash-and-burn method of agriculture. Instead, the people of Tikal grew breadnut trees, root crops, beans, and corn in high-yield household garden plots, on terraces, and in raised fields created by mounding up soil in low-lying swampy areas. Remote-sensing instruments, such as side-scan aerial radar, have revealed dense networks of raised fields and irrigation canals. This intensive agriculture supported Tikal's large urban population.

Thirty years of research are just beginning to unveil the intricate agricultural landscape of the ancient Maya. The ongoing study of Maya civilization at Tikal exemplifies the archaeological teamwork and technology that started to emerge in the 1940s. Today, digging plays only a small part in the study of the complex relationship between ancient peoples and their natural environment.

268

Elaborate murals in a Maya temple at Bonampak, Mexico, provided a wealth of new information about ancient Maya customs, dress, and social order. Guatemalan artist Antonio Tejeda Fonseca (above), part of a team sent by the Carnegie Institution in 1946, painted small-scale copies of the fragile murals as archaeologists surveyed and excavated the site. In a detail from a recent full-size copy (right), attendants dress a ruler in ceremonial jaguar skins and jade ornaments.

France, 1974: Divers use suction to uncover wine jars in a Roman cargo ship sunk off La Madrague de Giens between 60 and 50 B.C.

LOST SHIPS, SUNKEN CITIES

*T*he wind screamed in the rigging of the Roman ship. Heavy with cargo, she wallowed in the Mediterranean storm off southern Gaul. Waves crashed over the rail, filling the hold with seawater. At last the ship foundered. Sailors swam for dear life as the hull settled gently on the soft bottom, its cargo of wine jars intact.

Two thousand years later, in 1967, French navy divers off La Madrague de Giens near the French Riviera noticed wine jars among the eelgrass in 60 feet of water. Archaeologists in diving gear soon uncovered the ancient ship's well-preserved hull. Hovering like spacemen, they cleared the sand from a jumble of amphoras—big clay jars with large handles. Slowly, systematically, divers uncovered thousands of jars stacked in several layers and padded with rushes and heather. As the position of each jar was recorded, the archaeologists lifted it to the surface with an air-filled balloon.

Some of the amphoras still held a trace of wine. And some bore a name stamped in the clay: P. Veveius Papus. Years before, this same stamp had been found at a kiln site in the Caecuban region south of Rome, a district known in antiquity for its fine wines.

Next the divers studied the hull. The massive keel supported heavy frames, thick planks, and two masts set well forward. The ship could carry about 350 tons of cargo. This was a very large Roman merchantman, about 120 feet long with a beam of 27 feet and a depth of 13. For archaeologists the vessel was a treasure chest of information.

This is not the kind of treasure that beckons most salvagers into the sea. Spanish doubloons, treasure galleons, chests of jewels—rumors of such sunken riches have lured adventurers for centuries. Belatedly, more than 150 countries have enacted laws to protect wrecks in their waters, but enforcement is usually lax. Wrecks in shallow waters are vanishing at an alarming rate. Soon it may be impossible to find underwater sites worth excavating.

Ever since people ventured onto the oceans, there have been shipwrecks—and salvagers risking their lives for the cargoes. At first they used nets and grappling irons; in clear water they dived by holding their breath. They tried the diving bell in the 16th century, the sealed barrel in the 17th, and the diving suit and helmet in the 19th. But nothing offered

the dexterity and precision needed for an underwater dig.

Then in 1943 French diver Jacques-Yves Cousteau and a colleague developed the Aqua-Lung, a self-contained underwater breathing apparatus now better known by its acronym, scuba. Plunging into the Mediterranean Sea a decade later, Captain Cousteau recovered amphoras from a Greek wreck off the French Riviera. His divers simply dug out the cargo and drew no plans of the site. But such early ventures helped develop ways to dig and keep records underwater.

Now archaeologists work in the water almost as easily as on land. Some even prefer the sea, where they can swirl the sand off a fragile goblet a few grains at a time. With scuba gear, mini-submarines, and advanced electronics, they can probe sites hundreds, even thousands, of years old—Bronze Age ships, Roman merchantmen, Byzantine cargo carriers, Tudor warships, ancient ports now sunk beneath the waves.

In the summer of 1958 American photojournalist Peter Throckmorton and a Turkish photographer crowded into a 38-foot boat to share the life of Turkish sponge divers while looking for ancient wrecks. They located more than thirty. On one of them, underwater archaeology came of age.

A sponge-boat captain had seen artifacts of bronze in a pile off Cape Gelidonya in southwestern Turkey. He wanted to dynamite the pile and sell the metal for scrap but complained it was "rotten." Throckmorton realized his friend was talking about a very old site, for bronze deteriorates very slowly in seawater. Throckmorton stopped him from blowing the pile apart and the next summer located the site. He persuaded the University of Pennsylvania Museum to excavate the site according to standards used on land.

This was the first scientific underwater excavation ever planned. The museum appointed George F. Bass, a student

of Mycenaean civilization, as director of the excavation and sent him to the local YMCA to learn scuba diving.

The site proved to be a shipwreck lying on a bare, rocky bottom in about a hundred feet of water. The divers photographed the wreck and used ordinary pencils on sheets of frosted plastic to sketch the positions of artifacts. The cargo had fused together so firmly that the only way to remove it was to lift it in lumps. Bass used a jeep's jack to loosen big blocks, then winched them up to be dissected ashore.

Pottery and radiocarbon dating showed the ship had sunk about 1200 B.C., during the late Bronze Age. She carried copper ingots from Cyprus—four-handled slabs weighing about 44 pounds each—and tin, the two metals used in making bronze. Wicker baskets held bronze scrap. Many artifacts aboard closely resembled items from Syria and Palestine, so Bass surmised that the ship had sailed from Syria to Cyprus,

Ingenuity ushers humans into the silent sea. Jacques-Yves Cousteau, a French undersea pioneer (opposite), peers from a research submersible in 1953. Six years later, the Aqua-Lung he helped invent in 1943 lets him photograph a tiny two-person sub (above) that takes researchers to depths a free diver cannot reach.

American inventor Harold E. Edgerton (left) tests his underwater camera in 1959. He also developed a side-scan sonar that has found many a shipwreck on the bottom.

where she took on scrap metal. Because the few personal effects were also from Syria and Palestine, he felt the ship was Phoenician, or Canaanite, though scholars had assumed the Mycenaeans were the dominant sea traders of the time.

While Bass probed this ship of commerce, the Swedes studied a ship of war: the *Vasa*, a 1,200-ton galleon launched at Stockholm in 1628. Overloaded with 64 bronze guns and scores of crewmen, wives, and children, the 200-foot ship had embarked in a light breeze on her maiden voyage. Less than a mile from the dock, two powerful gusts billowed her sails. Top-heavy, the *Vasa* heeled sharply to port. Water gushed in through her open gunports, and she sank in 110 feet of water, taking 30 to 50 people with her. There she lay until the 1950s, when a Swedish engineer named Anders Franzén set out on a bold venture to raise her intact. He combed archives and dragged the murky harbor for years until he located oak timbers in a large mound on the seabed. Swedish navy divers went down for a look. "Can't see a thing," one reported. Then he "touched something solid . . . it feels like a wall of wood!" It was the *Vasa*.

Government, industry, and private subscribers banded together to raise the ship. With jets of water, divers bored six

tunnels under the hull. Working in near-zero visibility, they passed six-inch cables through the tunnels and attached them to two pontoons partly filled with water. Engineers then pumped out the water, and the *Vasa* rose gently from the mud. They towed her into shallow water, and there she stayed submerged for another two years while workers reinforced the hull. At last, in April 1961, the *Vasa* was raised and, in May, floated into a dry dock, where the timbers were kept wet while the process of preserving them began.

It took eleven workers five months to clear debris and excavate the interior. Twelve skeletons were found, one of a seaman wearing leather shoes, linen stockings, a bulky knit wool vest, and trousers with coins still in the pockets.

Once the waterlogged timbers had been soaked in a preservative, skilled carpenters restored large portions of the bow, the afterdecks, and the hull. The intricate jigsaw puzzle is now almost complete. Two of the *Vasa*'s cabins

Stockholm harbor in 1961 again hails the Vasa *(opposite), a doomed galleon that sank in these waters on her maiden voyage 333 years before. Cradled in a giant frame, the proud hulk follows a tug (lower) to a temporary berth for restoration. Excavation proved a daunting task for archaeologists who found her 'tween decks in shambles (upper). But from the mud and chaos came a cargo of finds as noble as an officer's lace-trimmed hat, as humble as a sailor's pipe of clay.*

have even been reequipped with their original furniture.

More than 25,000 artifacts came from the hull and from probings around the wreck site: pewter tankards and leather bottles, a wooden plane and other carpentry tools, wooden kegs, and a myriad of small, seagoing artifacts of the 17th century. It took most of the 1970s to catalog them all.

More than shipwrecks await the marine archaeologist. Earthquakes have cast seaside cities into the ocean; changing shorelines have inundated once busy ports. Now archaeologists can study these sites with the precision of a dig on land.

Between 1655 and 1671 Port Royal in Jamaica was a roisterous buccaneers' port, the "wickedest city on earth." Then piracy waned; beginning in the 1670s, the residents turned to lawful commerce in slaves, sugar, and other goods. More than 6,000 people lived in the town's 2,000 buildings. Their world came to an abrupt end on the morning of June 7, 1692, when a severe earthquake and resultant seismic sea waves toppled about two-thirds of Port Royal into water up to 40 feet deep. About 2,000 people were killed; disease and other aftereffects claimed at least that many more.

Looters dived on the ruins within hours, but not until 1956 did archaeological investigations begin. Edwin A. Link, an American inventor, was disappointed to find only a monotonous mud bottom where the city had fallen. Even building walls were hard to locate, except for a crown of coral.

With National Geographic support, Link returned in 1959 with a diving and salvage boat and surveyed the streets with an echo sounder. He attached buoys to walls, then recorded them on a map compiled from estate records. Divers endured poor visibility, sharks, and the danger of cave-ins to recover hundreds of artifacts, including spoons, glassware, a swivel gun, and a brass pocket watch. An X ray detected a ghostly trace of the watch's long-vanished hands, still pointing to the moment when it stopped forever: 11:43.

In the 1960s author-diver Robert F. Marx continued Link's work; his team salvaged thousands of items from the sunken port. In 1981 marine archaeologist Don L. Hamilton began a detailed study. His excavators cleared the site with a water dredge, breathing by air hoses attached to a floating compressor. Then they dug with trowels, brushes, and other land tools. They used a grid and measuring instruments to draw accurate plans. In 1982 they began to uncover a large brick building of at least six rooms. In one room they found two kegs, a gun and some lead shot, and more than 60 wine bottles, many still corked. A table and stool lay under a fallen wall with several bottles nearby. Surely this was a tavern.

The Port Royal excavators used conventional techniques, albeit underwater. The Cape Gelidonya wreck had also been a relatively straightforward dig. In 1961, aided by the first of his many grants from the National Geographic, George Bass dived deeper—to a Byzantine vessel some 120 feet down near Yassı Ada, an island off western Turkey.

The wreck was a mound of pot-bellied amphoras, with what appeared to be corroded anchors at one end. Bass worked slowly and carefully. Archaeologists brushed sea growth from the wreck, labeled every item with a numbered plastic tag, and set up a mapping frame and wire grids over

Height 15½"

Symbol of royal power and the ship carvers' skill, the Vasa's *stern flaunts wooden figures, flourishes, and lions holding the Swedish arms (opposite). As nails corroded, nearly 800 carvings and ornate pieces fell from the sunken hulk. But nail holes remained to show restorers which went where. The lion above hid on the lid of a gunport to snarl at the foe when the rope lifted the lid. Now a museum invites visitors to admire the great ship, her decks and decorations almost fully restored (lower).*

Everyday objects recall a day like no other: June 7, 1692, the day an earthquake hurled about two-thirds of Port Royal, Jamaica, into the sea. Once a notorious haven for pirates, the drowned port has become a magnet for explorers and archaeologists. Artifacts from a ten-week dig in 1959 (right) fill a table on a pier—bulbous wine bottles, long-stemmed churchwarden pipes, and at lower right, a copper pot still holding bones of beef and turtle, probably from a stew that was simmering for lunch when disaster struck. Beside the relics rides the *Sea Diver*, an archaeological research vessel whose divers brought them up. Wrecks and sunken ports all over the world (map) yield a priceless legacy, both in finds and in facts about humanity's long and uneasy partnership with the sea.

278

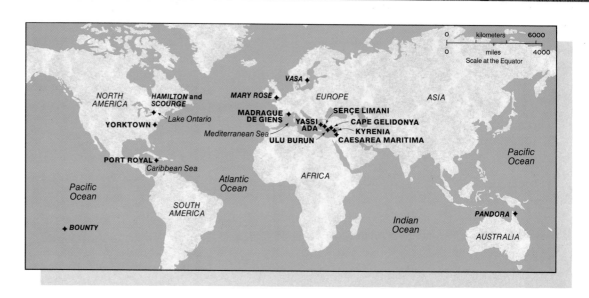

the site. Artists hovered above the grids with sheets of plastic squared off in corresponding grids, mapping the positions of the artifacts before divers carried them up to the surface. Archaeologists on the dive barge cleaned the artifacts and searched for others in piles of muck and shell sucked up in big hoses called air lifts. Bass devised two underwater towers for making a continual photographic record of the dig.

By the end of the second season, Bass had uncovered much of the visible portions of the cargo and the tile-roofed galley area. The galley was set deep in the hull, well appointed with a tiled cookstove, fine tableware, and a wide range of cooking utensils. Coins dated the wreck to the first half of the seventh century A.D. Marked on a balance used for weighing cargo was a name translated as George Elder Sea Captain.

The ship's timbers littering the site were so light that they could easily be swept away by divers or current, so Bass bought 2,000 bicycle spokes and sharpened one end of each; divers then used them to pin the wood fragments to the seabed. An assistant, Frederick H. van Doorninck, Jr., supervised the recording of every wood fragment, complete with each nail hole, bolt hole, score line, and mortise. From these he drew the lines of the 70-foot vessel. His drawings make the Yassı Ada ship look well preserved, but in fact van Doorninck had used every scrap of evidence he could find to reconstruct on paper a ship whose bow had vanished and whose stern was, at best, a shattered fragment.

As an iron object decomposes, it bonds with the sand and shells around it and thus builds up a crustlike concretion, a natural mold of the original object. Bass found such concretions all over the site. Team member Michael L. Katzev carefully sawed through the lumps, then filled them with a synthetic rubber compound. When the mold was broken away, an "iron" implement appeared—a cast of the original, covered with a thin layer of rust. Katzev conjured up double-bladed axes, adzes, hammers, woodworking gouges, even a caulking iron and some files with their ridges perfectly preserved. With these the ship's crew would have been virtually self-sufficient and able to make almost any repair.

The 3,575 dives on the Yassı Ada ship laid to rest any notion that underwater archaeology could not achieve the same precision as a land dig. As the technology matured, Bass and other marine archaeologists could concentrate not on diving but on studying the wrecks as time capsules that tell about ancient seafaring and life ashore as well.

A Roman wine amphora, for example, was often sealed with a stopper bearing the supplier's mark—a sort of label rarely found intact on land, because it had to be smashed to pour the wine. But during the ten-year excavation of the Roman cargo ship at La Madrague de Giens, some of the seals were found unbroken. They told where the wine came from and thus helped trace a thread in the ancient web of trade.

With the measurements and construction details of that vessel in hand, French archaeologist Patrice Pomey spent months in libraries looking for examples of ships like her. He found one portrayed in a bathhouse mosaic from Tunisia. The Madrague de Giens ship sank in the first century B.C.— but the mosaic dated to the third century A.D., proof that such

A diver in 1983 (upper) hovers above a brick floor that felt its last footstep nearly three centuries before. Here stood a brick building—like much of Port Royal, "Shaken and Shattered to Pieces, Sunk . . . and Covered . . . by the Sea," in the words of an eyewitness. The diver wears no tanks but breathes by a hookah system that pumps air down a hose from the surface—a useful device in shallow water. A dashed line in this aerial view of Port Royal traces its western waterfront before the disaster.

large merchant vessels were in use for at least two centuries. Thus the project helped show the enormous volume of Roman trade 2,000 years ago.

The main differences between land and underwater archaeology are in survey methods. Bass and his colleagues relied on sponge divers to find wrecks in shallow water of, say, 170 feet or less. Such wrecks are now becoming scarce, because they are easier to find and excavate. But ships go down in deeper waters too—and sometimes artifacts from them come up in fish nets. To pinpoint such wrecks, scientists peer into the deep with the kinds of "eyes" used by military services and oil companies. One example is side-scan sonar. A device towed by a ship sends out sound waves on either side and plots the echoes from features on the bottom.

Bass first tried this sonar near Bodrum, a port in southwestern Turkey. He could scan a path 1,200 feet wide, so by crossing a selected area at 600-foot intervals, he scanned every part of the seabed twice. The survey revealed a likely target that turned out to be a pile of amphoras 285 feet down.

This was a dramatic discovery—but another, off Ulu Burun, a cape in southern Turkey, showed that the sponge diver can still rival high technology in shallower water. In 1982 a diver spotted "metal biscuits with ears" on the seabed near the town of Kaş. The biscuits turned out to be four-handled copper ingots from a wreck of about 1375 B.C. The ship's remains were strewn over the bottom from 141 to 167 feet down. Judging from the cargo, the vessel had probably loaded up at Syria, stopped at Cyprus, and was heading for Greece or western Turkey when she struck the rocks of Ulu Burun. This, the earliest shipwreck ever excavated underwater, was dated by her cargo and other artifacts, among which were two silver bracelets and a two-handled Mycenaean cup. Though only part of the ship's keel and planking survive, Bass thinks she was about 66 feet long.

The cargo is already telling much about Bronze Age trade. The ship carried Greek, Cypriot, and Phoenician pottery, some neatly stacked inside a large jar. Amphoras from Canaan held glass beads, pitch, and several kinds of seeds. The ship also carried raw materials—150 copper ingots and some of tin; blue glass ingots, the earliest ever found; and an   281

A weapon of war? A symbol of authority? On the seabed off Ulu Burun near the Turkish town of Kaş, a diver in 1984 ponders a mace head of stone (left) from a vessel that sank about 1375 B.C. The oldest shipwreck ever excavated, it sprawls down a slope to depths of 167 feet, deeper than any other site dug by scuba divers. George F. Bass (right), father of underwater archaeology and head of the project, briefs his team aboard a research vessel for another dive in a series that may take five more years.

elephant tusk and a hippopotamus tooth. Bronze daggers, spearheads, and a sword were found, as well as a gold goblet, a pectoral shaped like a bird of prey, and a medallion, the last two probably of Syrian origin. Nearly two centuries older than the Cape Gelidonya ship, the Ulu Burun wreck carried a much richer manifest that will take Bass and others about five more years to excavate and still more to interpret.

Thousands of years and thousands of miles separate the Ulu Burun vessel from the *Scourge* and the *Hamilton,* two United States Navy schooners overwhelmed by a violent squall on Lake Ontario in the early hours of August 8, 1813. All but 16 crew members perished as the ships capsized and sank in minutes. Some 160 years later, marine historian Daniel A. Nelson found a reference to the location of the disaster in the log of H.M.S. *Wolfe,* a British ship in sight of the Americans. Working with Nelson, a Canadian government agency used advanced electronic equipment to search an area off Port Dalhousie, Ontario. Then in 1982 the team lowered a remotely piloted vehicle fitted with television cameras and designed to be operated at great depths from a surface vessel.

The lake is deep, cold, and fresh; wooden wrecks are safe from warm-water organisms and salt corrosion. Nelson sat transfixed before the screen as the ships came into view. The two wrecks lay 290 feet deep in almost perfect condition, the hulls intact, the spars fallen to the decks, the masts still upright—a vignette of warship life in 1813. The vehicle's cameras saw and recorded cutlasses and boarding axes in their proper places, the ships' figureheads intact, human skeletons scattered over the lake bed. At such deep-water wreck sites, video documentation has given a priceless first glimpse of finds that may later be recovered.

The state of the art in marine archaeology is shown by an excavation funded in part by National Geographic off Kyrenia, Cyprus, where a Greek vessel sank in about a hundred feet of water in the fourth century B.C. Michael Katzev directed the project in 1968-69, but interpretation and the testing of a reproduction under sail continue to this day.

The ship had settled on her port side and eventually split open near the keel. Three-fourths of her timbers survived. The divers were puzzled by concretions under the

Copper ingots leave the Ulu Burun ship the same way they boarded her 34 centuries ago: on the shoulders of cargo handlers. These "stevedores" (above) heft more than trade goods; they may be off-loading a cargo of insights about sea trade in the Bronze Age—a cargo made richer by the find of a golden goblet (right).

Another wreck surrenders her secrets as a team (opposite) cleans items with dental tools at Serçe Limanı in Turkey, where a cargo of glass went down a thousand years ago.

Archaeologists a hundred feet down uncover an ancient Mediterranean wreck in this artist's conception. Some methods are like those on land; others are unique to the sea.

A light on a metal detector (1) alerts divers to what may be a buried artifact. Gold, copper, iron? Hovering over the spot, one of them fans debris toward the suction of the air lift (2)—the pick and shovel of the deep.

Under a grid of plastic (3), beams and artifacts are tagged and their positions plotted. Overhead, a special camera (4) maps the site in three dimensions. A photographer (5) and an artist (6) record details, ever mindful that creatures such as the moray eel can be dangerous.

Hookahs (7), named for the Turkish water pipe, use air pumped from the surface for longer, but less mobile, dives. And the air-filled telephone booth (8) offers refuge where swimmers breathe without gear and talk to co-workers above.

Various transports haul objects topside. The consta lift (9) hoists centuries-old wine jars. Air bubbling from its vent equalizes pressure to keep its cargo from rocketing to the surface. Finless divers walk a timber-laden wire basket (10) up a rocky slope; a balloon eases their burden. Cables (11) from a crane lift heavy items, while divers carry small pieces in wicker baskets (12).

Last stop: decompression. Dangling from a barrel at 20 feet, a diver (13) breathes off nitrogen that can accumulate in body tissues during a dive. The gas causes crippling bends, or bubbles in the blood, if a diver rises too quickly. This diver will rest again at 10 feet before boarding the project's lifeline, the dive barge (14).

284

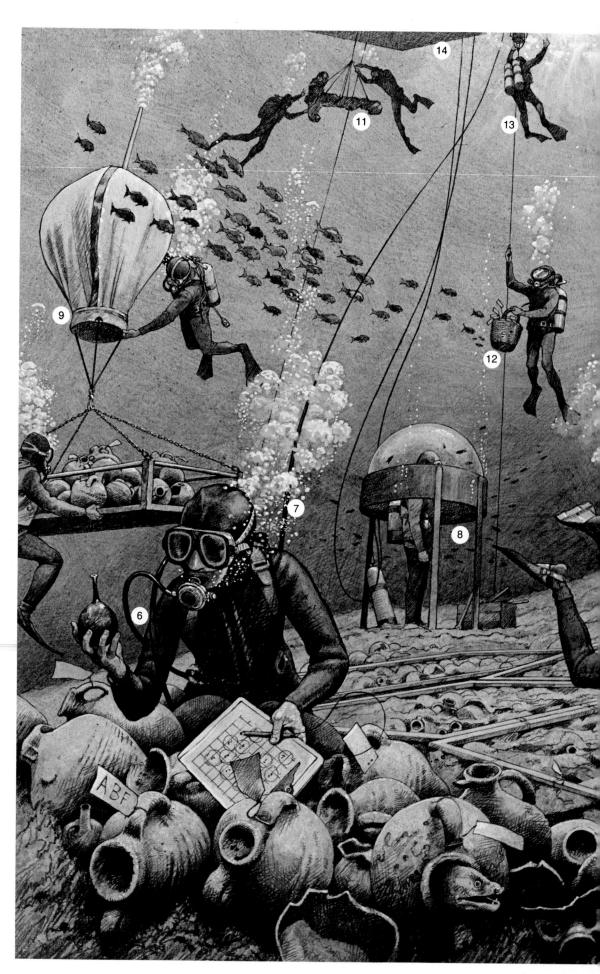

hull. These turned out to be eight iron spearheads, some of them bent. The ship had apparently been attacked by pirates.

The 48-foot merchantman carried about 25 tons of cargo: some 10,000 almonds, perhaps from Cyprus; nearly 400 amphoras of wine and olive oil, popular exports in the eastern Mediterranean; millstones from the island of Nisyros, probably the leftovers from a batch that had been sold off at various ports, leaving these to be used as ballast. Cabins in the bow and stern held four place settings of wood and pottery. There were two portable grills but no sign of a hearth; the crew probably cooked on beaches ashore and ate fresh foods on board. Katzev believes the Kyrenia ship came from Samos to Nisyros and Rhodes before stopping at Cyprus, where one of the few coins found on board was minted.

J. Richard Steffy, a specialist in ancient ship construction, had long been interested in ancient seafaring when he joined Katzev's team. Steffy has spent more than a decade researching and reconstructing the Kyrenia ship from detailed drawings and photographs of 6,000 wooden fragments. He soon realized that every ancient ship was a unique production and that the best way to study one was not by making drawings of it but by building a scale model.

Steffy showed how the ancient shipbuilders had hewn the keel from a single log, then added the curved stem and stern. They fitted the bottom planks next, then the floor timbers and side planking, half frames, and topsides. This took a lot of labor and timber. But the ship was well built; each plank edge was joined to its neighbors with oak tenons and locked in place with wooden pegs. She was very old when she sank and had been repaired several times. Steffy chronicled repairs both major and minor, as well as replacements of rotted planks, a second layer of bow planking, and a large

Becalmed in time, the sunken schooner Hamilton *sits for a ghostly portrait (opposite) by side-scan sonar in 1975, her hull in black, her acoustic shadow in white. She and the* Scourge, *caught in a Lake Ontario squall in 1813, sank 290 feet—too deep for scuba divers. A research barge in 1982 sends down a robot unit (above) with cameras and lights—and brings up images like this one of an anchor (left). Such robots may replace manned submersibles and divers for observation work.*

Overleaf: *The Kyrenia ship bares her frames and planks under the archaeologist's grid. For 23 centuries this Greek cargo ship lay on the seabed off Kyrenia, Cyprus, preserved in the mud under a mound of jars called amphoras that once were filled with wine. "When I saw that pile of amphoras," recalled Cypriot diver Andreas Cariolou, "the hair stood up on my neck like a hedgehog's." Divers brought up the cargo and other relics from the wreck he discovered, then later raised the ship.*

patch where the keel had cracked. The ship had been hauled up on land for overhaul at least twice. Eventually her owner sheathed her with lead to ward off worms and keep out water. Much of the lead had vanished, but Steffy traced the sheathing pattern from tiny tack shafts in the planks. His trend-setting research, which will take years more to complete, shows how the Greeks built the ships on which they depended for commerce, defense, and colonization.

Underwater archaeologists now work all over the world on wrecks large and small. Some are diving on the remains of the 24-gun frigate *Pandora,* which sank north of Australia in 1791, taking with her four captured *Bounty* mutineers who had been manacled in a cage on deck. And at Yorktown, Virginia, a cofferdam now encircles the hulk of a ship scuttled in the York River by Lord Cornwallis, commander of the British redcoats in the American Revolution. Filters clarify the muddy water for diver-archaeologists at work 20 feet below. Here advanced computer-assisted sensing equipment has been used to map even tiny objects on the bottom.

One of the most spectacular projects in recent years was the recovery of King Henry VIII's *Mary Rose,* a magnificent warship that sank off Portsmouth, England, on July 19, 1545. King Henry was in trouble; he faced a French attack force of 235 ships and 30,000 troops. The king had only 60 vessels, but they were ready. The 35-year-old *Mary Rose* had been rebuilt and rearmed to engage the foe at long range.

The day was almost dead calm as the *Mary Rose* ghosted down The Solent with her 415 crewmen, plus 285 soldiers and longbowmen who added even more weight to the overladen ship. Then a gust caught her; the *Mary Rose* heeled and swerved to starboard. "I have the sort of knaves I cannot rule," cried the vice admiral. The king ashore watched aghast as the top-heavy vessel dipped her open gunports under, shipped water in torrents, and sank in less than a minute. Only about 30 men scrambled to safety.

There the *Mary Rose* still lay in 1971, when British diver-journalist Alexander McKee and British archaeologist Margaret Rule located her after a six-year search for wrecks in The Solent. By chance, winter storms had disturbed the bottom and exposed the massive stubs of the ship's ribs like a row of

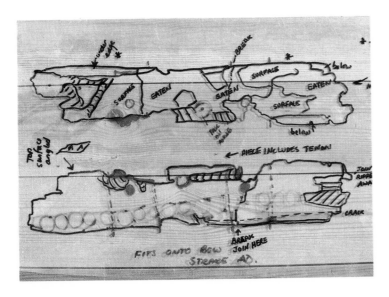

In a gallery of the crusader castle on Cyprus, the Kyrenia ship (opposite) floats on a sea of scaffolding as experts piece together her hull. "The wood," recalled archaeologist Michael L. Katzev, "was like soft, soggy bread" until it was brought to the surface, little by little, and treated for months with preservative. Drawings (left) recorded 6,000 fragments, even noting eaten areas where shipworms had done their work. Enough survives to guide craftsmen in Piraeus, the port of Athens, as they build by hand a reproduction of the Kyrenia ship (above). Like the ancient shipwrights, they build the hull shell first, adding ribs to stiffen the hull once the shape is formed. An earlier scale model, complete with a square sail and two steering oars, surprised her builders with her ability to sail fairly close into the wind.

black gravestones. She lay on her starboard side in 40 feet of swift current. The lower part of the hull had filled with fine silt that sealed its contents from marine erosion and rot. Tools, weapons, clothing, skeletons—nearly everything that went down with the ship was preserved. It took four years and 30,000 dives to bring up some 17,000 artifacts. The ship broke the surface on October 11, 1982. Now she rests in dry dock only a hundred yards from where she was built almost five centuries ago.

The *Mary Rose*'s four decks bristled with cannon. Some were old breech-loaded weapons of wrought iron that hurled missiles of lead, stone, or cast iron. Others were new muzzle-loaders of bronze, their mighty barrels resplendent with sculptures, ornamentation, and the royal insignia of rose and crown. Cast-iron guns were hooked over the rails to shower boarders with hailshot; at close quarters they could

inflict terrible casualties on an enemy ship's crowded decks.

Removable blinds protected the ship's gunners and archers. Her trained bowmen could shoot 12 arrows a minute at ranges of up to 270 yards; even the French admitted that English archers such as these were the world's best. Among many skeletons on board, divers found one of a sturdy man in his 20s who had worn a leather jerkin and a holder of arrows. Two vertebrae were displaced forward and to the left, as if he had applied frequent pressure on his backbone from that side—as right-handed archers would. His left arm was enlarged and a joint flattened from years of drawing a bow.

He may have drawn his bow that very day, for the *Mary Rose* probably saw action before she sank. The divers found skeletons on straw mattresses in the bowels of the ship. Very likely, these men had been wounded, then hustled below so their suffering would not demoralize their shipmates.

History runs in reverse as the Mary Rose *(opposite, upper) rises from the seabed near Portsmouth, England. Once the flagship of King Henry VIII's fleet, the big carrack— drawn by a chronicler with pennants flying (opposite, lower)—went down in 1545. Half her hull survives, bathed in sprays (center) lest it dry too fast and warp. Much that sank with her was retrieved intact. British archaeologist Margaret Rule (above) holds one of 139 longbows found aboard, some still supple enough to shoot.*

The *Mary Rose* was a microcosm of 16th-century English society. The seamen wore sturdy leather shoes, quaffed ale, and ate off wooden plates. Their sea chests held fishing lines and clothing; one had a gimballed compass in a box. The barber-surgeon shipped aboard with a chest of drug flasks and the tools of his trade, including an amputation saw, a blood-letting bowl, three brass syringes for treating bladder complaints and venereal disease, and a large wooden mallet, perhaps for applying force to an amputation knife— or knocking out his patients in the days before anesthetics.

Gentlemen of officer rank carried pocket sundials and wore richly decorated clothes; at least one took along a manicure set. They poured wine from flagons and dined off pewter dinnerware. The ship's company ate venison, mutton, beef, pork, and fresh vegetables and fruit. So did hordes of rats; their bones were found in many parts of the hull.

Spectacular ship-raisings such as the *Mary Rose* and the *Vasa* occur all too rarely in marine archaeology. Most projects involve the same sort of jigsaw puzzle of sonar readings, artifacts, and cargo inventories, but the wreck itself stays on the bottom. Either way, the findings deal with life ashore as well as at sea. Thus underwater archaeologists sometimes work with their land-based counterparts—as they do today at the ancient harbor of Caesarea Maritima.

Herod the Great, King of Judaea under the Romans, built two massive breakwaters at Caesarea Maritima, enclosing an artificial harbor of three and a half acres on the inhospitable coastline south of Haifa, Israel. Earthquakes long ago ravaged the breakwaters. But infrared aerial photographs and underwater surveys showed that Herod's engineers had built not just a simple harbor but a complex of inner and outer harbors and anchorages, a haven for merchant ships

around the time of Christ. A lighthouse had marked the entrance. Rows of warehouses lined the breakwaters. Broken jars suggested some of the cargoes stored inside, from Rhodian wine to pickled fish. Land archaeology rounded out the picture of a city of white marble, with a palace, amphitheater, elaborate aqueduct, sewers flushed by seawater, and a high defense wall. A temple to Emperor Augustus overlooked a harbor that once rivaled Piraeus, the seaport of Athens, in size. Small wonder Herod could afford this grandiose project; the revenues more than repaid his investment.

Underwater archaeology joined late in the quest for ancient societies. But at Caesarea Maritima, and scores of other sites across a planet that is more than two-thirds underwater, it has quickly earned its place. Among the varied techniques of archaeology, it contributes as no other can to an understanding of the human past.

Diameter ¾"

The ghost of a harbor darkens the sea at Caesarea Maritima in Israel (opposite), a port made great by King Herod at the time of Christ. A barge at the entrance serves as a tender for divers. Along the ruins of a breakwater, a diver (above) inspects huge concrete blocks cast underwater in wooden forms, a technique invented by the Romans. Diggers ashore uncovered public buildings, a theater, the governor's palace, and this gold areus, *a coin of about* A.D. *70 with the name of Herod's realm: Judaea.*

Tanzania, 1960: Members of the Leakey family—Mary, Louis, and young Philip—search for fossils of human ancestors at Olduvai Gorge.

TO THE ENDS OF EARTH & TIME

"*I* 've got him," cried Mary Leakey as she burst into the tent where her husband, Louis, lay sick with flu.

"Got what?" asked Louis.

"*Our* man," she exclaimed. "The one we've been looking for. Come quick. I've found a skull."

Illness forgotten, Louis got up from the bed and fumbled into his clothes. He and his wife then hurried to the gorge nearby where for 24 years they had searched for the remains of humanity's earliest ancestors. To date their quest had turned up an array of animal fossils—even some evidence of human handiwork, such as chips worked from larger stones and some crude implements. But so far the Leakeys had found no significant trace of early humans.

The scene of their activity was Olduvai Gorge, a remote, sun-baked ravine in the Serengeti Plain of northern Tanzania. Earlier on this scorching morning of July 17, 1959, Mary had left her husband in camp and had combed patiently over the stony surface of the gorge, as they both had countless times before, picking up small artifacts and animal fossils. Suddenly an unusual bone fragment caught her eye. Brushing away the loose soil, she exposed two large teeth still in place in the upper jaw of a fractured skull. These were *not* animal teeth. The years of searching had paid off.

"I turned to look at Mary, and we almost cried with sheer joy," Louis later recounted. "After all our hoping and hardship and sacrifice, at last we had reached our goal—we had discovered a hominid skull."

The unearthing of the skull of this early human ancestor established the Leakeys as international celebrities and brought paleoanthropology—the study of fossil humans—to the public's attention. Hominids, by definition, include humans and their immediate ancestors. The Leakeys named the owner of the skull *Zinjanthropus boisei,* "East African man," in honor of Charles Boise, a businessman who had sponsored their work. Later, the species would be renamed *Australopithecus boisei,* "southern ape-man."

The Leakeys' dramatic find came at a time when archaeologists first adopted a truly global perspective. Many had served overseas during World War II and, after the war ended, kept on working in remote parts of the world, including Africa and Southeast Asia.

The search for early human fossils had begun more than half a century earlier, when a Dutch physician named Eugène Dubois unearthed an apparently human skullcap near Trinil, Java. A year later, in 1892, he found a thighbone with many human characteristics. Dubois named his new hominid *Pithecanthropus erectus,* "upright ape-man." Critics accused Dubois of heresy and dismissed his claim to humanity for *Pithecanthropus.* But vindication came in 1929, when Chinese paleontologist W. C. Pei unearthed in Zhoukoudian cave near Beijing an almost complete skullcap closely resembling Dubois's find. Scientists soon reclassified both Java man and Peking man as *Homo erectus,* "upright man."

In 1924 Raymond Dart, an anatomy professor in South Africa, received two boxes of fossilized bones recovered from a limestone quarry near Taung. Inside one box Dart found a stone impression, or cast, of a skull interior. Another

rock held embedded the fossilized skull of a small apelike creature with a full set of almost-human milk teeth and the first molars just erupting. Because of the skull's balanced position atop the spine when its owner lived, Dart concluded that this child had walked upright.

Dart named his discovery *Australopithecus africanus,* "southern ape of Africa," and claimed it blended characteristics of apes and humans. Most scientists were skeptical of the ancestral relationship of the Taung child to humans. By the time Mary Leakey found *Zinjanthropus* 35 years later, other scientists had recovered dozens of *Australopithecus* fragments from caves around Johannesburg. Dart believed that his southern apes were toolmakers—that they had used chipped and broken animal bones as picks and scrapers to butcher game. Other authorities, including Louis Leakey, did not agree with Dart's claims. They felt that predators such as hyenas had fractured the bones and that *Australopithecus*

"We thought at first that he was exaggerating," recalled Mary Leakey (above, left) after an excavator told of a fossil footprint 12 inches long. But that print and others her team found in 1978 proved that hominids walked upright about 3.6 million years ago. The footprints remain at Laetoli in northern Tanzania, reburied to preserve them just as they were left in the soft volcanic ash (above).

At their base camp at Omo in Ethiopia, 23-year-old Richard Leakey and his father, Louis, *ponder a fragment of skull (opposite) in 1968. Louis doubted that the skull was a baboon's, as others supposed. "It was a large animal and he was wondering if it might not be a hominid," Richard wrote many years later.*

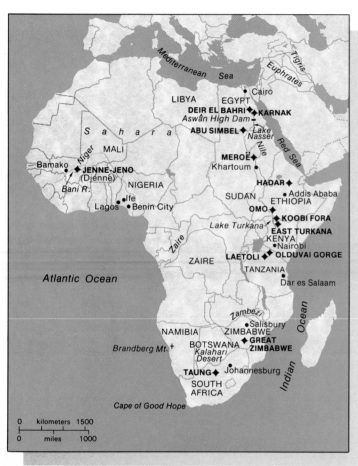

"The easiest part of camel riding is thinking about it before hand," wrote Richard Leakey after using the balky beasts during a search for fossils in 1969. He and team member Peter Nzube try the hard part (right) on a foray at Koobi Fora, a parched, fossil-rich lowland by Lake Turkana in Kenya. Meave Epps—now Mrs. Richard Leakey—halts in the saddle (opposite) for a drink of water, a precious cargo the camels needed only once a week. But they needed four hours a day to browse —and vigilance round the clock against lions and armed bandits. "By the end of each day we were absolute wrecks," Leakey recalled. After a few bone-wearying rides, team members walked and left the camels to haul baggage.

During one rest stop three days' march from their camp, Epps and Leakey spotted an Australopithecus skull while walking in a dry streambed. Hunting grounds for early human fossils abound in Africa (map), the continent where humans first evolved.

was only an aberrant offshoot unrelated to human evolution.

The Olduvai Gorge excavations marked the culmination of Louis S. B. Leakey's career. Born of missionary parents in Kenya's Kikuyu country, he referred to himself as a "white African." Leakey found himself somewhat of a misfit at Cambridge University in England, where he studied anthropology. In 1931 Hans Reck, a German geologist, introduced him to Olduvai Gorge. From the beginning Leakey sensed that Olduvai, with its layered beds of volcanic ash and clay, would prove a likely place to find fossils of early hominids, especially since it also preserved the shoreline of an ancient lake where Stone Age people had lived.

Leakey met his wife-to-be in 1933, while he was lecturing in London. Her talent for drawing and abiding interest in archaeology would lead to an auspicious partnership; Mary and Louis married three years later. For nearly a quarter century the Leakeys searched for human fossils at Olduvai. They retrieved thousands of animal fossils and small artifacts, many of them crude tools made of lava fragments. But hominid fossils continued to elude them, other than two insignificant skull fragments and two teeth.

Discovery of their first hominid skull in 1959 changed the Leakeys' lives. The National Geographic Society donated money to expand the excavations and to build a permanent camp staffed with geologists and paleontologists during the summer seasons. The camp on the gorge rim consisted of a thatched hut for working and eating—one side open to the breeze—and tents for sleeping. Whoever drove down from Nairobi, 216 miles to the northeast, brought fresh supplies.

Lions, leopards, rhinoceroses, and other wild animals frequently put in appearances at camp. Once a venomous tree snake called a boomslang appeared in the rafters over the lunch table and above a visitor's head. The Leakeys' son Jonathan, a reptile specialist, casually grasped the snake by its head and stashed it in a collecting bag.

The excavation team uncovered more hominids. One had a thinner skull and a larger, better developed braincase than the more robust *Zinjanthropus*. Louis Leakey claimed this was not one of Dart's australopithecine ape-men, which he believed was a dead-end line, but a true human. He called

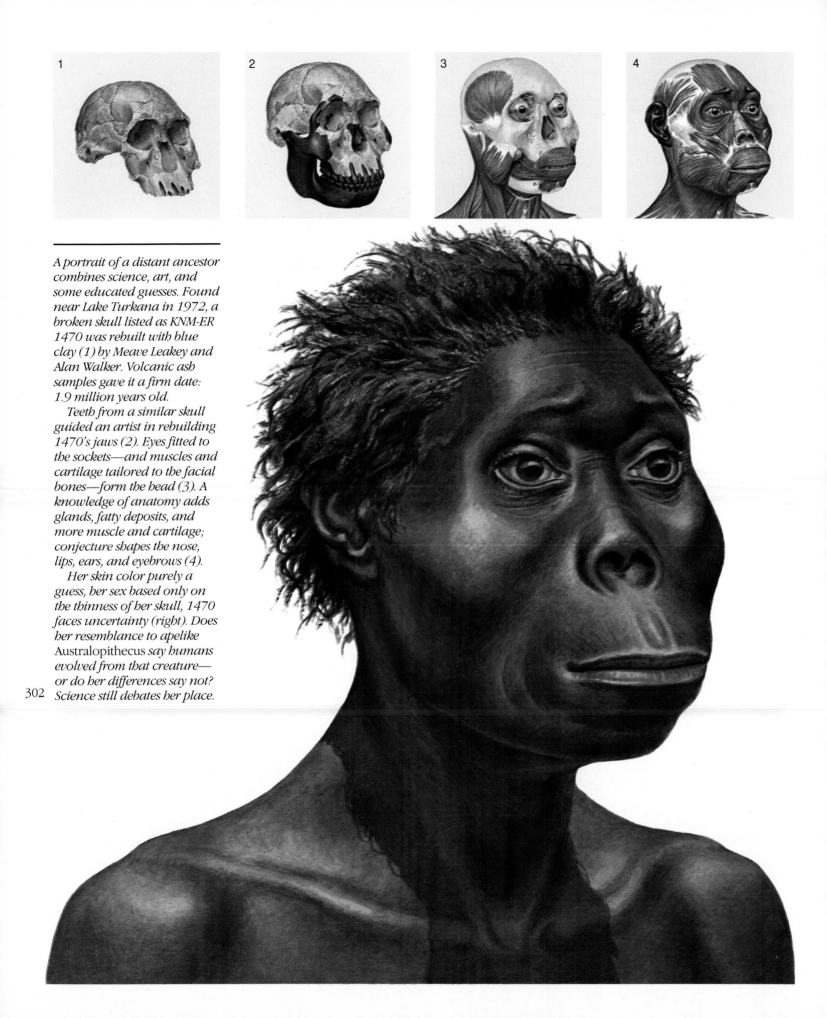

A portrait of a distant ancestor combines science, art, and some educated guesses. Found near Lake Turkana in 1972, a broken skull listed as KNM-ER 1470 was rebuilt with blue clay (1) by Meave Leakey and Alan Walker. Volcanic ash samples gave it a firm date: 1.9 million years old.

Teeth from a similar skull guided an artist in rebuilding 1470's jaws (2). Eyes fitted to the sockets—and muscles and cartilage tailored to the facial bones—form the head (3). A knowledge of anatomy adds glands, fatty deposits, and more muscle and cartilage; conjecture shapes the nose, lips, ears, and eyebrows (4).

Her skin color purely a guess, her sex based only on the thinness of her skull, 1470 faces uncertainty (right). Does her resemblance to apelike Australopithecus say humans evolved from that creature—or do her differences say not? Science still debates her place.

it *Homo habilis,* loosely translated as "handy man," because the bones of its fingers suggested dexterity suitable for making tools. Many of Leakey's colleagues contested his belief that *Homo habilis* was in the direct line to modern humans, contending that it was simply the most advanced australopithecine and not a "new" human ancestor.

The Leakeys provided geophysicists with samples from Olduvai's volcanic deposits for examination by the new potassium-argon dating technique, ideal for calculating the age of objects millions of years old. The Leakeys, unlike other scientists, had assumed that humans had lived on earth more than a million years but had no idea how much longer. The potassium-argon dates startled the scientific world by giving the early Olduvai sites an age of 1.75 million years, far older than anyone had previously imagined. The known antiquity of humans had suddenly almost doubled.

More surprises lay ahead. The Leakeys' son Richard, an expert safari leader and self-taught fossil hunter, wanted to take on a project independent of his parents. A chance flight over the desolate eastern shore of Lake Turkana in northern Kenya led him to promising fossil beds.

At the end of his first field season, in 1968, Richard had reconnoitered a 500-square-mile fossil site near Koobi Fora in the harsh, windy desert of East Turkana. To make a detailed survey of the trackless region, he rented camels. Reflecting on this youthful adventure, Leakey wrote: "I have to admit that I rather fancied my image as a camel-riding explorer of the great African desert.... Because of the many lions in the area, I always halted ... before nightfall.... After dinner, we drank coffee ... round the dying fire and this was the time to talk.... I find it difficult to describe the feelings of content that were generated by these evenings under the brilliant African starlit skies, listening to the rustle of the wind and the distant calls of jackals, hyenas and sometimes lions. To be sleeping on the warm ground without any shelter is perhaps as close as one can get to the conditions under which the people of our prehistoric past must have lived."

During another camel journey to Koobi Fora almost ten years after his mother's great discovery in 1959, Leakey spotted a skull staring up at him from a dry streambed. It was a complete australopithecine skull remarkably similar to his mother's discovery. Here was a prize indeed, for skulls normally break up long before they become fossilized. Only the teeth were missing from this one and, more important, it could be compared with the Olduvai skull.

Local assistants contributed greatly to Richard Leakey's work in Kenya. In 1972 Bernard Ngeneo found fragments of a fossil skull lying on the edge of a ravine. Richard's wife Meave and anatomist Alan Walker pieced together the skull. It proved to be 1.9 million years old, about the same age as the australopithecines. But Leakey reasoned that because its brain capacity was much greater than that of *Australopithecus,* the skull belonged to *Homo habilis,* the toolmaker. Thus he buttressed his father's earlier hunch after finding *Homo habilis* at Olduvai—that more advanced hominids had roamed East Africa about the same time as *Australopithecus.*

Louis Leakey, plagued with a heart problem, died two days after seeing the new skull.

While her son worked at Koobi Fora, Mary Leakey wound down the Olduvai excavations and turned to fossil beds at Laetoli, 30 miles south of Olduvai. Here in 1978 she uncovered a 75-foot-long trail of hominid footprints preserved in hardened volcanic ash about 3.6 million years old. A number of animals and erect hominids had walked on volcanic debris days before a nearby eruption rained ash on their tracks.

Of the three hominid trails, the prints on the left were smallest. Postulating that a child had made this track, Mary Leakey felt "a kind of poignant time wrench. At one point ... [the child] stops, pauses, turns to the left to glance at some possible threat or irregularity, and then continues to the north. This motion, so intensely human, transcends time. Three million six hundred thousand years ago, a remote ancestor—just as you or I—experienced a moment of doubt."

The Leakeys' discoveries inspired other scientists to search for the roots of human ancestry. In 1974 American paleoanthropologist Donald C. Johanson turned up a fragmentary skeleton at Hadar in the remote Afar region of northern Ethiopia. Dubbed Lucy, the female hominid had died in her twenties. She stood three and a half feet tall. A year later, with

Alan Walker (with pencil) and Richard Leakey inspect a skull discovered in pieces during an expedition they headed in 1984. The chance find of a fragment led to three weeks of patient digging by a fossil-hunting team dubbed the hominid gang. Bit by bit the stony soil yielded the skeleton of a 12-year-old boy who walked what is now the shore of Lake Turkana some 1.6 million years ago. His is the most nearly complete skeleton yet found of Homo erectus, *ancestor of modern humans.*

National Geographic Society support, Johanson recovered the "first family," the remains of at least thirteen hominids near rock deposits about three million years old. Commented his colleague, C. Owen Lovejoy: "When Don showed me the first knee joint, I told him to go back and find me a whole animal. He obliged with Lucy. So I told him to go back again and get me some variety. The next year he found Mom and Pop and the kids."

The Hadar hominids, who lived during the same geologic period as the creatures who made the footprints at Laetoli, aroused intense controversy. Johanson postulated that the Hadar bones, which he named *Australopithecus afarensis*, "southern ape-man from Afar," belonged to the same species as those found by the Leakeys. They were, he said, the ancestors of all other australopithecines and, indeed, humanity itself. The Leakeys and other scientists vehemently

disagreed, arguing that the Hadar hominids encompassed separate species, as did the fossils found at Lake Turkana. Such contention is hardly surprising, at least partly because knowledge of early human evolution hinges on such a sketchy fossil record—like trying to plot Tolstoy's *War and Peace* from a dozen random pages, as one scientist puts it.

In 1984 the search for a new hominid site on the western shore of Lake Turkana, again supported by the National Geographic Society, produced yet another major discovery. Kamoya Kimeu, the head of Richard Leakey's fossil-collecting team, was strolling near the base camp on his day off when he spotted a skull fragment. During three weeks of excavation in the blistering heat of a Kenyan summer, the digging crew recovered a nearly complete skeleton of a young *Homo erectus* male who had lived about 1.6 million years ago. Probably a descendant on the evolutionary branch from

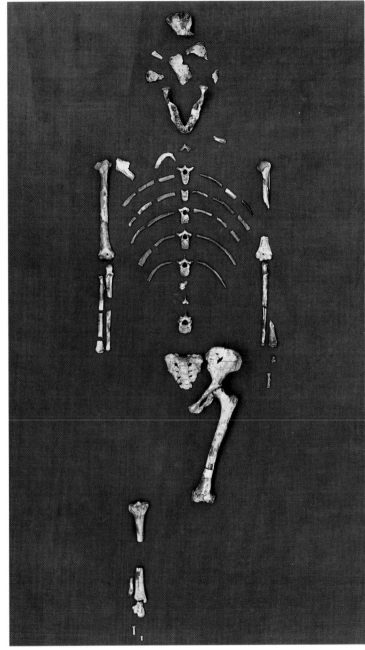

Fossil hunters comb a gully at Hadar in Ethiopia (above). Here American scientist Donald C. Johanson and student Tom Gray were ending a day's vain search in 1974. Johanson glimpsed a bone: "That's a bit of a hominid arm." Gray saw more: "Look at that. Ribs." The back of a skull, two vertebrae, a piece of pelvis—and soon "in that 110-degree heat," recalled Johanson, "we began jumping up and down . . . sweaty and smelly, howling and hugging" over what Gray touted as "something big."

It was something small—a female hominid three and a half feet tall (above, right). But Lucy looms large in the debate over human origins.

Johanson (right) displays a bit of femur in 1975 as he and scientist Becky Sigmon meet the "first family," thirteen hominids from Lucy's era, three million years ago. Johanson sees them all as one species, Australopithecus afarensis—a direct ancestor of humans. Other scientists class them as several species far back in human lineage.

Height 9"

Homo habilis, Homo erectus has been generally recognized as a direct ancestor of modern humans.

Although it lacked the left arm and hand, the lower right arm, and most of both feet, the skeleton Leakey described was a "youth that died at about the age of 12 years . . . a strapping lad. . . ." It provided information about early hominid anatomy that previous skulls and jaws could not. Had the boy lived to maturity, Leakey reported, "he would have reached a height of about six feet. For the first time, here [was] evidence that some of our distant ancestors were as tall as we are, not smaller, as had commonly been believed."

From the earliest days of its exploration and settlement by European colonists, Africa has provided clues to its human past. The first discoveries came in the south.

Dutch explorers and settlers had pushed north from South Africa's Cape of Good Hope in the 17th and 18th centuries and had come in contact with indigenous peoples, among them the San, whom they called Bushmen. Short-statured hunter-gatherers, the San led nomadic lives throughout southern Africa. European settlers chased them from homelands they had occupied for thousands of years, and in time the San died out in South Africa. Today nearly 60,000 of their descendants survive, primarily in the Kalahari Desert. But the San left behind an artistic legacy painted on the walls of caves and rock-shelters where they once lived.

San artists depicted the abundant herds of game that supported them—fat eland and other antelopes, giraffes, and elephants. In a typical scene, ostriches graze peacefully, but one of them clasps a bow and arrow under its belly—a hunter in disguise. Sticklike figures run across cave walls; women gather honey and sit around campfires. With the coming of Europeans, the artists painted full-rigged ships and the red-jacketed British soldiers who hunted down the San.

Another clue to Africa's artistic heritage turned up in 1897, when a British punitive force marched through the Nigerian forest to the kingdom of Benin. Their purpose: to avenge the massacre of a diplomatic mission. The invading troops ransacked the ruler's palace, burned the capital to the ground, and carried away carved ivory tusks and bronze

Pottery sherds get a scrubbing near a mosque in Djénné (opposite), a town on Mali's Bani River. These sherds, plus iron tools, copper ornaments, and other artifacts, came from the nearby ruins of Jenne-Jeno—"ancient Djénné"—sub-Saharan Africa's oldest known city, first settled about 250 B.C. The digs Roderick and Susan McIntosh led here in 1977 and 1981 revealed that at its peak from A.D. 700 to 1000, Jenne-Jeno supported up to 20,000 people and a rich economy based on fish, rice, and trade with the rest of West Africa.

Archaeologists in the 20th century have also turned their attention to other early African cultures, among them the kingdom of Benin, now part of Nigeria. Beginning about 500 years ago, Benin metalworkers cast elegant sculptures in bronze and brass, most notably heads such as the one above. The royal city of Meroë in Sudan used its wealth from iron production to build pyramids (right) over the graves of its kings more than 2,000 years ago.

307

treasures, among them elegant heads and plaques that depict the world of the Benin court until the end of the 19th century. The Benin heads gave Europeans another inkling of the rich legacy of African art that would influence Picasso and other 20th-century artists. Masterpieces of bronze casting, the Bronze Age busts symbolized royal ancestors—stylized, aristocratic images distinguished by different fashions in headdresses and neck-ring collars.

More naturalistic were the clay and bronze sculptures from the Nigerian city of Ife, dug up by British archaeologist Frank Willett in the 1950s and 1960s. Some date from the 12th century A.D. Realism animates many of the nearly life-size subjects—a gagged victim destined for sacrifice, a ruler and his consort with linked arms and legs.

Recent excavations have shown that Africa south of the Sahara nurtured several distinctive cultures. Trade routes crisscrossed the southern edges of the desert more than a thousand years ago. West African states traded with desert caravans coming down from the north, offering slaves as well as gold, ivory, and other goods in exchange for salt and manufactured products from Europe. The kings of Mali became Europe's major suppliers of gold in the 13th and 14th centuries. In the late 10th century, traders from the Persian Gulf founded merchant settlements on the East African coast. But the origins of African trade have roots deeper in history.

The search for West Africa's oldest cities led two American archaeologists, Roderick and Susan McIntosh, to the bustling market town of Djénné on Mali's Bani River in 1975. About two miles from town they surveyed the daunting site of Jenne-Jeno—"ancient Djénné"—an expansive, 26-foot-high hill dotted with scores of foundations for mud-brick houses. They found remains of a massive wall that had girded the city. "Composed entirely of the debris of human occupation," the McIntoshes wrote, "this tell is a maze of eroded house walls, the surface littered with potsherds, glass beads, fragments of stone bracelets, and bits of corroded metal."

A Namibian archaeologist traces a zebra figure from the wall of a Stone Age cave in his country's Brandberg Mountain. Remote and dry, Brandberg harbors many rock paintings, some of the best of thousands scattered throughout southern Africa. Until as recently as a hundred years ago, hunter-gatherers such as the San, or Bushmen, used mineral oxides for paint and wildebeest hair for brushes to sketch ebullient, enigmatic scenes of human figures hunting, fighting, and performing rituals—a unique record of an early people.

The 1972 discovery of eight 500-year-old mummies in western Greenland, including a baby first thought to be a doll (right), has yielded clues and questions about another group of hunters—the Inuit. One mummy's intestines contained traces of typical arctic foods plus bits of wood from an evergreen tree that does not grow in Greenland.

The archaeologists and their 20 workmen from Djénné probed deep into the mound and obtained charcoal from a hearth. Radiocarbon dates showed that Jenne-Jeno had been occupied as early as 250 B.C., making it the oldest known city in Africa south of the Sahara.

Jenne-Jeno reached its prime between A.D. 700 and 1000. From its tightly clustered house foundations and the great spread of the living area, the McIntoshes estimated that perhaps 20,000 people had lived in the city and its neighboring settlements. Scattered test pits yielded pottery, terra-cotta statuary, and crucibles for smelting copper and gold. A delicate gold earring and necklaces of semiprecious stones gave proof of the skills of local artisans. Remains of ironworking shops emerged—and the iron knives, bracelets, fishhooks, and spearheads they produced. Raw materials for stone and metal crafts, as well as salt—all absent in the floodplain—

could only have come from distant sources. In exchange Jenne-Jeno exported rice, dried fish, and other foods, which the fertile lowlands and waterways abundantly supplied.

The McIntoshes' crew uncovered a round mud-brick house with adjacent cooking ovens, garbage dumps, and burial urns. Apparently a principal wife had lived there. Within a ring of connecting apartments, the McIntoshes speculated, dwelled the husband and his other wives. Similar compounds crowded close by. In a wall niche the diggers found the torsos of two terra-cotta statuettes. Similar niches, with statuettes of revered ancestors, occupied places of honor in Djénné houses up until the early 1900s.

The arrival of Arab merchants in the ninth century reinforced Jenne-Jeno's position as a major West African trade and market center. Then, around A.D. 1400, its original inhabitants unaccountably abandoned their homes. The city

fell into decay, perhaps because the new Islamic elite considered the city tainted by pagan practices. As ancient Jenne-Jeno declined, modern Djénné arose nearby.

While some archaeologists worked to unearth Africa's past, others took interest in another area long regarded as a cultural backwater: Southeast Asia. In 1966 Stephen Young, an American student doing sociological research, tripped over a tree root while walking down a road cut through a mound in Ban Chiang, a village in northeastern Thailand. Young landed face-to-face with a pot protruding from the soil. He could see dozens more clay vessels in the sides of the road cut. Guessing that lack of glaze on the sherds indicated great age, Young showed samples to Thai officials in Bangkok and to a collector of Thai antiquities. Soon villagers descended on the site, pillaging artifacts to sell to wealthy patrons in Bangkok and to Americans at a nearby air base.

A trainee (above) exposes parts of a child's fragile skeleton for photographing in a burial at Ban Chiang in northeastern Thailand. The joint University of Pennsylvania-Thai dig in the mid-1970s uncovered 2,200-year-old pottery with painted swirls (opposite) and bronze artifacts from perhaps 2000 B.C. The discovery of metal objects that old has caused "scientists to rethink traditional theories about the development of civilization in Southeast Asia," observed a Pennsylvania archaeologist.

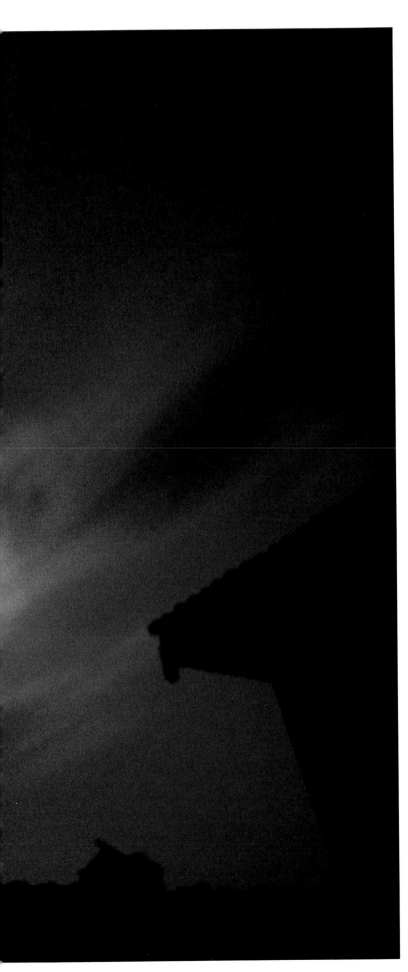

When Chester Gorman, an archaeologist from the University of Pennsylvania, arrived to excavate at Ban Chiang eight years later, he found the mound cratered and heaped with dirt piles. The following year he dug in one of the few remaining undisturbed places—the middle of a village street—and sent home 18 tons of material for study.

Postholes, revealed by cylinders of earth darker than surrounding deposits, indicated that Ban Chiang had been a settlement of houses on wooden stilts as early as 4000 B.C. By 1000 B.C. it had grown into a much larger community of rice farmers: Pottery held impressions of rice husks presumably added as a temper to the clay. The inhabitants of Ban Chiang also kept domesticated water buffalo, probably for plowing irrigated paddies. The forelimb bones of buffalo showed deformation, suggesting the animals' use for pulling plows.

What most interested Gorman about Ban Chiang was its bronze metallurgy. Burials contained bronze anklets, bangles, bracelets, necklaces, and a spearpoint dating to about 2000 B.C. Until Ban Chiang's antiquity was revealed, many scholars believed that metallurgy had first developed in the Near East, then spread to Southeast Asia around 500 B.C. Gorman's excavations proved that Ban Chiang smiths had crafted

Shimmering moonlight bathes the finely sculptured figure of a young man at Aphrodisias, a Greco-Roman city in western Turkey. Settled during the fifth millennium B.C., the metropolis flourished under Roman rule as a sanctuary of the goddess Aphrodite and the home of gifted and prolific sculptors whose works graced the empire. Unlike other ancient Mediterranean sites (map), Aphrodisias remained largely unexcavated until 1961, when Kenan T. Erim, a classics professor at New York University, began to dig here. "Imagine coming upon a city of antiquity so rich . . . that choice sculptures roll out of the sides of ditches, tumble from old walls, and lie jam-packed amid colonnaded ruins," he wrote.

bronze tools about 1,500 years earlier, at a time when Europeans themselves had only recently begun to use the metal.

Did metallurgy develop on its own in Southeast Asia? Perhaps so, perhaps not. But one thing is certain: Thailand's northeastern region contains rich deposits of copper and tin, the two parent metals of bronze, and it is possible that metallurgy developed independently in more than one location.

In the Mediterranean, archaeologists studied the ruins of cities that had flourished about the same time as Ban Chiang. Spyridon Marinatos, a Greek archaeologist, spent most of his long career studying the Minoans, whose civilization had peaked on the island of Crete around 1550 B.C.

Study of building destruction and volcanic deposits in an ancient Cretan port convinced Marinatos that a massive eruption on the nearby island of Thíra had wiped out the Minoan civilization around 1500 B.C. He had read about the

1883 volcanic explosion of Krakatau, an Indonesian island that had burst apart with a roar heard more than 2,000 miles away; waves a hundred feet high claimed more than 36,000 lives. Marinatos calculated that the Thíra explosion struck with four times the violence of Krakatau, unleashing 300-foot-high waves that traveled the 70 miles from Thíra to Crete at more than 200 miles an hour.

Setting to work on Thíra in 1967, Marinatos zeroed in on the present-day village of Akrotíri, where erosion had removed as much as 65 feet of the overlying pumice and ash—still 200 feet deep in places. His crew sank trenches into a deep ravine and soon uncovered the ruins of a buried city dating to about 1500 B.C. Building by building, Marinatos uncovered a village of narrow streets lined with buildings that contained brightly painted frescoes. One bedroom scene depicts swallows darting above red lilies that seem to nod in

Against a fresco of lilies and swallows, a restorer brushes volcanic ash from the plaster cast of an ancient bed frame on Thíra, an island in the Aegean Sea. About 1500 B.C. a volcanic eruption blanketed the island, sending ash and possibly a seismic sea wave toward nearby Crete, whose Minoan civilization had ruled the Mediterranean since 2000 B.C. Some scientists think that this cataclysm explains how Minoan culture vanished.

In 1967 Greek archaeologists dug trenches in the volcanic ash and pumice at Thíra's southern edge and discovered Akrotíri, a well-preserved city that is still under excavation (left). Its two- and three-story houses (opposite), dazzling frescoes, and large storage jars bespeak wealth and Minoan influence. The absence of skeletons and precious articles shows that Thíra's citizens escaped before the eruption.

The bones inside this gold casket from the Greek village of Verghina sparked a raging controversy. Did they belong to Alexander the Great's father, Philip II of Macedonia, who was slain in 336 B.C., or to a later ruler?

Years of digging in the Verghina area had convinced Greek archaeologist Manolis Andronicos (opposite) that here lay Aegae, ancient Macedonia's first capital. In 1977 he excavated a large mound that had long piqued his curiosity and came upon two burial chambers; one had been looted, the other had not. Inside, Andronicos gasped. Amid royal funerary objects was a solid gold casket bearing Macedonia's sunburst symbol. Covers shield "Philip's" tomb (1), its looted neighbor (2), and a site that may be another royal tomb (3).

316

Length 16⅛"

the breeze. In another, two boys with long, black hair pummel one another with boxing gloves—the earliest known picture of boxing gloves. One mural, a 20-foot-long scene taken from an elaborately decorated room, depicts ships arriving at anchorage amid frolicking dolphins.

Until he died in a fall at Akrotíri in 1974, Marinatos pieced together the minute details of everyday life during the Bronze Age. Using methods developed at Pompeii, his technicians made casts of a wooden table and other pieces of furniture, filling with plaster the hollows in the pumice left by the burned-out wood. Experts from an Athens museum restored the masterly frescoes.

The idyllic town of Akrotíri died in a few hours. All the other communities on the volcano's slopes were obliterated. Earth tremors may have brought the inhabitants some premonition of disaster. Apparently they had enough warning to gather up their valuables and flee: The excavators so far have retrieved no jewelry and few metal weapons, tools, utensils—and no human skeletons. As the eruption began, pumice and ash rained down on Akrotíri, and it vanished from sight for more than 3,400 years.

The Thíra eruption ranks as a disaster of stupendous proportions. It seriously weakened, and perhaps even destroyed, Minoan civilization. Many scholars believe that memories of the eruption persisted into classical times, perpetuated by Plato and the Greek geographer Strabo as the legend of lost Atlantis, the continent supposedly swallowed by the sea in a mighty catastrophe.

Discoveries that shed light on biblical history spark a high level of excitement. In 1964 Italian archaeologist Paolo Matthiae, supported by a team of experts, dug into little-known Tell Mardīkh, a 50-foot-high mound in northwestern Syria. The first trenches revealed the massive main gate of a city and a great protective wall that once rose 50 feet.

Year after year Matthiae's team uncovered dwellings, cisterns, and fortifications that belonged to a major city of the early Bronze Age. Courtyards and chambers of a temple came to light; so did a palace embellished with terraces, shell-inlaid stairways, and plaster-walled antechambers.

317

Andronicos scrutinizes a gold quiver from the disputed royal tomb. "Who else but a king would own this?" he asked. Philip II may have captured the elaborate case in his campaign of 339 B.C. against the Scythians, a nomadic tribe in southern Russia whose chiefs carried similar ones.

Other objects discovered inside the tomb—shown at left exactly as Andronicos found them—include a gold-and-silver diadem, a bronze shield cover, and a sponge, center, that is still resilient.

Then came the first clue to the city's identity. In 1968 Matthiae unearthed a headless statue that bore a 26-line inscription. He summoned from Rome an expert in ancient writings, Giovanni Pettinato, who identified the statue as that of a king of Ebla. Could this, Matthiae wondered, identify the city as Ebla, seat of a Semitic kingdom that had flourished in Syria 2,400 years before Christ? Ancient tablets recorded the conquest of the city around 2300 B.C. by Sargon the Great, founder of a powerful Mesopotamian dynasty. But Matthiae did not yet have enough evidence to support his hypothesis.

Then in 1974 Matthiae discovered 42 cuneiform tablets in another palace. Again he called upon Pettinato, who was surprised to find the tablets written in Sumerian and an unknown language. Intensive study disclosed the script as Old Canaanite, a direct forerunner of Hebrew.

The next year Matthiae's crew recovered an entire library of cuneiform tablets scattered across the floor of a room that fire had gutted when invaders destroyed the palace. When he gazed on this cache, the greatest archive of third-millennium texts ever unearthed, Matthiae "suddenly felt like an archaeologist of the last century . . . like Hilprecht [discovering] the tablets of Nippur," as his wife recalled.

Eventually Matthiae's laborers assembled more than 15,000 tablets and photographed them on site. At the base camp they piled the clay plaques everywhere—on tables, in bedrooms, in storerooms. Two teams of students worked round the clock to catalog the archives. Working 18 hours a day for 20 days, Pettinato classified some 5,000 tablets into four categories: economic and administrative, historical and diplomatic, cultural, and literary and religious. But the key to full understanding came with the realization that one group of the tablets listed 3,000 Sumerian words and their Old Canaanite equivalents—the first known bilingual dictionary.

Pettinato confirmed that Tell Mardīkh did indeed entomb ancient Ebla and that the city had engaged in international trade with a host of states competing with one another for political and commercial advantage. The city's trade network reached to Cyprus, Israel, and numerous cities along the Tigris and Euphrates Rivers. Ebla became, for its time, a megalopolis, with 30,000 inhabitants living within its walls—

Some 15,000 cuneiform tablets (right) and fragments found among the ruins of a royal palace divulged the secrets of a hitherto unknown civilization from the third millennium B.C. In 1975 Italian archaeologist Paolo Matthiae uncovered the clay tablets while excavating 50-foot-high Tell Mardīkh in northwestern Syria. Written mostly in Sumerian but partly in the oldest known Semitic tongue, they recounted wars, treaties, and trade matters in Ebla, a city-state of about 260,000 people that rivaled Mesopotamia and Egypt for power in the ancient world.

The discovery of Ebla "alters forever our perception of ancient history," observed Matthiae, seen above as he catalogs potsherds at the site. An excavator (opposite) sifts earth for further clues to one of archaeology's most sensational finds since World War II.

11,700 of them functionaries serving the palace—and a regional population of more than a quarter million.

Pettinato learned that one of Ebla's greatest kings, Ebrium, who ruled around 2400 B.C., bore a name similar to Eber, a patriarch of the Hebrews and a direct ancestor of Abraham. Pettinato also found that the city's residents worshiped a god whose name, Ya, resembled the name for God (Yahweh) in the Old Testament—a clear connection, he felt, between the culture of Ebla and that of Israel and the Old Testament. But Matthiae and other scholars disagreed. They believed the only solid connection with the Bible was linguistic. A bitter controversy ensued; today most scholars reject the biblical claims Pettinato made for the tablets.

It will take many years to translate all the Ebla tablets, but their discovery has already added an important chapter to the history of the Near East. Never before have modern scholars had such a wealth of written information from so early a period of human history. "These discoveries," wrote Ignace J. Gelb of the University of Chicago's Oriental Institute, "reveal a new culture, a new language, a new history. Ebla was a mighty kingdom, treated on an equal footing with the most powerful states of the time."

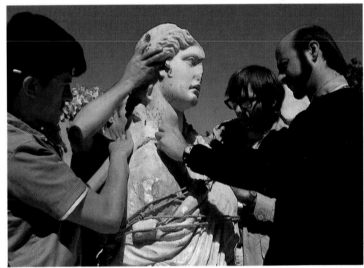

A small marble concert hall called the Odeum aired the performing arts at Greco-Roman Aphrodisias, but it was its brilliant sculptures that brought the city acclaim. Aphrodisias continued to prosper as a Byzantine center, then finally succumbed by the 13th century to repeated earthquakes and invasions.

Today restorers repair the many broken statues. Kenan T. Erim, the Turkish-born archaeologist who leads the dig, helps reunite one statue's head and body (above).

The Ebla excavations typify the painstaking, long-term projects that are yielding rich dividends at other Near Eastern sites, including Aphrodisias in western Turkey. Excavations here over the last quarter century have revealed that the earliest settlers arrived in the area some 7,000 years ago. Over the millennia the settlement grew in size and importance, eventually becoming a major cult center for Ishtar and a host of other Mesopotamian fertility goddesses. Later it prospered as an outpost of ancient Greece.

By Julius Caesar's time Aphrodisias had gained renown as a sanctuary dedicated to Aphrodite, the Greek goddess of love and beauty. The Romans built a temple to honor her. Beloved by Roman emperors and protected by their legions, Aphrodisias flourished from the first century B.C. to the fourth century A.D. It grew into a metropolis famed for its writers, poets, orators, philosophers—and above all for its

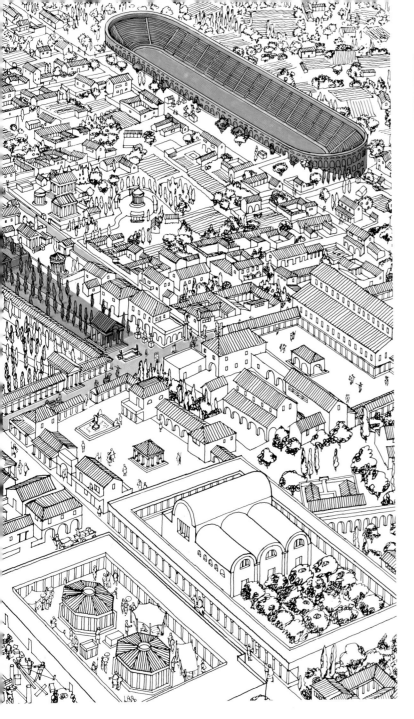

sculptors. Their works graced the uttermost reaches of the Mediterranean world. In admiration of its splendor and achievements, the Roman emperor Augustus declared Aphrodisias his chosen city "from all of Asia." Senatorial decrees provided the citizens of Aphrodisias with privileges and granted them rights of self-rule and tax exemption.

An arduous jeep journey took Kenan T. Erim to Aphrodisias in 1959. "I noticed chunks of marble—some inscribed in Greek and Latin, some obviously sculptured—embedded in walls and houses," wrote the New York University archaeologist of the site. "All about me, past met present. . . ." Aphrodisias enchanted Erim; he has dug there ever since 1961, supported in part by the National Geographic Society.

Erim and his workers excavated the only mound on the plain. Part of the village of Geyre sprawled across its slopes. But the settlement had been damaged by an earthquake in

"I have selected this one city from all of Asia as my own," wrote Emperor Augustus. At its height in the second century A.D., Aphrodisias housed more than 50,000 people, their life reflecting faraway Rome's. Excavated areas, tinted in this artist's rendition, reveal an affluent city partly planned on a grid. The semicircular theater echoed with wrestling matches, dramas, and dances. Vaulted roofs covered Roman baths. In the rectangular Agora, or central market, goldsmiths, cobblers, potters, and sausage makers cried their wares. To its right stand the Odeum and the columned Temple of Aphrodite. A gateway from the Agora led to the three-storied Sebasteion, built to honor Aphrodite and Rome's early emperors. The oblong stadium could hold much of the city's population.

In 1966 the village of Geyre (opposite), now relocated, sat atop the buried city. Erim and his team members have dug up less than a fifth of the city's 250 acres and assembled fragments of many structures (above) for restoration.

1957, and most of the residents had moved to a new village built nearby. More than a hundred workmen removed the modern houses and dug down some 25 feet to the floor of a theater that once seated 8,000 spectators. Gladiators fought here, actors performed, and acrobats entertained. On the theater's walls Erim found imperial edicts inscribed. One from the emperor Hadrian absolved Aphrodisias from a tax on nails: "Knowing that your city deserves honor for other reasons and is exempted from the tax roll of the province."

Gradually the jumbled earth gave up sculptures of citizens who had brought credit to the city. Erim and his team disinterred marble statues of individuals, some identified by inscriptions: C. Julius Zoilos, a freed slave and magistrate who won special privileges for his city from the emperor Augustus; Aristocles Molossus, who helped beautify the theater precincts; and Theodorus, who dedicated a relief of Aphrodite. The archaeologists recognized humbler folk as well, including pugilists, gladiators, and a market overseer.

"Marble seemed almost malleable in their hands," wrote Erim of Aphrodisias's sculptors. As if greeting old friends, he welcomed each new face emerging from the earth. Heads rejoined bodies centuries after being parted—priests, gods, even boxers with battered noses. "What have we found?" Erim would wonder. "A hero, an emperor, some personage who dominated history?... And, as I brush the last of the dirt away, we see the face of a fellow man whose memory lives still in this bit of stone, a fellow man whose image we have resurrected from centuries of darkness."

Aphrodisias declined with the advent of Christianity. By the 13th century invaders had ravaged the city, earthquakes had devastated it, and time inevitably drew its shroud of silt and dimming memories over the shattered buildings.

At Aphrodisias and Ebla, Akrotíri and Ban Chiang, Olduvai and Jenne-Jeno, patient detective work is creating a new, detailed picture of early world history. Archaeology, once confined to Europe, the Near East, Egypt, and the Americas, ripened into a global activity in the 1960s and 1970s, spanning nearly every country and every millennium.

An emperor and his lady (opposite) who once graced Aphrodisias's Sebasteion escaped the destructive wrath of early Christian reformers. The marble pair will join other imperial and mythological figures in a new addition to the museum on the site. A river god's lifelike form (right) from the early second century A.D. *exemplifies the powerful yet subtle way that Aphrodisias's sculptors handled marble. Restorers clean the blue-gray marble columns of the baths near the theater (above).*

Mexico, 1978: Found by a utility company ditchdigger in Mexico City, a stone disk portrays the dismembered body of the Aztec moon goddess.

THE FUTURE OF THE PAST

*I*t was a morning like any other in a busy, modern metropolis, that February day in 1978. Workmen for a utility company in Mexico City had set out to dig a ditch for a new electric cable. But when one man struck stone in the damp earth, when he saw that the stone was decorated in relief, the cable was forgotten. Two days later archaeologists began to uncover what turned out to be a stone disk about ten feet in diameter. Upon it was carved the body of Coyolxauhqui, the Aztec moon goddess, dismembered by her brother Huitzilopochtli, the war god.

The Aztec civilization was only 200 years old when, in 1519, Hernán Cortés led Spanish conquistadores into its spiritual and political heart—the city of Tenochtitlán. There the Spaniards found a religious center dominated by the Templo Mayor, or Great Temple. They climbed 114 steps to the temple's summit to gaze at a statue of Huitzilopochtli. "It had a very broad face and monstrous and terrible eyes . . . the body was girdled by great snakes made of gold and precious stones," wrote Spanish soldier Bernal Díaz del Castillo. The dark dried blood of thousands of human sacrifices caked the walls of the temple.

A Spanish friar named Bernardino de Sahagún told of Aztec captives led to their deaths before the statue of Huitzilopochtli. Priests grasped each victim "by the arms and legs to draw him taut. Thereupon they gashed his breast open, seized his heart . . . then rolled . . . his body over, cast it hence, bounced it down. It fell to the base [of the pyramid]." On one occasion the ritual killings had gone on from daybreak to nightfall for four days. The Spaniards vowed to erect a cross where the diabolical idol of Huitzilopochtli stood.

Within three years the Spaniards had reduced Tenochtitlán to ruins and had begun to build Mexico City from the rubble. For four and a half centuries the Aztec city lay buried. Then, after the stone carving of Coyolxauhqui was exhumed in 1978, excavations directed by Mexican archaeologist Eduardo Matos Moctezuma uncovered long-forgotten offerings in Huitzilopochtli's temple.

In cavities and stone-walled chambers the diggers found more than a hundred ceremonial offerings: idols, sacrificial knives, ceramic vessels, braziers containing copal incense, and gifts of tribute from as far away as Veracruz in the

Mexican lowlands. One stone-lined pit held the skulls of 34 children, from three months to eight years of age. They had been sacrificed to the rain god Tlaloc, whose shrine stood beside Huitzilopochtli's at the top of the temple.

Though the Spanish conquest annihilated the Aztec civilization, Aztec history and traditions play an important role in modern Mexican culture. "Mexicans, look at yourselves in the mirror of this splendor," says the inscription in Spanish over the entrance to the National Museum of Anthropology in Mexico City. Today a million Mexicans speak Nahuatl, the Aztec language, and some, though Christian, also pay homage to the ancient gods. Legend says that Huitzilopochtli told the Aztecs to search for an eagle on a cactus devouring a snake and there to build Tenochtitlán. Mexico's national emblem bears a cactus; upon it an eagle devours a snake.

At the National Palace, only a block from the Templo

Mayor, a series of epic murals by Mexican artist Diego Rivera commemorates Mexico's history: In a teeming Aztec market, nobles mingle with shopkeepers, a prostitute promenades, and a dentist examines a boy's teeth. Scenes of slaughter recall the Spanish conquest and the colonial era.

Mexico spends vast sums on the excavation and restoration of major sites—not only to attract tourist dollars but also to preserve symbols of national pride. But at a site named Great Zimbabwe in the former African country of Rhodesia, now called Zimbabwe, national pride, national politics, and archaeological findings combined to fuel a bitter conflict.

In 1552 a Portuguese historian named João de Barros described a "fortress, masonry within and without, built of stones of marvellous size. . . ." It is likely that de Barros spoke of Great Zimbabwe. Here, spread over a hundred acres of hill and valley in southern Africa, stand a variety of structures.

The fortress de Barros is thought to have described is larger than many African villages. A vaguely elliptical stone wall —830 feet long and varying from 16 to 35 feet in height— encloses a labyrinth of lower walls and passages dominated by the Conical Tower. A superb example of dry-stone masonry, the tower is 30 feet tall and 18 feet in diameter. It was originally decorated with a frieze. The tower could not have been inhabited, for it is solid within.

It did not occur to early Portuguese historians that Africans might have built stone walls of such superior workmanship. They proposed that the ruins had been part of the biblical region of Ophir, famous for the mines that yielded King Solomon's gold. "King Solomon made a navy of ships," says the Old Testament, "And they came to Ophir, and fetched from thence gold, four hundred and twenty talents, and brought it to king Solomon."

Surely no Africans could have built the stone walls of Great Zimbabwe (above)—or so said white settlers of the colony they called Southern Rhodesia. In 1902 colonials used Shona tribesmen (opposite) to dig— in vain—for Semitic remains. Scientific researchers now say that Shona forerunners built the mysterious structures, the largest around A.D. 1400. But the reckless early dig destroyed clues to the nature of the site, thwarting African scholars of the nation now named for the ruins—Zimbabwe.

In 1871 a German geologist named Karl Mauch visited the ruins of Great Zimbabwe and immediately attributed them to the Phoenicians who returned with Ophir's gold. So too did Cecil Rhodes, the region's administrator. The British South Africa Company, together with other institutions, invited British explorer James Theodore Bent to dig at the ruins in 1891. Bent, believing that the architects must have been a civilized and ancient people, concluded that "a northern race coming from Arabia" had built the stone structures.

In 1902 the company appointed journalist Richard Hall as curator of Great Zimbabwe. To Hall and many of his European contemporaries, the monumental stone structures exemplified civilization. Indeed, Great Zimbabwe was the political, commercial, and religious center of a kingdom whose economy was based on the gold trade. But white settlers in the early 20th century justified their own economic and political encroachment by promoting a concept of black backwardness. Africans were not civilized, they said, and so could not have created Great Zimbabwe.

Hall's idea of preserving the ruins was to obliterate archaeological deposits by what he called "recent and timely preservation work" that removed "the filth and decadence of the Kaffir [black] occupation." Hall declared that Great Zimbabwe had been built by Semitic colonizers 3,000 to 4,000 years ago, then later occupied by Phoenicians, and in modern times inhabited by "bastard races" descended from the original builders and local Africans.

Hall's opinions were generally accepted, but his reckless digging infuriated archaeologists interested in Africa's past. Hall's crew cut down trees and discarded fallen stones, spoil heaps, and in some places up to 12 feet of stratified archaeological deposits. In 1905 the British Association for the Advancement of Science invited David Randall-MacIver, a specialist in ancient Egypt, to dig at Great Zimbabwe. When he arrived at the site, he described Hall's work as "reckless blundering . . . worse than anything I have ever seen."

Randall-MacIver investigated the ruins and recovered such artifacts as spindle whorls, coils of copper used for bracelets, and household pottery. He concluded that the ruins were "essentially of African construction and 331

Its tranquillity undisturbed, a giant Buddha has slept for 750 years at Dazu in China's rugged Sichuan Province. Looters once plundered more accessible sites, but the Chinese now take pride in methodical excavations. Many digs yield spectacular Bronze Age finds. A 3,000-year-old ritual wine ewer (left) displays Shang Dynasty craftsmanship: Unlike Europeans who cast bronze and then hammered it, the Chinese worked their ornate designs into the mold, then cast the vessel in one piece.

Height 15⅜"

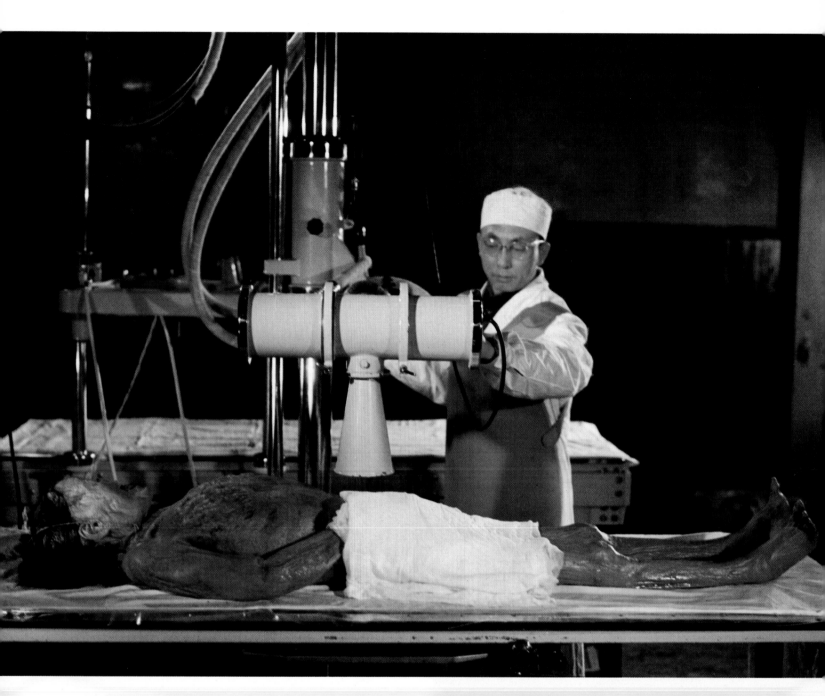

Cause of death: heart attack—2,100 years ago. Helping with the belated autopsy (above), a Chinese radiologist X-rays Lady Dai, a Han Dynasty noblewoman who died in 141 B.C. Her well-sealed tomb, opened in 1972, kept her almost perfectly preserved. The examining doctors concluded she was about 50, had borne children, and had gallstones and a bad back. A Chinese report on the find observed, in ideological idiom, that her elaborate burial demonstrated "the extravagance of the feudal rulers and their exploitation of the people."

Two other Han nobles of the time, Prince Liu Sheng and Princess Dou Wan, tried to defy eternity with jade, thought then to prevent decay. Both corpses wore fabulous burial suits (at right, Dou Wan's, restored). Each suit—hundreds of jade wafers linked with gold thread—probably took ten'man-years to make. To no avail: All that remained of the royal couple when disinterred in 1968 were teeth and dust— and jumbles of jade and gold.

of no great antiquity." In 1929 British archaeologist Gertrude Caton-Thompson studied the site. She, too, concluded that black Africans had built Great Zimbabwe in medieval times.

Later excavations and radiocarbon dating indicated that Africans had erected the major stone buildings of Great Zimbabwe in the 14th and 15th centuries on a site occupied during the Iron Age. And in 1980 the newly independent nation of Zimbabwe took its name from that of its great ruins: *zimbabwe*, derived from *dzimba woye*—venerated houses.

Quite different from the brash manipulation by Rhodesian settlers is today's marriage of archaeology with nationalist interests in China. During the late 1920s and 1930s scholars, skeptical of written records, began to search in the ground for the truth about ancient Chinese civilization.

In 1928 archaeologists at the National Academy's Institute of History and Philology launched a search for remains of the Shang civilization near Anyang, a town north of the Yellow River. For a decade they excavated royal residences and tombs. They found evidence of a 3,200-year-old civilization of farmers and skilled bronze workers who had been ruled by kings and nobles living in separate compounds.

Legend said that the Shang king served as intermediary to the ancestors, and only he could perform the sacrificial rites of ancestor worship. From a royal grave excavated in 1965 at Yi-tu in eastern China came harsh evidence of human sacrifice at the death of a king or regional lord. At the bottom of an 80-foot shaft lay a wooden burial chamber, and beneath the spot where the coffin had stood was a pit containing the bones of a human victim and a sacrificial dog. Human skulls and skeletons lay stacked at the main entrance. In all, 48 humans and 6 dogs had been buried along with furnishings of bronze and jade as a final tribute to the ruler who lay within.

"China has one of the oldest civilizations in the world [with] a recorded history of nearly 4,000 years," wrote statesman Mao Tse-tung. "Make the past serve the present." Today the notion that accumulated human experience is a useful guide for the future generates tremendous popular concern in China for preserving ancient cultural objects. The Chinese government touts the legacy of the working masses who built the nation, and everyone is taught to participate in preserving the past—bureaucrats, soldiers, workers, students, and entire local communities.

In 1968 a detachment of the Chinese People's Liberation Army discovered an enormous underground tomb south of Beijing. Within, their flashlights shone upon bronze, iron, earthenware, and jade. Another tomb nearby, sealed with boulders and once molten iron, had to be blasted open by army demolition experts. The tombs contained the sepulchers of a Han prince, Liu Sheng, and his wife, Princess Dou Wan, who had lived in the late second century B.C. Digging teams removed more than 2,800 funerary objects: bronze and gold vessels; gold, silver, and jade ornaments; pottery urns; lacquered vases; fragments of silk. Liu Sheng's tomb housed 6 chariots, 17 horses, and 11 dogs, as well as a grindstone and enough food and wine for a long journey.

Chinese archaeologists in recent years have begun to

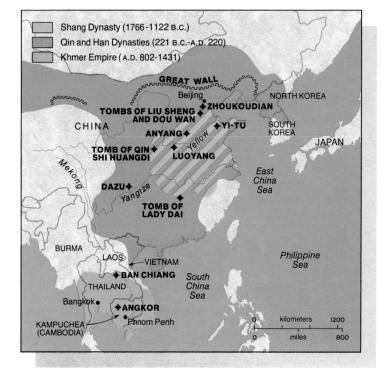

333

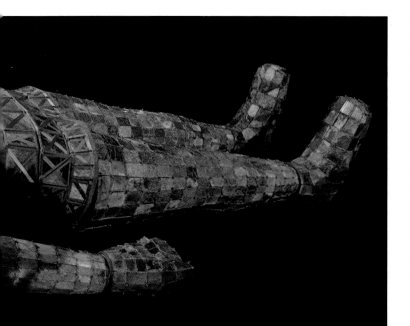

A trail of tombs guides Chinese archaeologists into their past (map). Graves at Anyang and elsewhere contained inscribed artifacts proving the Shang Dynasty ruled here well before the fall of Troy. The Shang state held only part of the country; a millennium passed before Qin Shi Huangdi, the First Emperor, unified China and built a huge tomb for himself to celebrate his power. Qin also created the Great Wall, which his Han successors extended. In total land area, wealth, and sophistication, the
Han Empire ranked with its far-off contemporary, Rome.

Far to the south, in another realm and time, the temple city of Angkor began presiding over Indochina's Khmer Empire about A.D. 900. The Khmers abandoned it to jungle after a Thai attack in 1431.

sort legend from historical fact. So important is their work that the Chinese government has made its own all ancient artifacts dug from the earth, no matter who owns the land from which an object is recovered.

Elsewhere traffic in antiquities flourishes. A multimillion-dollar art market nourished by wealthy collectors and private museums finances a booming, worldwide trade in artifacts. Tomb robbers keep track of New York auction prices and changing market values. They have reason to. A piece of pottery from an American Indian cemetery can bring hundreds of dollars. A Maya vase or a Mimbres picture bowl from New Mexico might be worth thousands of dollars. Ancient African art is so highly prized by collectors that many of the best pieces have long vanished. Modern African art is equally prized—a crate of masks from Zaire that costs several hundred dollars in Africa can translate into a sizable tax deduction when donated to a museum in the United States.

Many collectors argue that the objects they collect are too valuable to be preserved in countries where museums are nonexistent or inadequate. Lord Elgin made the same claim in the early 1800s after his agents had removed many of the Parthenon's marble sculptures. But today most countries have museums and caretakers for their antiquities.

Still, there is not always enough money to protect even major sites. So collectors' agents lurk in obscure towns and villages, buying up loot from peasant tomb robbers. Divers plunder sunken ships. Thieves in a Guatemalan jungle hack ancient religious carvings from their bases at Maya sites. In Utah commercial vandals bulldoze an Indian burial site. In a similar incident "the remains of children were tossed in the garbage heap," lamented the state archaeologist.

Laws now prohibit such exploitation. A United Nations

Silent legions of clay (above, left) escorted China's first emperor through the afterlife for 2,200 years. Pottery found by some well-diggers in 1974 led to discovery of a three-acre underground vault near Qin Shi Huangdi's tomb complex. It held one of archaeology's most stunning finds: a terra-cotta army of about 6,000 warriors, with horses and war chariots. No assembly line made these life-size soldiers (above); each bears a different face, possibly modeled after actual people. Looters, vandals, and the collapse of the roof shattered many figures, which restorers now piece back together.

In the suburbs of Luoyang, workers open a late Han crypt (left), nearly 2,000 years old. Hundreds of such tombs dot the area, but the government requires checking each one for artifacts before modern buildings go up. Some tombs succumb to today's urban sprawl; others are saved.

Squatting amid contraband history (opposite), a trader in Mali, West Africa, displays his artifacts—many probably poached from Jenne-Jeno, a local mound dating from the Iron Age. A grave robber probes for pre-Columbian tombs in Peru (above), seeking gold. Demand from wealthy collectors, mostly foreigners, supports them both. Many Third World governments try to stop the trade, a threat they see as trafficking not just in stolen relics, but in sherds of their nations' souls.

agreement of 1970 calls for the protection of cultural property that is of historical and scientific interest. In 1983 the United States became the first major art-importing nation to be a party to that agreement. U. S. legislation gives the President the authority to impose emergency import restrictions on illegally exported material. Individual countries have passed legislation as well. A law passed in Egypt in 1983 decrees that all objects made before 1883 belong to the state, and declares illegal the sale, exportation, and even the unauthorized possession of such artifacts. Laws such as Egypt's may impede illegal traffic, but looting and smuggling continue. Some archaeologists and officials fear that those who could sell artifacts to the government for fair prices will choose instead the higher prices offered on the black market.

Quite apart from the ravages of collectors and tomb robbers, what remains of the past diminishes daily in the shadow of 20th-century industrial growth. Freeways, housing developments, industrial parks—all gnaw at the finite archives of the past. Archaeologists scramble to save what they can, but lack of funding hinders them at every step.

The picture, though, is not uniformly bleak. In Japan developers are required by law to see that any archaeological site slated for new construction is excavated first and that the results are reported publicly. And in Greece, where the cumulative effects of natural and man-made disasters threaten to destroy the Parthenon, the government is spending millions of dollars to restore the temple built in the fifth century B.C. to honor Athens' patron goddess, Athena.

The national concern about saving classical Greece's greatest architectural achievement is not new. According to folklore, it was not long after the Greeks began their battle for independence from Turkish rule in 1821 that the Turks took shelter atop the Acropolis, the massive rock upon which the Parthenon stands. Out of ammunition, they began to disassemble the temple columns to extract the ancient metal dowels that held them together; from these they peeled the lead coating to use for making bullets. The Greeks, all thought of victory temporarily gone, demanded an immediate cease-fire and hastily dispatched fresh supplies of ammunition to the Turks. The Parthenon's columns were safe, and the battle was resumed.

Today the Parthenon faces a foe even more destructive than bullets. Deterioration from without and within threatens to mar and weaken its marble columns. The acid skies of Athens, polluted by industry and the fumes of nearly 800,000 motor vehicles, contain sulfur dioxide and other corrosive agents, all wrapped in a cloud of toxic haze that blankets the Acropolis and damages the Parthenon's marble surfaces. And, ironically, 40 years' worth of restorative attempts—in the form of iron bolts and braces meant as reinforcements—have only hastened the internal decay.

The unwitting perpetrator was a Greek engineer named Nicholas Balanos, who spent the first half of the 20th century dismantling the Parthenon and its smaller neighbor on the Acropolis, the Erechtheum, to insert the metal reinforcements. His instincts were correct, but he used raw iron that swelled with corrosion and fractured the marble.

Now the damage is being undone by architect Manolis Korres, who heads the restoration project. Korres's team will again take down each shattered stone, this time replacing the rusted bolts and braces with fasteners of titanium, stronger and more corrosion resistant than stainless steel.

Once Korres is satisfied that the Parthenon will stand indefinitely, he will begin a massive face-lift. Equipped with descriptive drawings made by past observers and with his own keen observations, Korres will fit together what he calls "a huge jigsaw puzzle where the image is not given, and where the player doesn't have all the pieces." What he does have is an assortment of nearly a thousand stones, some weighing more than ten tons, that were blasted off the Parthenon when Venetians bombarded the building with cannonballs in 1687 in a successful attempt to blow up Turkish gunpowder supplies inside.

To re-create missing pieces of fragmented stone blocks, a team of two dozen marble carvers makes plaster casts of broken surfaces, then uses the plaster models as guides for chiseling identical contours in marble. Each newly carved surface fits snugly against its mate in the old block; cement bonds the pieces together to form a new, full block.

Korres must also fortify the Acropolis itself, its natural stone foundation badly eroded and weakened further by vegetation. This he does by drilling into the rock cliffs, sometimes to a depth of 50 feet, and inserting stainless steel rods.

Nothing short of a perfect restoration will satisfy Korres and the citizens of Greece. "The Acropolis is us," proclaimed Georges Dontas, a member of the restoration committee. He believes the Greeks must keep full control of their own archaeological heritage. So the Greek government has been very cautious about accepting financial assistance from such

A monumental move at Abu Simbel in Egypt: In 1964 the colossal statues of Pharaoh Ramesses II, endangered by the rise of the Nile behind the new Aswân High Dam, gain a bulldozed pillow of sand—an early step in the task of moving the ancient shrine to higher ground. The sand protected the statues as workers cut into the surrounding cliff. Numbers on blocks (left) helped them to reassemble the 1,050 pieces, including this 19-ton face (above). The massive rescue, funded by Egypt, the United States, and dozens of other UNESCO countries, cost almost 40 million dollars and took four and a half years to finish —the most spectacular moving job so far undertaken.

Overleaf: Floodlights hold back the dusk as workers and heavy equipment reassemble the 3,200-year-old temples of Ramesses and his queen, Nefertari (at right), 212 feet above their old level. Arch-shaped trusses now hold up a new, artificial hill built over the temples' interiors.

international organizations as the United Nations Educational, Scientific and Cultural Organization (UNESCO) and the European Community. Similar statements echo throughout the world, but sometimes nations transcend their borders and band together to save a threatened site.

At Abu Simbel an international partnership launched by UNESCO raised almost 40 million dollars to rescue Pharaoh Ramesses II's temples from the rising waters of Lake Nasser. The lake was formed in the 1960s by the Aswân High Dam, built on the Nile 180 miles downstream from Abu Simbel.

Ramesses II ordered the two adjacent temples carved into a sandstone hillside around 1270 B.C., probably to commemorate the 30th year of his reign. Four colossal statues of the pharaoh loomed above the entrance to the larger temple. Centuries of sandstorms and neglect almost obscured it, but in 1817 Italian strongman Giovanni Battista Belzoni dug through to the entrance, and it was not long before Abu Simbel was drawing tourists.

Flooding the temples was unthinkable, even though the dam downstream would provide hydroelectric power and millions of arable acres. So Egyptian and European artisans sawed the statues into blocks and loaded them onto trailers. The workmen made narrow cuts into the painted walls and ceilings inside the temples, drove steel pins into the incisions, then cut the rock away from the back with power saws, using the pins as guides. All the cut blocks went into storage —Ramesses' 19-ton faces rested on soft sand, draped with mats that protected them from the elements. Finally, engineers reassembled the temples against an artificial hill—two concrete domes beneath an imitation of the original terrain—212 feet above their original location.

But the temples are not completely out of harm's way. Lake Nasser, and the increased cultivation it allows, have created a higher humidity than the sandstone monuments are used to. The water table no longer fluctuates with annual flooding; instead it has risen, allowing water and soluble salts to migrate more easily to the surface of the monuments. The water evaporates but the salts crystallize and crumble the stone, a process accelerated by the increased humidity.

No affordable treatment has so far been found that can

Researchers (above) work on a problem: How to match up thousands of photographs of decorated blocks, known as talatat, *from a wall torn down 33 centuries ago. A stand holds an enlargement of one block. The wall once formed part of a mile-long temple complex at Karnak, built by Pharaoh Akhenaten around 1350 B.C. to honor his sun god, Aten. A later pharaoh, Horemheb, demolished the shrine and used the talatat as rubble to fill his own monuments. Over the years*

some 45,000 talatat have turned up, including 6,000 recovered in the 1960s during repairs to a massive pylon Horemheb erected at Karnak.

Without modern technology, piecing them together would have been almost impossible. But a computer could sort through a list of the talatat— cataloged by details of appearance—and find close matches, such as the three blocks at left. They show twin images of Akhenaten's wife, Nefertiti, making an offering to the sun god.

343

Vintage technology rises to the occasion—flamboyantly—during a 1982 flight to map the tombs and temples of Thebes in Egypt. This hot-air balloon, one of two used by University of California scientists, hovers before Queen Hatshepsut's temple at Deir el Bahri. The balloons gave the advantages of slowness and stability needed for careful camera work. One result of their flights here: Discovery of a Coptic shrine carved high in the face of a cliff during the seventh century A.D.

fully protect Egypt's sandstone from salt damage. The creation of accurate records may be the only recourse. An American archaeologist named James Henry Breasted realized the importance of records and in 1924 organized a long-term survey of the reliefs and inscriptions on the walls of ancient Egyptian monuments that continues to this day. Temple by temple, room by room, Egyptologists from the Oriental Institute of the University of Chicago clean, restore, and copy. They take photographs, then draw additional details directly on the surfaces of the photographs. They bleach out the prints to leave black-and-white drawings. It takes weeks to complete even a single drawing.

Computers can help, as they did at Karnak in east-central Egypt. Around 1350 B.C. Pharaoh Akhenaten built a temple here to his sun god, Aten. Twenty years later one of his successors razed and cannibalized the structure for building stone. In 1965 Ray Winfield Smith, a research fellow at the University of Pennsylvania Museum, decided to reconstruct the temple. He and his team, with support from the National Geographic Society, located tens of thousands of decorated blocks in Egypt, Europe, and the United States. They assigned each stone a number, photographed it, and recorded every decorative detail from the photographs on coding sheets. They fed the information to a computer, which categorized it. Then the scientists could ask for every block containing a right foot or a sunray falling at a particular angle, and the computer would provide the identification numbers of all the appropriate photographs.

After years of patient work, Smith's research team had drawn on paper a lavish pillared courtyard dedicated to Queen Nefertiti, the wife of Akhenaten. It was part of a mile-long temple complex decorated with more than a thousand scenes. The temple itself will probably never be completely rebuilt because of the tremendous expense involved, but thanks to a computer, scholars can now study accurate drawings of an ancient Egyptian masterpiece.

Technological advances useful to archaeologists extend beyond the computer. In the tropical lowlands of northern Guatemala, the all-seeing eye of side-scan aerial radar, which bounces signals off the ground at an oblique angle, revealed irregular networks of gray lines amid vast stretches of swampy, apparently impenetrable forest. The lines may be all that remain of canal systems that once threaded through ancient swamp gardens. These gardens might have fed tens of thousands of ancient Maya.

At the Parthenon restoration project in Greece, an ultra-powerful X-ray device peers through marble to locate the corroding iron reinforcements that riddle the temple's columns. A laser shatters the metal so that it can be removed. Sculptures eroded by atmospheric sulfur dioxide have been resolidified with chemicals and installed in pure nitrogen environments within display cases.

Scientists probe more than ancient stone with modern methods. Paleopathologists rehydrate desiccated tissue taken from mummies prepared deliberately and from those formed naturally in the cold or dry climates of places such as Alaska and Egypt. By analyzing the restored tissue, scientists

are able to study the effects of disease on ancient humans.

In 1985 Svante Pääbo, a molecular biologist in Sweden, extracted and cloned DNA from the 2,400-year-old mummy of an infant Egyptian boy. That same year scientists drained a small pond in Titusville, Florida. In the peat on the bottom, they discovered several 7,000-year-old human skulls—two of them complete with preserved brains. They have extracted DNA from one brain and, like Pääbo, hope to learn more about evolutionary changes in genetic structure.

Experimentation in archaeology is not limited to state-of-the-art technology. "New archaeologists" seek innovative ways to study living societies in order to construct models that describe the behavior of past ones. Jeremy Sabloff of the University of New Mexico said, "We've gone beyond filling up museums with art objects. The objects are not an end in themselves but a means to inform us about the social and

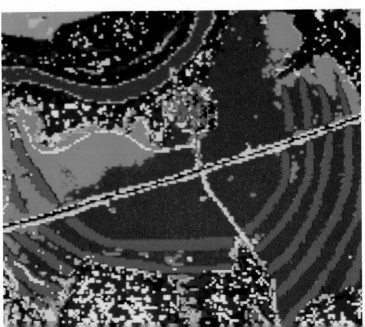

Archaeologists at Copán in Honduras map Maya ruins with a transit and plumb bob (above, left). Technology offers newer tools as well. Before fully opening a 1,500-year-old Maya tomb at Río Azul in Guatemala, diggers check for fragile contents by scanning the interior with a tiny video camera (above) funded by the National Geographic Society.

Remote sensing mixes visible and infrared light to form a computerized aerial image of Poverty Point, Louisiana (left). Dating from 1600 B.C., the vast site is the oldest of its size yet found in the United States. A people known simply as the Poverty Point Culture ringed a central plaza with low ridges 150 to 175 feet wide, seen in red. A bayou, at top, is purple; modern asphalt roads appear yellow. What may be prehistoric fill, discovered by this image, shows as light blue at the ends of the ridges.

economic behavior of ancient people." In the 1970s Lewis R. Binford of the University of New Mexico observed Alaska's Nunamiut Eskimos, a modern hunter-gatherer society. Binford watched the Eskimos set up hunting camps and saw how they hunted, killed, butchered, and ate animals. His insights gave him a fuller understanding of how ancient hunter-gatherers chose their campsites, and helped him analyze the animal bones found at such sites.

William Rathje, a University of Arizona archaeologist, has spent more than a decade studying the modern garbage of Tucson. Twice a week, city sanitation workers turn over a sampling of garbage bags to Rathje and his students, who sift carefully through the contents, classifying, weighing, and recording everything. They compile statistical profiles of what different households throw away—meat, vegetables, canned goods, and paper products. "Archaeologists study ancient garbage to learn about past civilizations," said Rathje. "Here we look at our own refuse to learn about our own civilization.... Our trash is the unvarnished imprint of our life-styles." Nicknamed "garbology," this new discipline has shown that "what people say they throw out and what they actually do can be two different things."

Sunbeams alone parade where philosophers once walked and talked in the Agora, Athens' ancient marketplace. The American School of Classical Studies, which has worked here since 1931, rebuilt this stoa, or colonnaded portico, from rubble. The school razed acres of modern houses to reach the ruins—an unusual feat at urban sites, where rescue archaeologists typically race jackhammers, not wield them. Amphoras (above) number among the tens of thousands of items found.

To gain insight into Iron Age societies, archaeologists in Britain recently experimented with agricultural and domestic practices from that distant era. In 1972 archaeologist Peter Reynolds began a project that would reconstruct an Iron Age farm of about 300 B.C. on Butser Hill in southern England. The purpose, wrote Reynolds, "is to explore all the aspects of such a farm, the structures and processes, the plant cultivation and animal husbandry, and to consider not only how each particular aspect itself [might] operate but also how all the aspects integrate together."

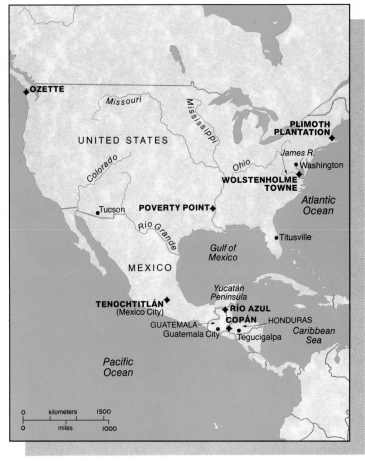

Reynolds built a communal round-house from wattle and daub—hazel rods and a binding mixture of clay, earth, animal hair, grass, and hay. Reynolds and researchers for the Butser Ancient Farm Project Trust baked bread, fired pottery, worked deerskin with flint scrapers, wove wool, smelted iron in clay-lined furnaces, and grew prehistoric cereals. They kept a selection of livestock—cows, pigs, sheep, chickens, a goat, and a pony—that resembled Iron Age breeds. Everything they built and did was grounded in archaeological evidence. Even the soil was ideal; it had never been treated with artificial pesticides, herbicides, or fertilizers.

The types of food the animals ate, the effect of farming on the soil, and other details of this unusual experiment have helped archaeologists toward a better understanding of the Iron Age sites they excavate. Reynolds found, for example, that the wheat yield at the farm far exceeded what had been considered likely, and that grain could be stored for long

Murder! What weapon split the skull now emerging from the mud of colonial Wolstenholme Towne, Virginia? Records of a massacre in 1622 offered Ivor Noël Hume, excavator of the lost village (map), an answer: Indians had turned settlers' tools against them—perhaps a spade in this case. To extract another find, Noël Hume (in center, above left) helps lift a plaster cast that holds soil with a thin shell of rust embedded in it: the helmet from a suit of armor. At right, the helmet after laboratory restoration.

Height 11″

periods in underground pits without rotting. Such findings could lead to revised estimates of Iron Age cereal acreage and of the population it could support.

Yesterday's symbols of archaeology were the pick and trowel; tomorrow's will probably be the computer and other tools of science. But nothing will replace the old-fashioned flair for detective work exhibited by such archaeologists as Ivor Noël Hume, who, funded in part by the National Geographic Society, excavated Wolstenholme Towne in Virginia during the 1970s. The settlement of 30 to 40 people was part of the Martin's Hundred plantation along the James River, where 220 English settlers made their homes in 1619.

The citizens of Wolstenholme Towne built a palisaded fort for protection against Indians and Spaniards. But on March 22, 1622, an Indian attack razed the village and most of the outlying farms. The survivors fled as their houses burned. No one rebuilt on the site, and it was soon forgotten—a time capsule of life in the early 17th century.

Noël Hume's team set to work at Martin's Hundred in 1976 and spent five years unraveling a puzzle of postholes, graves, and rubbish pits. The archaeologists had few written records from the settlement itself, but at every step they referred to such sources as the 17th-century transcripts from the court books of Virginia and the Virginia Company of London to help interpret the significance of their finds.

The houses uncovered were defined by series of holes that had once held framing posts. Postholes indicated that the first house excavated had originally been a small rectangle, then had grown with later additions. An earth-filled pit nearby looked like a cellar. This seemed a strange sort of house at first, but a description written by the secretary of the Dutch city of New Amsterdam and published in 1650 disclosed that poor farmers in New England and the Dutch colony of New Netherland lived in pit houses, with the roof eaves resting on the ground. Once the farmers could afford more conventional houses, they would fill in their pit houses and build new homes nearby.

The Martin's Hundred house seemed to have been constructed in a similar way, but Noël Hume wanted to know more than just *how* houses were built; he wanted to know *who* had built them. Near the foundation of the pit house, diggers found a short length of twisted and woven gold—the type of decoration sported by the gentry and military officers of the early 17th century. Researchers turned up a 1621 resolution that forbade anyone in Virginia to wear gold in their clothing except the "Council & heads of hundreds." William Harwood, the head administrator of Martin's Hundred, had signed the resolution. Could this have been his property?

Another clue indicated that it might well have been. Excavators dug up a cannonball and checked a 1625 census that listed Harwood as the only person at Martin's Hundred who owned a "peece of Ordnance." The cannonball, no doubt, was meant for the cannon once mounted on the bastion of Wolstenholme Towne's fort.

"As a rule," wrote Noël Hume, "it is history that provides archaeologists with a reason to dig, but in Martin's Hundred it was the other way around." Here, archaeologists

Wolstenholme Towne

- • Posthole
- ○ Tree hole
- ▮ Grave
- — Slot for support timbers

COMPANY BARN

FORT

Store

Dwelling

Well

Watchtower

Pond

Gate

Shed

Gate and Pathway

Later Fence

Gun Platform

Longhouse

Gate

Gate

Pond

Storehouse

Shed

Shed

Gate

COMPANY COMPOUND

Gate

DOMESTIC UNIT

James River

Cliff

N

0   meters   25

0   feet   100

A blueprint in postholes (opposite) traces the walls of Wolstenholme Towne's wooden fort; foreground holes mark a watchtower. From such finds Noël Hume could outline a preliminary plan of the oldest English-American village yet excavated (left), re-created above by the artist's brush.

Noël Hume, a leader in the young field of American historical archaeology, excels at tying slim clues from the site into a network of supporting evidence—centuries-old artwork, museum pieces, and items from shipwrecks. At Graz, Austria, he found helmets like those dug up in Virginia— look-àlikes in an arsenal of armor Europeans had used to fend off the Ottoman Turks. The English wore such armor as well, but it was to prove cumbersome against Indian guerrilla tactics.

Even a grisly English murder in 1979 helped; the pathologist on the case verified that the Wolstenholme skull bore marks similar to those on the modern victim, killed by his wife—with a garden spade.

had no historical chronology to guide them; they worked with a finite capsule in time. They reconstructed history by using documents of the same period to help them identify and interpret their discoveries.

Richard Daugherty, an anthropologist at Washington State University, had few written records to consult when he excavated buried remains at Ozette, a tiny, abandoned coastal village in the northwestern corner of Washington. But in piecing together the history of the Makah Indians, who inhabited Ozette until half a century ago, he had their modern descendants to help him.

By the 1930s, because the federal government had decreed that all Indian children must attend school and there was none at Ozette, the Makah had moved to another Makah village nearby. But tribal elders kept the legends of their ancestral home alive. One of the tales told of a great disaster—a huge mountain of mud that had buried their village long ago.

Daugherty suspected that there was truth to the legend, and in 1970, when violent winter storms sent tides raging up the broad beach at Ozette, his suspicions were confirmed. Part of a bank washed away to reveal an abundance of artifacts—a canoe paddle, fishhooks of wood and bone, parts of inlaid boxes, a harpoon shaft, a woven hat—all dating to about the time of Columbus's arrival in America. They had survived the centuries under a layer of dense mud.

Conventional techniques would not do for the waterlogged and mostly wooden remains of Ozette. The excavators devised an elaborate pumping system to provide jets of water of various intensities to remove mud from objects as small as combs and spindle whorls and as large as house planks. The archaeologists treated artifacts with chemicals to prevent them from drying out and cracking. They also used a

freeze-drying technique to preserve a wooden bowl that was still saturated with seal oil.

Makah artisans helped Daugherty and his students replicate the basketry and wood carvings discovered on the site. They wove a wool blanket on a loom similar to those excavated. Perfectly preserved tool kits indicated how the ancient Makah had made fishhooks.

The Makah Tribal Council built a museum to house the cultural remains. The dig has been closed for the present in order to work with the nearly 55,000 artifacts already recovered. Say the Makah: "We . . . look in a special way at what [has come] from the mud at Ozette, for this is our heritage."

Today's archaeologists can work miracles with skilled excavation, patient detective work, and judicious use of science and technology. Often, these miracles never leave the pages of obscure scientific journals. But some archaeologists

Pilgrim settlers—costumed museum staffers—raise a beam (far left) for a 1620s-style cottage at Plimoth Plantation in eastern Massachusetts. They work into place the frame for the twig-and-clay chimney (above) and add a thatched roof (center).

In growing numbers such living-history museums give visitors a sample of past lifestyles. Plimoth is only a copy of the original settlement, yet so authentic that history students have often moved in, the better to know their subject.

transform dry, forbidding pages of detailed records into vividly accurate reconstructions.

Under the streets of bustling, modern York in northeastern England lie the remains of Jorvik, a Viking city of perhaps 10,000 people that thrived during the tenth century A.D. When extensive urban redevelopment began in York during the 1970s, the York Archaeological Trust for Excavation and Research Ltd. took the opportunity to excavate everywhere possible—in deep sewer trenches, at sites slated for bank vaults, and between 1976 and 1981 in a large, open area that was known as Coppergate, the street of the woodworkers called coopers. The damp, peaty soil had preserved the remains of buildings, ovens, rubbish pits, even an entire cooper's workshop. From human feces and animal bones, the archaeologists were able to study such minutiae as meat preferences among the Viking inhabitants of Jorvik.

More than half a million people visited the excavation. As the dig ended, the trust built an exhibition area beneath a new shopping center. Here visitors ride electric cars past costumed mannequins of the past ten centuries. Arriving in Jorvik, they see, hear, even smell a Viking commercial precinct complete with workshops, houses, and a wharf. They watch Vikings unload cargoes of herring and furs, cook food, tan leather, and play; they listen to gossip in the Old Norse language. Beyond, they pass from the living settlement into the dead one. They see the excavated evidence—timber buildings, occupation layers, artifacts as they were found by the diggers. Visitors watch archaeologists at work, excavating, drawing, and recording, then ride through a site laboratory where the finds are cleaned, labeled, and stored.

Peter Addyman, the director of the York Archaeological Trust, believes that the Jorvik Viking Centre is a powerful way of introducing people to archaeology and to the forgotten past. He is right, for here, and at similar reconstructions around the world, visitors can follow the steps of painstaking excavation and witness a past as authentic as the science of archaeology can make it. To all who visit, it becomes clear that the finite remains of the past must be preserved—not for museums or art collectors, not for archaeologists, not even for proud nations, but for all humanity.

355

A stone face gazes into its own clouded future at the temples of Angkor in Kampuchea (Cambodia). During the 1930s archaeologists rolled back centuries of jungle growth to reveal this jewel of the Khmer Empire, carved with visions of Vishnu, of Buddha, of heavens and hells. But the domestic holocaust that engulfed the nation in the 1970s brought bullets and neglect to Angkor, and now conservators seek ways to save past from present.

Worldwide, such efforts issue a challenge well worth meeting. For the past offers more than relics and wonders; it unveils the range of human experience, of human deeds—and so helps us to know ourselves. That is the real adventure of archaeology, found not in carved stone or cast bronze, but in ideas, forged in the minds of living people, long ago.

356

EUROPE

1985

1982: Margaret Rule raises the Tudor warship *Mary Rose* off Portsmouth, England.

1981-84: The York Archaeological Trust re-creates a Viking settlement at York, England.

1980s: Sara Bisel studies first human remains from the Roman era at Herculaneum, Italy.

1972: Peter Reynolds begins to reconstruct an Iron Age farm at Butser Hill, England.

1967-1974: Spyridon Marinatos digs at buried city of Akrotíri on Thíra, an Aegean island.

1956: Anders Franzén locates 17th-century Swedish warship *Vasa* in Stockholm harbor.

1950s: Carlo Lerici uses modern technology to investigate Etruscan tombs in Italy.

1950

1950: Peat diggers uncover 2,200-year-old Tollund man in Denmark's Tollund fen.

1940: Four boys find 15,000-year-old Lascaux cave paintings near Montignac, France.

1939: Charles Phillips unearths an Anglo-Saxon ship burial at Sutton Hoo, England.

1934-37: Mortimer Wheeler perfects the grid system at prehistoric Maiden Castle, England.

1900: Arthur Evans claims discovery of the palace of King Minos at Knossos, Crete.

1900

1879: Marcelino Sanz de Sautuola identifies Stone Age cave paintings at Altamira, Spain.

1876: Heinrich and Sophia Schliemann find gold-filled graves at Mycenae, Greece.

1875-1900: Gen. A. H. Pitt Rivers conducts systematic excavations in southern England.

1863-68: Édouard Lartet and Henry Christy dig up Stone Age artifacts in France.

1860s: Giuseppe Fiorelli makes plaster casts of ancient victims at Pompeii, Italy.

1857: Quarrymen uncover a humanlike skull and bones near Neandertal, Germany.

1850

1840s-1880s: Jens Jacob Worsaae applies the Three Age System in the field in Denmark.

1837: Jacques Boucher de Perthes begins to find stone hand axes with the remains of extinct animals in France's Somme Valley.

1801-1804: Lord Elgin directs the removal of sculptures from the Parthenon in Athens.

1700

1719-1725: William Stukeley measures Avebury and Stonehenge in England.

AFRICA

1984: Kamoya Kimeu, a member of Richard Leakey's team, finds a nearly complete *Homo erectus* skeleton at Lake Turkana, Kenya.

1978: Mary Leakey uncovers 3.6-million-year-old hominid footprints at Laetoli, Tanzania.

1974-75: Donald Johanson unearths a three-million-year-old hominid (dubbed Lucy) and the "first family" at Hadar in Ethiopia.

1964: Louis Leakey's discovery of *Homo habilis* at Olduvai Gorge, Tanzania, doubles known antiquity of humans to 1,750,000 years.

1963-68: UNESCO project rescues Pharaoh Ramesses II's temples at Abu Simbel, Egypt.

1959: Mary Leakey finds a fractured skull of *Australopithecus boisei* at Olduvai Gorge.

1950s-1960s: Frank Willett recovers clay and bronze sculptures from Ife, Nigeria.

1929: Gertrude Caton-Thompson concludes that black Africans built Southern Rhodesia's Great Zimbabwe in medieval times.

1924: Raymond Dart defends relationship to humans of Taung child, an australopithecine skull found near Taung, South Africa.

1922: Howard Carter and Lord Carnarvon discover Tutankhamun's treasure-filled tomb in Egypt's Valley of the Kings.

1897: A British punitive force removes ivory and bronze treasures from Benin, Nigeria.

1894-1942: W. M. Flinders Petrie conducts the most extensive research about Egypt before the reign of the pharaohs.

1881: Émile Brugsch, Gaston Maspero's assistant, exhumes more than 40 royal mummies at Deir el Bahri, Egypt.

1874: Amelia Edwards tries to "face-lift" Ramesses II's statue at Abu Simbel, Egypt.

1858-1881: Auguste Mariette carries out widespread excavations on behalf of the Egyptian government.

1842-45: Karl Lepsius collects thousands of artifacts in Egypt for the king of Prussia.

1822: Jean-François Champollion deciphers the Rosetta Stone and later journeys to Egypt to read temple inscriptions (1828).

1816-19: Giovanni Belzoni plunders ancient Egyptian temples and tombs along the Nile.

1799: Napoléon Bonaparte's troops find the Rosetta Stone in the Nile Delta.

NEAR EAST

1980s: George Bass investigates a Bronze Age shipwreck off Ulu Burun, Turkey.

1969: Michael Katzev raises a fourth-century B.C. Greek ship off Kyrenia, Cyprus.

1964-1980s: Paolo Matthiae unearths the city-state of Ebla in Syria–a hitherto unknown civilization from the third millennium B.C.

1961-1980s: Kenan Erim digs up and restores Roman statuary at Aphrodisias, Turkey.

1952-58: Kathleen Kenyon finds evidence of agriculture around 8000 B.C. at Jericho, Jordan, the world's oldest known walled town.

1952: Max Mallowan recovers Assyrian ivory plaques and ornaments at Nimrud, Iraq.

1950s: Robert and Linda Braidwood learn that people were farming at Jarmo in Iraq as early as 6750 B.C.

1947: A Bedouin youth discovers some Dead Sea Scrolls in a cave at Qumrān, Jordan.

1920s: Leonard Woolley reveals details of 16 mass suicides at Ur's Royal Cemetery in Iraq.

1912-14: Leonard Woolley and T. E. Lawrence probe Carchemish, a Hittite city in Syria.

1906: Hugo Winckler begins to excavate the ancient Hittite capital of Boğazköy in Turkey.

1899-1917: Robert Koldewey reveals Babylon, Nebuchadnezzar II's capital in Mesopotamia.

1888: J. Peters and H. Hilprecht begin to dig at Nippur, a Sumerian city in Mesopotamia.

1878: Alexander Conze sets Karl Humann to work on the citadel at Pergamum, Turkey.

1877: Ernest de Sarzec finds archives of cuneiform tablets at Telloh in Mesopotamia.

1872: George Smith locates fragment missing from Flood Tablet at Nineveh, Mesopotamia.

1871-1882: Heinrich and Sophia Schliemann search for ancient Troy at Hissarlik, Turkey.

1845-1850: Austen Henry Layard tunnels into Nimrud and Kuyunjik in Mesopotamia in his quest for the Assyrian capital of Nineveh.

1843: Paul-Émile Botta unearths an Assyrian palace at Khorsabad in Mesopotamia.

1835-1847: Henry Rawlinson copies trilingual inscriptions on the Persian Rock of Bīsotūn.

1820-21: Claudius Rich looks for Nineveh at Kuyunjik but dies before he can excavate.

ASIA, AUSTRALIA, & OCEANIA

1977: Divers locate the remains of the 18th-century frigate *Pandora* off Australia.

1974-75: Chester Gorman probes a Bronze Age village at Ban Chiang, Thailand, and recovers 4,000-year-old bronze artifacts.

1974: Well-diggers discover the huge tomb complex of Qin Shi Huangdi, who reigned as China's First Emperor 2,200 years ago.

1972: Chinese archaeologists open the sepulcher of Lady Dai, a Han Dynasty noblewoman who died in 141 B.C.

1968: A Chinese army detachment finds the second century B.C. tombs of a Han prince, Liu Sheng, and his wife, Princess Dou Wan.

1965: The grave of a Shang ruler at Yi-tu, China, reveals evidence of human sacrifice at the death of a king or regional lord.

1940s, 1950: Mortimer Wheeler's digs at Mohenjo Daro and Harappa in India uncover the oldest known examples of town planning.

1930s: Archaeologists roll back centuries of jungle growth to unveil temple city of Angkor, Cambodia, the capital of the Khmer Empire.

1929: W. C. Pei discovers a nearly complete skullcap, now called Peking man *(Homo erectus)*, in China's Zhoukoudian cave.

1928: Chinese archaeologists find evidence near Anyang of the 3,200-year-old Shang civilization of farmers and bronze workers.

1920s: John Marshall excavates at Mohenjo Daro and Harappa in India and concludes that the Harappan civilization was peaceful.

1891-92: Eugène Dubois finds a humanlike skullcap and thighbone, known today as Java man *(Homo erectus)*, near Trinil, Java.

NORTH AMERICA

1982: Daniel Nelson uses robot submersible with cameras and lights to record two sunken U. S. Navy schooners in Lake Ontario.

1980s: Don Hamilton salvages 17th-century artifacts at sunken city of Port Royal, Jamaica.

1976-1980: Ivor Noël Hume digs at Virginia's Wolstenholme Towne, the oldest English-American village yet excavated.

1973-1980s: William Rathje studies the modern garbage of Tucson, Arizona.

1970s: Richard Daugherty pieces together Makah Indian history at Ozette, Washington.

1970s: Lewis Binford studies modern hunter-gatherers—Alaska's Nunamiut Eskimos.

1959: Edwin Link traces the sunken streets of Port Royal, Jamaica, with an echo sounder.

1940s: Willard Libby develops radiocarbon dating to calculate age of organic substances.

1935: Andrew Douglass extends the tree-ring record in the Southwest back to A.D. 11.

1927: Discovery of the Folsom point near Folsom, New Mexico, proves that hunters lived in New World at least 10,000 years ago.

1926: John D. Rockefeller, Jr., agrees to fund the restoration of Williamsburg, Virginia.

1915-1929: Alfred Kidder uses stratigraphy to reconstruct the prehistory of the Southwest.

1911: Ishi, the last known Yana Indian, wanders into the 20th-century world.

1906-1961: John Harrington studies the customs of vanishing American Indians.

1890s: Excavations at Jamestown, Virginia, pave the way for historical archaeology.

1888: Richard Wetherill first explores Anasazi cliff dwellings at Mesa Verde, Colorado.

1880: Adolph Bandelier records tribal histories about Pecos Pueblo, New Mexico.

1879-1884: Frank Cushing lives with Zuni Indians at New Mexico's Zuni Pueblo.

1845-47: Ephraim Squier and Edwin Davis open more than 200 prehistoric Indian mounds in Ohio and nearby states.

1810s: Caleb Atwater surveys dozens of Indian mounds in the Ohio River Valley.

ca 1780: Thomas Jefferson excavates a burial mound near Charlottesville, Virginia.

LATIN AMERICA

1984: Archaeologists find an undisturbed Maya tomb at Río Azul, Guatemala.

1978-1982: Eduardo Matos Moctezuma excavates the Templo Mayor, the main Aztec temple-pyramid, in Mexico City.

1969-1973: M. Moseley and C. Mackey study the Chimú capital at Chan Chan, Peru.

1962: René Millon begins to map America's earliest city–Teotihuacán in Valley of Mexico.

1960: Richard MacNeish discovers the earliest cultivated corn at Tehuacán, Mexico.

1956: The Tikal Project, an ongoing study of a large Maya site, begins in Guatemala.

1952: Alberto Ruz Lhuillier penetrates the tomb of a Maya ruler inside the Temple of the Inscriptions at Palenque, Mexico.

1946: Giles Healey first sees the vivid Maya murals at Bonampak in Mexico.

1940-46: Matthew Stirling unearths Olmec altars and stone heads in southern Mexico.

1932: Alfonso Caso finds Mixtec treasures at Monte Albán in Mexico's Valley of Oaxaca.

1924-1940: Sylvanus Morley excavates and rebuilds Maya city of Chichén Itzá in Mexico.

1911: Hiram Bingham first journeys to the Inca city of Machu Picchu in highland Peru.

1905-1910: Leopoldo Batres recklessly clears Pyramid of the Sun at Teotihuacán, Mexico.

1904-1911: Edward Thompson recovers nearly 30,000 Maya sacrificial offerings from the Sacred Cenote at Chichén Itzá, Mexico.

1893: John Owens makes papier-mâché molds of the Great Hieroglyphic Stairway at Copán, an ancient Maya city in Honduras.

1881-1894: Alfred Maudslay conducts the first serious study of Maya ruins in Mexico and Central America.

1857-1861, 1880-86: Désiré Charnay photographs Chichén Itzá and other Maya sites in Mexico with his primitive camera.

1839-1841: John Lloyd Stephens and Frederick Catherwood describe and draw Maya ruins in Mexico and Central America.

1805-1807: Guillermo Dupaix investigates Maya sites in Mexico for the king of Spain.

1787: Antonio del Río clears the Maya ruins at Palenque in Mexico.

1985

1950

1900

357

1850

1700

JOURNEY THROUGH THE AGES

A Calendar of World Cultures

EUROPE	AFRICA	NEAR EAST
A.D.		
ca 1455: Johannes Gutenberg prints Bible.	1488: Bartolomeu Dias rounds the Cape of Good Hope at Africa's tip.	1500s-early 1900s: Ottoman Empire holds sway in the Near East.
1337: Hundred Years' War breaks out.	ca 1450: Benin sculptors begin casting stylized bronze heads in West Africa.	1453: Constantinople falls to Ottoman Turks.
ca 1300: Early stirrings of the Renaissance.	ca 1400: Timbuktu prospers as a trading and intellectual center in West Africa.	ca 1300: Osman I wages war against the Byzantines and founds the Ottoman Empire.
1215: Magna Carta establishes the foundation of English constitutional rights.	1300-1500: Great Zimbabwe develops into a political, commercial, and religious center in southern Africa.	1099: Islamic defenders lose Jerusalem to the crusaders.
1095: Pope Urban II launches First Crusade.	1100s: Ife artisans of West Africa begin to make naturalistic bronze and clay sculptures.	1054: Byzantine church breaks with the Roman church.
800: Pope Leo III crowns Charlemagne the emperor of the Romans on Christmas Day.	late 900s: Traders from the Persian Gulf found settlements on Africa's east coast.	ca 570: Prophet Muhammad is born in Mecca.
790-1000: Vikings colonize the British Isles, continental Europe, Iceland, North America.	700-1000: Jenne-Jeno in Mali becomes a West African market center.	70: Romans demolish Herod's Temple in Jerusalem when Jews revolt against Rome.
476: Fall of the Roman Empire.	297: Roman emperor Diocletian crushes an uprising in Alexandria, Egypt.	68: Qumrān sect hides Old Testament scrolls in caves near the Dead Sea.
5th century: Anglo-Saxons settle in Britain.	ca 1: Iron Age begins in southern Africa.	ca 30: Jesus Christ is crucified at Jerusalem.
79: Vesuvius buries Pompeii, Herculaneum.		1-300: Aphrodisias flourishes as a Roman religious sanctuary in western Turkey.
43: Claudius I renews the Roman invasion of Britain almost a century after Julius Caesar's battles with the Celts.		
B.C.		
300-50 B.C.: Iron-using Celts dominate much of Europe. Within their ranks are Druids, a privileged class serving as priests.	30 B.C.: After Cleopatra's death, Egypt becomes a Roman province.	ca 520 B.C.: Darius I founds the Persian capital of Persepolis.
432 B.C.: Athenians complete the Parthenon.	ca 250 B.C.: Royal city of Meroë in Sudan uses wealth from iron production to build pyramids over the graves of its kings.	605-562 B.C.: Neo-Babylonian Empire prospers in the Fertile Crescent under Nebuchadnezzar II.
616-509 B.C.: Etruscan kings rule Rome.	335-327 B.C.: Alexander the Great conquers Egypt and Persia, then invades Indus Valley.	883-859 B.C.: Ashurnasirpal II conquers Mesopotamia and expands Assyrian Empire.
776 B.C.: Greeks host first Olympic Games.	ca 400 B.C.: Bantu people from West Africa develop agriculture and ironworking.	1200-1000 B.C.: Iron Age begins in Near East.
8th or 9th century B.C.: Homer's *Iliad* recounts sack of Troy in 12th century B.C.	ca 450 B.C.: Greek historian Herodotus tours Nile Valley and describes Egyptian customs.	1300-1190 B.C.: Hittite Empire controls Anatolia and northern Syria.
ca 800 B.C.: Iron Age begins in Europe.	ca 500 B.C.: Iron Age begins in East and West Africa.	1792-1750 B.C.: Hammurabi, ruler of first Babylonian Empire, sets down his law code.
1450-1100 B.C.: Mycenaeans rule Aegean.	ca 800 B.C.: Greeks and Phoenicians colonize the Mediterranean coast.	ca 2400 B.C.: Ebla challenges Ur, the richest and most powerful city in Mesopotamia.
ca 1500 B.C.: Volcano erupts on Thíra.	1361 B.C.: Tutankhamun ascends Egypt's throne during the New Kingdom.	ca 3000 B.C.: Bronze Age begins in Near East.
ca 2000 B.C.: Minoans start to build Knossos, one of Europe's first cities, on Crete.	1991-1780 B.C.: Middle Kingdom pharaohs exploit Sinai and Nubia for minerals.	ca 3000 B.C.: Sumerian scribes devise cuneiform, or wedge-shaped, writing.
ca 2000 B.C.: Bronze Age begins in Europe.	2200-2000 B.C.: Bronze Age begins in the Nile Valley.	ca 3500 B.C.: Sumerians build the world's first known cities in Mesopotamia.
ca 2800 B.C.: Construction of Stonehenge begins in southern England.	ca 2500 B.C.: Old Kingdom rulers build the colossal pyramids at Gîza.	ca 6000 B.C.: Copper Age begins in Near East.
ca 2900 B.C.: Stone Age farmers build village of Baigneurs at edge of Lake Paladru, France.	ca 3000 B.C.: Hieroglyphic writing develops in the Nile Valley.	ca 6500 B.C.: Farming spreads in Near East.
ca 3000 B.C.: Stone Age peoples of Europe begin to use copper.	ca 3100 B.C.: Upper and Lower Egypt unified.	ca 8000 B.C.: Sheep and goats domesticated in the Zagros Mountains.
ca 5500 B.C.: Agriculture spreads north and west from southeastern Europe.	ca 5000 B.C.: Cultivators begin to harvest grains in the Nile Valley.	ca 8000 B.C.: Fortified settlement founded at Jericho in Jordan.
ca 8000 B.C.: Hunter-gatherers start to build shelters, live in settlements, bury their dead.		ca 8500 B.C.: Hunter-gatherers in the Levant harvest wild grain, live in year-round villages.
ca 13,000 B.C.: Stone Age artists paint animals on the walls and ceiling of Lascaux cave.		

ASIA, AUSTRALIA, & OCEANIA

1521: Ferdinand Magellan crosses the Pacific.

1498: Vasco da Gama reaches India.

1368: Chinese drive out the Mongols and found the Ming Dynasty.

1279: Kublai Khan completes the conquest of China and ascends the Chinese throne.

1271-1295: Polo family travels across Asia to China, then returns to Venice.

1211-1227: Genghis Khan invades China and builds a great empire in northern Asia.

1100-1200: Easter Islanders erect gigantic stone statues on temple platforms.

ca 1040: Chinese use movable type made of hardened clay to produce books.

ca 900-1451: Temple city of Angkor reigns as capital of Khmer Empire in Southeast Asia.

845: China bans foreign religions.

ca 800: Colonization of New Zealand marks the peak of major settlement in Polynesia.

ca 400: Widespread migration of tribes displaces peoples in much of Eurasia.

ca 100: Pilgrims and merchants introduce Buddhism to China and northern Asia by way of the Silk Route.

206 B.C.-A.D. 220: Han Dynasty consolidates and extends its empire in China.

221-210 B.C.: Qin Shi Huangdi unifies Chinese states, builds empire and Great Wall.

ca 500 B.C.: In China, Confucius teaches the doctrine of harmony based on filial piety.

ca 528-483 B.C.: The Buddha spreads his faith in the Ganges region.

ca 600 B.C.: Iron Age begins in China.

1000-800 B.C.: Iron Age begins in India.

ca 1300 B.C.: Shang capital is established at Anyang, China.

ca 2000 B.C.: Villagers at Ban Chiang in Thailand begin to work bronze, grow rice.

ca 2500 B.C.: Harappans build sophisticated, planned cities in the Indus Valley.

3000-2500 B.C.: Bronze Age begins in Asia.

ca 5000 B.C.: Copper Age begins in China.

ca 8000 B.C.: Hunter-gatherers populate Southeast Asia.

NORTH AMERICA

1699: Williamsburg becomes the second capital of colonial Virginia.

1619: English settlers make their home at Wolstenholme Towne in Virginia.

1607: Englishmen settle Jamestown, Virginia.

ca 1585: English colonist John White makes accurate paintings of Indians.

1540: Spaniard Francisco Vásquez de Coronado finds Zuni pueblos in Southwest.

1539-1542: Spaniard Hernando de Soto explores parts of the Mississippi Valley.

1500s-early 1900s: Makah Indians fish and hunt whales at Ozette in Pacific Northwest.

1492: Columbus reaches the New World.

ca 1200: Anasazi abandon their homes in the Chaco Canyon region of the Southwest.

ca 1000: Vikings establish short-lived villages on the northern coast of North America.

ca 1000: Thule Eskimos, ancestors of the Inuit, settle in Greenland.

900-1300: Anasazi build huge, multiroomed pueblos in the Southwest.

700-1700: Mound Builders farm, trade, build flat-topped mounds in the Mississippi Valley.

ca 200 B.C.: Farmers and potters establish small settlements in the mountains and deserts of the Southwest.

400 B.C.-A.D. 500: Hopewell Indians bury their elite in huge earthen mounds scattered throughout the Ohio Valley.

1000-300 B.C.: Adena people of the Ohio Valley build mounds over the graves of their leaders, make first religious art in the East.

ca 1600 B.C.: Artisans and traders construct extensive geometric earthworks at Poverty Point in the lower Mississippi Valley.

ca 2000 B.C.: North America's earliest known pottery is produced along the southern Atlantic and Gulf coasts.

ca 3000 B.C.: Peoples of the Great Lakes area hammer native copper into tools.

ca 3000 B.C.: Predecessors of the Eskimos adapt to the climate of western Alaska.

ca 6000 B.C.: Arctic hunters roam the Aleutian Islands and the Pacific Northwest.

ca 8000 B.C.: Big-game hunting declines with the onset of a warmer, drier climate.

LATIN AMERICA

1537: Prince Manco Inca flees from the Spanish to the last Inca refuge, Vilcabamba.

1532: Fall of Inca Empire in South America.

1521: Fall of Aztec Empire in Mexico.

1519 and later: Spanish conquistadores and missionaries open the Americas and threaten the native cultures.

1492: Columbus reaches the New World.

1428-1521: Aztecs rule much of Mexico.

1325: Aztecs establish their capital, Tenochtitlán, in the Valley of Mexico.

ca 1200: Incas found their capital at Cuzco in highland Peru.

ca 900: Chan Chan emerges as the capital of the Chimú kingdom on Peru's north coast.

ca 900: Toltec establish their capital at Tula in Mexico's central highlands.

ca 700: Mixtec invaders force the Zapotec from Mexico's Valley of Oaxaca and turn Monte Albán into a vast burial site.

250-900: Lowland Maya civilization flourishes in much of Mexico and Central America.

ca 100: Teotihuacán in the Valley of Mexico emerges as the New World's first city.

ca 500 B.C.: Paracas weavers of coastal Peru produce elaborate burial garments.

ca 600 B.C.: Zapotec flatten a mountaintop and build a ceremonial center at Monte Albán.

ca 1000 B.C.: Region between South America and Mexico emerges as a cultural crossroads.

1200-400 B.C.: Olmec develop Mexico's first known civilization.

ca 3000 B.C.: Western Hemisphere's earliest known pottery is produced in settlements along the Pacific and Caribbean coasts.

ca 3000 B.C.: Agriculture spreads from the Andean highlands to the coast.

3500-2000 B.C.: Agriculture spreads through much of Mexico and Central America.

ca 5000 B.C.: Hunter-gatherers begin to cultivate plants in Mexico's Tehuacán Valley.

ca 6000 B.C.: First evidence of domesticated plants—corn, beans, squash, potatoes—in South America.

ca 9000 B.C.: Hunters slay sloths, guanacos, and horses at southern tip of South America.

A.D.

B.C.

359

BIBLIOGRAPHY

General References. A nontechnical introduction to archaeology, C. W. Ceram's classic *Gods, Graves, and Scholars* (NY: Bantam, 1976) outlines the development of this science. A companion volume, *The March of Archaeology* (NY: Knopf, 1966), was the first picture book illustrating the history of archaeology. In *Hands on the Past* (NY: Knopf, 1966), Ceram highlights discoveries in Central America and the Mediterranean through writings by archaeologists.

Another popular author is British archaeologist Glyn Daniel. In *Man Discovers His Past* (NY: Crowell, 1968), Daniel looks at early treasure hunters and modern scientists, noting that "Man's past has still a great future." *A Hundred and Fifty Years of Archaeology* (Cambridge: Harvard U. Press, 1976) updates a 1950 classic with a look at postwar advances. *A Short History of Archaeology* (London: Thames & Hudson, 1981) gives India, China, and the Americas their due in a global view of the science's growth. Writings by archaeologists blend with Daniel's commentary in *The Origins and Growth of Archaeology* (NY: Crowell, 1967).

Pioneering archaeologists tell of their work in Robert F. Heizer's *Man's Discovery of His Past* (Sunnyvale, Calif.: Peek, 1969). News reports by archaeologists make interesting reading in *The Great Archaeologists* (NY: State Mutual Book, 1981), edited by Edward Bacon. Brian M. Fagan chronicles nine great archaeological discoveries in *Quest for the Past* (Reading, Mass.: Addison-Wesley, 1978). Fagan's *In the Beginning* (Boston: Little, Brown, 1985) details the history of archaeology and the techniques now used to illuminate the human past.

Other general works and their editors are *The Times Atlas of World History,* Geoffrey Barraclough (Maplewood, NJ: Hammond, 1979); *The Atlas of Archaeology,* Keith Branigan (NY: State Mutual Book, 1982); *Larousse Encyclopedia of Archaeology,* Jean Charles-Picard (NY: Larousse, 1983); *The Encyclopedia of Ancient Civilizations,* Arthur Cotterell (NY: Smith, 1980); *The Atlas of Ancient Archaeology,* Jacquetta Hawkes (NY: McGraw-Hill, 1974); *The Cambridge Encyclopedia of Archaeology,* Andrew Sherratt (NY: Cambridge U. Press, 1980); and *The Facts on File Dictionary of Archaeology,* Ruth D. Whitehouse (NY: Facts on File, 1983).

Egyptology references include Brian M. Fagan's *The Rape of the Nile* (NY: Scribner's, 1977), which shows how plundering evolved into the science of Egyptology. Leslie Greener writes entertainingly of Egyptology from tomb robbers to scholars in *The Discovery of Egypt* (London: Cassell, 1966). F. Gladstone Bratton saw his *A History of Egyptian Archaeology* (London: Robert Hale, 1967) as "a romantic and exciting detective story." Illustrations and first-person narratives in Peter A. Clayton's *The Rediscovery of Ancient Egypt: Artists and Travellers in the 19th Century* (London: Thames & Hudson, 1983) depict Egypt as visitors saw it then. Detailed biographies tell *Who Was Who in Egyptology* (London: The Egypt Exploration Society, 1972) by Warren Dawson and Eric Uphill.

Books on Mesopotamia include Brian M. Fagan's *Return to Babylon* (Boston: Little, Brown, 1979), an account of 19th-century archaeologists and their discoveries in the Near East. André Parrot's *Nineveh and Babylon* (London: Thames & Hudson, 1961) is both a detailed history and a trove of photographs of Assyrian art. In *Ancient Mesopotamia* (Chicago: U. of Chicago Press, 1977), A. Leo Oppenheim highlights the cultures of Assyria and Babylonia. *The Sumerians* (Chicago: U. of Chicago Press, 1963) by Samuel Noah Kramer is now a bit dated but still a classic. *Foundations in the Dust* by Seton Lloyd (London: Thames & Hudson, 1980) summarizes the history of archaeology in Mesopotamia.

New World sources include the richly detailed *A History of American Archaeology* (San Francisco: W. H. Freeman, 1980) by Gordon R. Willey and Jeremy A. Sabloff, and Willey's two-volume *An Introduction to American Archaeology* (Englewood Cliffs, NJ: Prentice-Hall, 1966 and 1971). Ivor Noël Hume's *Historical Archaeology* (NY: Knopf, 1974) takes beginners and veterans alike through the step-by-step planning and execution of a dig at a historical site.

Brian M. Fagan's *Elusive Treasure* (NY: Scribner's, 1977) looks at American Indian cultures and the explorers and archaeologists who studied them. *In Search of the Maya* and *Pursuit of the Ancient Maya,* both by Robert L. Brunhouse (Albuquerque: U. of New Mexico Press, 1973 and 1975), present lively portraits of the adventurers and scientists who investigated Maya culture. In *Ancient Maya Civilization* (New Brunswick, NJ: Rutgers U. Press, 1982), Norman Hammond reviews current knowledge about the Maya. Recent work is also detailed in Robert J. Sharer's edition of Sylvanus G. Morley's classic work, *The Ancient Maya* (Stanford, Calif.: Stanford U. Press, 1983).

The Aztecs (NY: Freeman, 1984) by Brian M. Fagan and *The Aztecs: A History* (Norman: U. of Oklahoma Press, 1980) by Nigel Davies view the Aztecs' rise to power and their tribute empire. Wider coverage appears in *The Aztecs, Maya, and Their Predecessors* (NY: Academic Press, 1981) by Muriel Porter Weaver and *A History of Mexican Archaeology* (NY: Thames & Hudson, 1983) by Ignacio Bernal.

The monthly magazine *Archaeology* contains timely articles about the science and its projects around the world. The *National Geographic Index* lists many articles and maps on archaeology from the pages of the NATIONAL GEOGRAPHIC magazine.

The Society has also published a number of related books, including the atlas *Peoples and Places of the Past;* the large volumes *Splendors of the Past, Ancient Egypt,* and *Lost Empires, Living Tribes;* the Special Publications *The Mighty Aztecs, The Mysterious Maya, The Incredible Incas and Their Timeless Land, Clues to America's Past,* and *Discovering Man's Past in the Americas;* the children's book *Secrets from the Past;* and chapters on underwater archaeology in *Exploring the Deep Frontier, World Beneath the Sea,* and *Undersea Treasures.*

Chapter 1: "The Adventure Begins." In *The Ancient History of Wiltshire* (Wakefield, England: EP Publishing, 1975), Sir Richard Colt Hoare describes Stonehenge and other sites in the early 1800s. Christopher Chippindale reviews centuries of theories in *Stonehenge Complete* (London: Thames & Hudson, 1983).

Ole Klindt-Jensen portrays both archaeologists and the science they fostered in *A History of Scandinavian Archaeology* (London: Thames & Hudson, 1975). In *The Establishment of Human Antiquity* (NY: Academic Press, 1983), Donald Grayson traces efforts to answer the question: How old is humankind?

Frontiers in the Soil (Atlanta: Frontiers Publishing, 1979) by Roy S. Dickens, Jr., and James L. McKinley is a charming how-to for novice excavators.

Chapter 2: "The Treasure Hunters." In *Sir William Hamilton* (London: Faber & Faber, 1969), Brian Fothergill describes the collector and his antiquities. Roland Morris, who found the wreck that held some of these artifacts, tells of the excavation in *HMS Colossus* (London: Hutchinson, 1979).

Lord Elgin's *Memorandum on the Subject of the Earl of Elgin's Pursuits in Greece* (London: Miller, 1811) is his apologia for taking sculptures from the Parthenon. William St. Clair offers a more recent view in his scholarly but readable *Lord Elgin and the Marbles* (Oxford: Oxford U. Press, 1983).

The story of the Rosetta Stone is told by Sir E. A. Wallis Budge in *The Rosetta Stone in the British Museum* (London: Religious Tract Society, 1929). Baron Dominique-Vivant Denon captures the wonder of an alien culture in the two-volume *Travels in Upper and Lower Egypt* (NY: Campbell, 1803). Art by Denon and others fills 14 of 24 volumes of *Description de l'Égypte* (Paris: Imprimerie impériale, 1809-1828), a first-rate historical document.

Giovanni Belzoni trumpets his deeds in *Narrative of the Operations and Recent Discoveries Within the Pyramids, Temples, Tombs, and Excavations in Egypt and Nubia* (London: Murray, 1820). Stanley Mayes tells the tale in *The Great Belzoni* (London: Putnam, 1959).

Chapter 3: "In Search of Buried Cities." Austen Henry Layard's two-volume *Nineveh and Its Remains* (NY: Putnam, 1849) outlines his excavations at a site he later learned was Nimrud. He recounts his expedition to the actual Nineveh in *Discoveries in the Ruins of Nineveh and Babylon* (London: Murray, 1853). In *Layard of Nineveh* (London: Murray, 1963), Gordon Waterfield profiles Layard as archaeologist and diplomat.

Richard Brilliant's *Pompeii, A.D. 79* (Kent, Ohio: Volair, 1979) brings to life the city's history, archaeology, and art. *The Shadow of Vesuvius: Pompeii A.D. 79* (London: Joseph, 1979) by Raleigh Trevelyan shows the impact of archaeology on art and literature.

Chapter 4: "From Sport to Science." Geoffrey Bibby's *The Testimony of the Spade* (NY: Knopf, 1956) is an engaging account of the pioneers of archaeology in northern Europe. In *The Story of Archaeology in Britain* (London: Joseph, 1964), Ronald Jessup places the science in its historical context in the British Isles.

The Lake Dwellings of Switzerland and Other Parts of Europe (London: Longmans, Green, 1866) is a treatise by Ferdinand Keller, first to study them. Jens Jacob Worsaae's *The Prehistory of the North* (London: Trübner, 1886) chronicles cultural growth in northern Europe. John Lubbock offers an early look at how cultures evolve in *Prehistoric Times* (NY: Holt, 1913). M. W. Thompson's *General Pitt-Rivers* (Bradford-on-Avon, England: Moonraker, 1977) is a brief biography of this pioneering archaeologist.

Chapter 5: "Tombs, Texts, and Trophies." Jean-Philippe Lauer views more than a century of excavations at Egypt's first royal cemetery in *Saqqara* (NY: Scribner's, 1976). Amelia Edwards retraces her trip *A Thousand Miles up the Nile* (NY: Hippocrene Books, 1983) with great Victorian charm.

Neil A. Silberman tells archaeologists' own adventures in the Holy Land in *Digging for God and Country* (NY: Knopf, 1982). Firsthand reports include George Smith's *The Chaldean Account of Genesis* (San Diego: Wizards, 1977), a fact-filled narrative of his discovery and study of the Flood Tablets. In *By Nile and Tigris* (NY: AMS, 1975), Sir E. A. Wallis Budge narrates his journeys in these regions.

Heinrich Schliemann's saga comes to life in his extravagant *Mycenae* (Salem, NH: Ayer, 1967) and in Leo Deuel's more objective *Memoir of Heinrich Schliemann* (NY: Harper & Row, 1977). *Progress into the Past* (NY: Macmillan, 1967) by William A. McDonald summarizes archaeology's probings into Mycenaean civilization.

Chapter 6: "Seeking the First Americans." Two of the earliest views of the New World were the account written around 1555 by Bernardino de Sahagún, *Florentine Codex: General History of the Things of New Spain* (Santa Fe: School of American Research, 1982), and the art of John White, reprinted in Paul Hulton's *America 1585* (Chapel Hill: U. of North Carolina Press, 1984).

Words by John L. Stephens and illustrations by Frederick Catherwood in the mid-1800s became *Incidents of Travel in Central America, Chiapas, and Yucatan* and *Incidents of Travel in Yucatan* (NY: Dover, 1969). Victor W. von Hagen tells the tale in *Search for the Maya* (Westmead, England: Saxon, 1973). Early views of Maya sites in Mexico fill Keith F. Davis's biography of a late 19th-century photographer, *Désiré Charnay* (Albuquerque: U. of New Mexico Press, 1981).

In 1848 E. G. Squier and E. H. Davis published *Ancient Monuments of the Mississippi Valley* (NY: AMS, 1973); many of its accounts are all that is left of lost sites. Robert Silverberg views the mounds from a modern perspective in *Mound Builders of Ancient America* (Greenwich, Conn.: New York Graphic Society, 1968). Students of Pueblo cultures still rely on Frank H. Cushing's trailblazing *My Adventures in Zuñi* (Palmer Lake, Colo.: Filter Press, 1967), written a century ago.

Hiram Bingham's *Lost City of the Incas* (NY: Atheneum, 1963) is an engaging memoir of the discovery and excavation of Machu Picchu, with a history of the Incas. In *Antisuyo* (NY: Simon & Schuster, 1970), Gene Savoy seeks lost cities in the jungles of Peru.

Chapter 7: "Putting Time in Order." Herman V. Hilprecht narrates—a bit extravagantly—his excavations at Nippur in *Explorations in Bible Lands*

(Philadelphia: Holman, 1903). Robert Koldewey writes in detail of *The Excavations at Babylon* (London: Macmillan, 1914). *Babylon* (London: Thames & Hudson, 1979) by Joan Oates updates work at this pivotal site.

W. M. Flinders Petrie, a founder of Egyptology, recounts his *Seventy Years in Archaeology* (NY: Holt, 1932). Kurt Bittel's *Hattusha: The Capital of the Hittites* (NY: Oxford U. Press, 1970) tells of an empire that rivaled Egypt. Sir Leonard Woolley shares the adventure of his discoveries in Egypt, Italy, and northern Syria in *Dead Towns and Living Men* (London: Lutterworth, 1954).

In *Time and Chance* (Westport, Conn.: Greenwood, 1974), Joan Evans describes her father, John, and her half-brother, Arthur, both eminent archaeologists. Sir Arthur Evans is also portrayed by Sylvia L. Horwitz in *The Find of a Lifetime* (NY: Viking, 1981). Sinclair Hood's *The Minoans* (NY: Praeger, 1971) depicts the ancient civilization that Evans discovered.

Chapter 8: "A New Look at the New World." René Millon uses diagrams, maps, and photographs to illustrate *Urbanization at Teotihuacán, Mexico* (Austin: U. of Texas Press, 1973). A landmark narrative is Alfred P. Maudslay's five-volume *Archaeology* (London: Porter, 1889-1892), with precise descriptions and drawings of his Maya discoveries. In *People of the Serpent* (NY: Houghton Mifflin, 1932), Edward H. Thompson tells of his work and adventures in the land of the Maya. Another pioneer is profiled in Robert L. Brunhouse's *Sylvanus G. Morley and the World of the Ancient Mayas* (Norman: U. of Oklahoma Press, 1971). A Peabody Museum catalog, *Cenote of Sacrifice* (Austin: U. of Texas Press, 1985), includes essays on Chichén Itzá and its sacred well.

Richard Wetherill: Anasazi (Albuquerque: U. of New Mexico Press, 1966) by Frank McNitt portrays this explorer and his spectacular finds in the American Southwest. George E. Webb's *Tree Rings and Telescopes* (Tucson: U. of Arizona Press, 1983) pays tribute to astronomer A. E. Douglass and his work on tree-ring dating. Ivor Noël Hume probes a nation's roots in *Here Lies Virginia* (NY: Knopf, 1963). Theodora Kroeber's *Ishi* (Berkeley: U. of California Press, 1976) portrays this lone Indian thrust into the modern world. In *Encounter with an Angry God* (Banning, Calif.: Malki Museum Press, 1975), Carobeth Laird takes a close look at life in the field with her eccentric former husband, ethnologist John Peabody Harrington.

Chapter 9: "Scientists in the Field." Howard Carter takes readers on one of archaeology's great quests in *The Tomb of Tutankhamen* (NY: Dutton, 1972). I. E. S. Edwards offers an objective account in *The Treasures of Tutankhamun* (NY: Penguin, 1973), and Christiane Desroches-Noblecourt reconstructs the young pharaoh's era in *Tutankhamen* (NY: New York Graphic Society, 1976). History and reminiscence blend in Herbert E. Winlock's *Excavations at Deir el Bahri 1911-1931* (NY: Macmillan, 1942).

Digging up the Past (Westport, Conn.: Greenwood, 1977) by Sir Leonard Woolley outlines various field methods. His memoir, *Spadework in Archaeology* (NY: Philosophical Library, 1953), reveals "how very alive . . . archaeology is" in digs from England to the Fertile Crescent. In *Ur 'of the Chaldees'* (Ithaca, NY: Cornell U. Press, 1982), P. R. S. Moorey updates Woolley's milestone report on Ur.

Sir Mortimer Wheeler probes the Indus and other ancient cultures in his *Early India and Pakistan* (NY: Praeger, 1959). This great pioneer is vividly portrayed by Jacquetta Hawkes in *Adventurer in Archaeology* (NY: St. Martin's, 1982).

Rupert Bruce-Mitford describes the grave of an Anglo-Saxon ruler in *The Sutton Hoo Ship Burial: A Handbook* (London: British Museum, 1979).

Chapter 10: "When, Where—and Why." David Wilson looks at remote sensing, pollen analysis, and other innovations in *The New Archaeology* (NY: Knopf, 1975). *Dating Methods in Archaeology* (NY: Academic Press, 1973) by Joseph W. Michels tells how scientists calculate an object's age. In *The Science of Archaeology* (Belmont, Calif.: Wadsworth, 1978), Richard S. MacNeish uses the Tehuacán Project in Mexico to show how a dig can be run.

Peter V. Glob's engrossing *The Bog People* (Ithaca, NY: Cornell U. Press, 1969) recounts the discovery and study of these Iron Age humans and portrays them in haunting photographs.

John C. Trever's *The Untold Story of Qumran* (Westwood, NJ: Revell, 1965) gives a firsthand report of the discovery of the Dead Sea Scrolls and the intrigues that followed. Kathleen Kenyon presents a readable account of her work in *Digging Up Jericho* (London: Benn, 1957) and brings the story up-to-date in *Archaeology in the Holy Land* (NY: Norton, 1979).

Mallowan's Memoirs (NY: Dodd, Mead, 1977) by Sir Max Mallowan blends archaeology and life with his wife, Dame Agatha Christie. His two-volume *Nimrud and Its Remains* (NY: Dodd, Mead, 1966) concentrates on archaeology and includes color photographs of his discoveries.

Chapter 11: "Lost Ships, Sunken Cities." George F. Bass, the founder of marine archaeology, depicts his specialty in *Archaeology Under Water* (NY: Praeger, 1966) and recounts his own adventures in *Archaeology Beneath the Sea* (NY: Walker, 1975). Bass also edited the comprehensive *A History of Seafaring Based on Underwater Archaeology* (NY: Walker, 1972). Another undersea pioneer, Peter Throckmorton, relates his experiences in *The Lost Ships* (Boston: Little, Brown, 1964) and looks at both present and future in *Shipwrecks and Archaeology* (Boston: Little, Brown, 1969).

Anders Franzén describes his triumphant obsession with raising a great Swedish galleon in *The Warship Vasa* (Stockholm: Norstedt, 1974). Margaret Rule tells of excavating King Henry VIII's warship in *The Mary Rose* (London: Conway Maritime, 1982).

General sources include a UNESCO treatise, *Underwater Archaeology* (Paris: UNESCO, 1972), and *Archeology Under Water: An Atlas of the World's Submerged Sites* (NY: McGraw-Hill, 1980), edited by Keith Muckelroy.

Chapter 12: "To the Ends of Earth and Time." Sonia Cole's biography, *Leakey's Luck* (NY: Harcourt Brace Jovanovich, 1975), is full of fascinating detail about Louis Leakey's life, while his own book, *By the Evidence* (NY: Harcourt Brace Jovanovich, 1976), focuses on his discoveries to 1951. In *Disclosing the Past* (Garden City, NY: Doubleday, 1984), Mary Leakey tells of her life and pivotal finds at Olduvai Gorge, both with her husband, Louis, and after his death. Their son Richard E. Leakey describes his boyhood and his discoveries of fossil hominids in *One Life* (London: Joseph, 1983).

In *Lucy: The Beginnings of Humankind* (NY: Warner Books, 1982), Donald C. Johanson recounts his discovery of the fossil hominids he named *Australopithecus afarensis*. Controversy surrounds the search for human ancestors; an unbiased view can be found in John Reader's *Missing Links* (Boston: Little, Brown, 1981).

Ebla: A Revelation in Archaeology (NY: Times Books, 1979) by Chaim Bermant and Michael Weitzman tells of the discovery of more than 15,000 clay tablets at this ancient city and the dispute about their connection with the Old Testament. *Archaeology of the Bible* (NY: Simon & Schuster, 1977) by Magnus Magnusson takes a wider view, examining Old Testament stories in the light of archaeological evidence.

Chapter 13: "The Future of the Past." "That which I have myself seen," writes Spanish conquistador Bernal Díaz del Castillo as he reports the defeat of the Aztecs in *The Discovery and Conquest of Mexico* (NY: Farrar, Straus & Cudahy, 1956). Peter S. Garlake's *Great Zimbabwe* (London: Thames & Hudson, 1973) details the history of this African site and its excavations. *Shang Civilization* (New Haven, Conn.: Yale U. Press, 1980) by Kwang-Chih Chang portrays this artistic culture of ancient China, while *Anyang* (Seattle: U. of Washington Press, 1977) gives a description of the Shang capital by the site's chief excavator, Li Chi.

In *The Plundered Past* (NY: Atheneum, 1973), journalist Karl E. Meyer surveys the illicit international traffic in antiquities and its disastrous effects. Peter J. Reynolds describes a working reconstruction in *Iron-Age Farm* (London: British Museum, 1979). Ivor Noël Hume writes with wit and authority of excavations at the 17th-century plantation of *Martin's Hundred* (NY: Knopf, 1982). *Hunters of the Whale* (NY: Morrow, 1974) by Ruth Kirk with Richard D. Daugherty recounts his excavation of a buried Makah village on the Washington coast and its meaning to tribal descendants.

A wealth of finds—Viking, Anglo-Saxon, Roman—came to light under modern York in England; Richard Hall depicts this project in *The Viking Dig* (London: Bodley Head, 1984).

AUTHOR BRIAN M. FAGAN is an archaeologist whose work has taken him from Zambia to California. A native of England, he received his doctorate in archaeology from Cambridge University. In Central Africa he excavated early farming villages and studied Iron Age societies of a thousand years ago. He came to the United States in 1966 and is now a professor of anthropology at the University of California, Santa Barbara.

Dr. Fagan has written a number of books about archaeology; several are cited above. He is also a well-known lecturer and an expert sailor. He has sailed thousands of miles in Europe, the Caribbean, and California, and has written a guide to yacht chartering.

ACKNOWLEDGMENTS

We are grateful to many individuals and organizations who contributed to *The Adventure of Archaeology.* Our special thanks go to J. Lawrence Angel, Smithsonian Institution; William M. Calder III, U. of Colorado, Boulder; and James F. Romano, Brooklyn Museum.

We are also indebted to Susan Heuck Allen; William P. Beaman; Philip Betancourt, Temple U.; Aimé Bocquet, U. of Grenoble; H. W. Catling and J. A. MacGillivray, British School at Athens; John D. Broadwater and Alain C. Outlaw, Virginia Research Center for Archaeology; Todd Carrel; Benjamin B. Citarelli; Michael D. Coe, Yale U.; Margaret Conkey, State U. of New York, Binghamton; William Connelly; Brian Cook, Angela Care Evans, Katharine Johns, Terence C. Mitchell, Kenneth Painter, and A. J. Spencer, British Museum; Glyn Daniel; Hester A. Davis, U. of Arkansas; Harm de Blij, Valerie Mattingley, Jennifer Moseley, and Mary G. Smith, National Geographic Society; Roy S. Dickens, U. of North Carolina, Chapel Hill; Christos Doumas, Akrotíri Project; Robert H. Dyson, Zahi Hawass, Sue Levy, Phoebe Resnick, and Joyce White, The University Museum, U. of Pennsylvania; Judith A. Franke, Dickson Mounds Museum; Robert S. Freideman; Alwyn Gentry, Missouri Botanical Garden; Susan Gregg and Eleanor Mannikka, U. of Michigan, Ann Arbor; Richard A. Hall, York Archaeological Trust; Norman Hammond, Rutgers U.; Susan D. Hanna and Diane G. Stallings, Colonial National Historical Park; Evelyn B. Harrison and Randall K. White, NYU; Frank Hawke, Unison International; Robert L. Hohlfelder, U. of Colorado, Boulder; John Hopkins, Society of Antiquaries; J. Paul Hudson; Rebecca C. Hyman; W. James Judge, Fort Burgwin Research Center; Alice Jugie; Jeffrey Kao, Harvard U.; Susan Womer Katzev and Harry E. Tzalas, Kyrenia Ship Project; Donald H. Keith, Institute of Nautical Archaeology; William M. Kelso, Thomas Jefferson Memorial Foundation; David Madsen, Utah State Historical Society; Lady Mallowan; William J. Murnane and Richard L. Zettler, The Oriental Institute, U. of Chicago; National Geographic Administrative Services, Library, Translations Division, and Travel Office; Jorgen Nordquist, Danish National Museum; Douglas W. Owsley, Louisiana State U.; Achilles Paparsenos, Greek Embassy; Wolfgang Radt, Deutsches Archäologisches Institut, Istanbul; Alain Raffray, UNESCO; Michael Rhodes, Museum of London; Donald M. Rosencrantz, Naval Ocean Systems Center, San Diego; Jacob Rothenberg, City U. of New York; Yannis Sakellarakis, Herakleion Museum; Thomas Schäfer, Deutsches Archäologisches Institut, Athens; Thomas L. Sever, NASA; Joseph Shaw, U. of Toronto; T. Leslie Shear, Jr., American School of Classical Studies, Athens; David L. Thompson, Howard U.; Jan Timbrook, Santa Barbara Museum of Natural History; William B. Trousdale and Gus Van Beek, Smithsonian Institution; R. Lindley Vann, U. of Maryland, College Park; Michael Vickers, Ashmolean Museum; John Witek, Georgetown U.; Cary Wolinsky.

ILLUSTRATIONS CREDITS

The following abbreviations appear in this list: (t)-top; (c)-center; (b)-bottom; (r)-right; (l)-left; AMO-Ashmolean Museum, Oxford; BA-The Bettmann Archive; BM-British Museum; DAI-Deutsches Archäologisches Institut; EA-Ekdotike Athenon S.A.; LC-Library of Congress; MCL-Mansell Collection, London; MMA-Metropolitan Museum of Art; NGC-National Geographic Collection; NGL-National Geographic Library; NGP-National Geographic Photographer; NGPA-National Geographic Publications Art; NGS-National Geographic Staff; NMC-National Museum, Copenhagen; NYPL-New York Public Library; PMHU-Peabody Museum, Harvard University; RHPL-Robert Harding Picture Library; SAL-Society of Antiquaries, London; SC-The Searight Collection; UMP-University Museum, Philadelphia. WMS-Wasa Museum, Stockholm.

Cover stamping, Gerard Huerta. 2-3, NYPL. 7, Jonathan Blair. 8-9, James L. Stanfield, NGP. 10, Kerry Hayes. 10-11, Keith Philpott. 11, Gordon W. Gahan. 12-13, Michael A. Hampshire. 14, Otis Imboden, NGP. 15-16, Michael A. Hampshire. 17, Georg Gerster. 18, Adam Woolfitt. 19(t), SAL. 19(b), NGPA. 20, from *The Ancient History of Wiltshire* by Sir Richard Colt Hoare; LC. 20-21, Patrick Ward. 22-23, NMC. 23, "John Tradescant the Younger with Roger Friend" by Emanuel de Critz; AMO. 24(t), Columbia University, New York: Lee Boltin. 24(b), from *The Hornet,* March 22, 1871; Ardea London. 24-25, John Reader. 25, NMC. 26, Owner unknown. 27, from *Voyage Au Cambodge* by Louis Delaporte, 1880; LC. 28-29, Thomas Blackshear. 30, after C. H. Kniep from *Collection of Engravings from Ancient Vases*... by Sir William Hamilton, 1791; Virginia State Library. 31(t), Ira Block. 31(b), BM. 32-33, by Thomas Horner; Benaki Museum, Athens. 34, RHPL. 35, "Temporary Elgin Room" by A. Archer; BM. 36-37, BM: Ira Block. 37, Michael A. Hampshire. 38, NGPA. 38-39, Gordon W. Gahan. 40(t), from *Views in Egypt*... by Luigi Mayer, 1804; LC. 40(b), Fred J. Maroon. 40-41, by David Roberts; BM: RHPL. 42, SC. 43(t), from *Voyages en Egypt* by D. Denon; Bibliothèque Nationale, Paris. 43(c), by M. H. Orange; BA. 43(b), BM. 44-45, Farrell Grehan. 46(t), BM: RHPL. 46(b), from *The Great Belzoni* by Stanley Mayes, 1959; NGL. 47, Georg Gerster. 48-49, from *Six New Plates*... by G. B. Belzoni, 1822; NYPL. 49(t), from *Researches and Operations of Giovanni Battista Belzoni in Egypt and Nubia,* 1820; NGL. 49(b), SC. 50-51, Georg Gerster. 52-53, "General Views of the Island of Philae, Nubia" by David Roberts; SAL. 53, Georg Gerster. 54, BBC Hulton Library. 54-55, British Library. 56-57, Thomas Blackshear. 58, James P. Blair, NGP. 58-59, Georg Gerster. 59, from *A Short History of Archaeology* by Glyn Daniel, 1981. 60-61, James L. Stanfield, NGP. 61, NGPA. 62-63, BM: Ira Block. 63, Georg Gerster. 64-65, Jean Dufour. 66, British Library. 67, BM. 68, SC. 68-69, MCL. 69(r), BM: Ira Block. 69(b), from *Illustrated London News,* February 28, 1852. 70, from *A Short History of Archaeology* by Glyn Daniel, 1981. 70-71, SC. 71, BM. 72-73, State Russian Museum, Leningrad: V. Dorokhov, VAAP. 73, NGPA. 74-75(t), from *Campi Phlegraei* by Sir William Hamilton, 1776; LC: Victor R. Boswell, Jr., NGP. 74-75(b), École Nationale Supérieure des Beaux-Arts. 76-77(t), Jonathan Blair, Black Star. 76-77(b), engraving by Charles François Mazois, DAI, Rom. 77, Wayne McLoughlin. 78, Mary Evans Picture Library. 78-79, O. Louis Mazzatenta, NGS. 80-81, Cheryl Nuss. 81-85, O. Louis Mazzatenta, NGS. 86-87, Thomas Blackshear. 88, NGPA. 88-89, Ian Berry, Magnum. 90, Ivor Noël Hume. 91, Museum of London. 92-93, Ira Block. 94-95, Centre de Documentation de la Prehistoire Alpine, Grenoble (94, H. Müller). 96, Albert Moldvay. 97(t), NGPA. 97(b), from *Reliquiae Aquitanicae* by Édouard Lartet and Henry Christy, 1875; LC. 98-99, Jean Vertut. 100, drawing by J. Kornerup, NMC. 101, Salisbury and Wiltshire Museum. 102(b), University Museum of National Antiquities, Oslo. 102-103, Ted Spiegel. 104-105, Thomas Blackshear. 106, Three Lions. 107, Robert Caputo. 108, NGPA. 108-109, "Outer Court of the Temple of Edfou, Egypt" by David Roberts; Family Collection of Frank Bicknell, Esq., London. 110, Farrell Grehan. 111(t), Egyptian Museum, Cairo: Émile Brugsch. 111(b), from *Century Illustrated Magazine,* May 1887. 112-113, Thomas J. Abercrombie, NGS. 113, from *The Manners and Customs of the Ancient Egyptians* by Sir John Gardner Wilkinson, 1883; NGL. 114, SC. 114-115, BBC Hulton Library. 115(b), Illustrated London News Picture Library. 116, from *A Thousand Miles up the Nile* by Amelia B. Edwards, 1888; NGL. 117, Photographer unknown; NGC. 118, Palestine Exploration Fund. 118-119, Jodi Cobb, NGP. 120, DAI, Athens. 121(l), MCL. 121(r), NGPA. 122-123, Ira Block. 124(t), Gordon W. Gahan. 124(b), EA. 125-127, DAI, Athens. 127, Ira Block. 128, National Archaeological Museum, Athens: Gordon W. Gahan. 128-129, EA. 130-131, DAI, Athens. 131, EA. 132-133, Thomas Blackshear. 134(l), from *Codex Borbonicus,* Akademische Druck-u. Verlagsanstalt, Graz; Dumbarton Oaks: Victor R. Boswell, Jr., NGP. 134(r), BM. 135(t), from *Ancient Monuments of the Mississippi Valley* by E. G. Squier and E. H. Davis, 1848; NGL. 135(b), Ohio Historical Society. 136, Georg Gerster, Photo Researchers. 137(t), NGPA. 137(b), PMHU. 138-139, John J. Egan; St. Louis Art Museum. 139, Denver Museum of Natural History (139(l), Jesse D. Figgins). 140-141, Danny Lehman. 142-143, "Broken Idol, at Copan" by Frederick Catherwood, 1844; NYPL. 143(t), "Archway, Casa del Gobernador, Uxmal" by Frederick Catherwood, 1844; NYPL. 143(b), PMHU. 144-145, from *Les Anciennes Villes du Nouveau Monde,* 1885; The Robert Goldwater Library, MMA: Victor R. Boswell, Jr., NGP. 145(r), Désiré Charnay; NYPL. 146(t), from *My Adventures in Zuñi* by Frank H. Cushing, 1970. 146(b) and 147, Smithsonian Institution (147, Joseph H. Bailey, NGP). 148, E. C. Erdis. 149-151, Hiram Bingham. 151(b), Yale Peruvian Expedition Papers, Yale University Library: Victor R. Boswell, Jr., NGP. 152-153, Hiram Bingham. 154-155, David Louis Olson. 156, Lee Boltin. 156-157, David Brill. 158-159, UMP. 160, Gordon W. Gahan. 161, DAI, Athens. 162, "Pergamon with Oxen" by Christian Wilberg, 1879; DAI, Istanbul. 162-163, Elisabeth Steiner, DAI, Istanbul. 163(b), Antikenmuseum, Berlin. 164, Photographer unknown; NGC. 165(t), NGPA. 165(b) and 166(t), Georg Gerster. 166-167, Geoffrey Biddle. 168-169, Georg Gerster. 170(l), Michael A. Hampshire. 170(r), Staatliche Museen zu Berlin. 170-171, BA. 171, Linda B. Meyerriecks, NGS. 172-173(t), Egypt Exploration Society. 172-173(b), from *Diospolis Parva* by W. M. Flinders Petrie, 1901; LC. 174-175, EA, Archaeological Museum of Herakleion, Crete. 176-177, Gordon W. Gahan. 177 and 178(t), AMO. 178(b), Gordon W. Gahan. 179(t), AMO. 179(b), Ira Block. 180(l), from *The Annual of the British School at Athens,* 1902-1903; LC. 180(r), EA, Archaeological Museum of Herakleion, Crete. 181, Ira Block. 182-183, Arthur E. Pierson, The Oriental Institute, University of Chicago. 183(r), Neilson C. Debevoise. 183(b), Gianni Tortoli. 184, MMA. 184-185, BM. 186-187, Matthew W. Stirling. 188, from *Urbanization at Teotihuacán, Mexico* by René Millon, Volume I, Part 2, 1973; NGL. 188-189, O. Goldner, Photo Researchers. 189(b), Photographer unknown; NGC. 190, NGPA. 190-191, Horst Munzig, Susan Griggs. 192(t), NGL. 192(b), Photographer unknown; NGC. 193, H. N. Sweet; NGL. 194, PMHU: Otis Imboden, NGP, and Hillel Burger. 195(t), Bates Littlehales, NGP. 195(b), F. P. Orchard, PMHU. 196, Carnegie Institution. 197(t), David Alan Harvey, NGP. 197(b), PMHU. 198-199, Richard H. Stewart. 200(t), Charles Martin. 200(b), O. C. Havens. 200-201, Walter Meayers Edwards. 201(b), NGPA. 202-203, Dewitt Jones. 204(t), Albert Moldvay. 204(b), American Museum of Natural History. 205, William Belknap, Jr. 206(t), Colonial Williamsburg Foundation. 206(b), Swem Library, College of William and Mary. 207, Linda Bartlett. 208, Colonial Williamsburg Foundation. 208-209, Linda Bartlett. 210-211, Kay Chernush. 211(b), Sisse Brimberg, Woodfin Camp. 212(t), Santa Barbara Museum of Natural History. 212(b), Smithsonian Institution. 212-213, Peter Howorth. 214-215, Griffith Institute, AMO. 216-217, MMA. 218, The Times Ltd. 219(t), Farrell Grehan, FPG. 219(b), Christopher A. Klein, NGS. 220-221, Wide World. 221(t), MMA. 221(c), NGPA. 221(b), MMA. 222, Egyptian Museum, Cairo: Émile Brugsch. 223, James E. Harris. 224-225, Georg Gerster. 226-227, BM. 227(r), UMP. 228-229, SAL. 229(l), Ira Block. 229(r), Council of the Dorset Natural History and Archaeological Society, Dorset County Museum, Dorchester, Dorset: Ira Block. 230(l), from *Mohenjo-Daro and the Indus Civilization* by Sir John H. Marshall, 1973; NGL. 230-232, Dilip Mehta, Contact from Woodfin Camp and Associates. 233(t), James P. Blair, NGP. 233(b), NGPA. 234-235, National Museum of Pakistan, Karachi: James P. Blair, NGP (234(bl), RHPL). 236, BM. 237, NGPA. 238, C. W. Phillips. 238-239, B. Wagstaff, BM. 239(b), BM. 240-241, Ira Block. 242-243, The Photo Source, Central Press. 244, Jean Vertut. 245, Rene Burri, Magnum. 246, Three Lions. 247(t), Silkeborg Museum, Denmark: Ira Block. 247(b), Moesgaard Prehistoric Museum, Aarhus, Denmark: Ira Block. 248(t), Illustrated London News Picture Library. 248(b), Scarborough Borough Council. 249, David Scharf, Peter Arnold, Inc. 250-251, Wayne McLoughlin. 252-253, Zbigniew Jan Lutyk, NGS. 253(c), NGPA. 253(b), State Archaeological Museum, Warsaw. 254(t), W. Robert Moore. 254-255, James P. Blair, NGP. 255(b), Villa Giulia, Rome: James P. Blair, NGP. 256-257, Palphot, Ltd., Israel: B. Rotenberg. 257, Père R. de Vaux, École Biblique et Archéologique Française, Jerusalem. 258-259, British School of Archaeology, Jerusalem. 259(b), Amman Archaeological Museum: Nathan Benn. 260, NGPA. 260-261, Georg Gerster. 262, David S. Boyer, NGS. 263, Gordon W. Gahan. 264-265, Steven C. Wilson, Entheos. 265, NGPA. 266-267, UMP. 268, PMHU. 268-269, Rob Blount, Florida State Museum. 270-271, CNRS, Centre Camille Jullian: Chéné. 272, The Cousteau Society. 272-273, Jacques Ertaud. 273, B. Anthony Stewart. 274-275, WMS. 275(t), WMS: Winfield Parks. 276-277, WMS: Ira Block. 278(t), Luis Marden. 278(b), NGPA. 279(t), D. D. Denton, Nautical Archaeology, Texas A&M University. 279(b), Luis Marden. 280-282, William R. Curtsinger. 283, Jonathan Blair. 284-285, Michael A. Hampshire. 286, Canada Centre for Inland Waters. 286-287, Emory Kristof, NGP. 287(b), Hamilton-Scourge Foundation, Hamilton, Ontario: Emory Kristof, NGP. 288-289, Bates Littlehales, NGP. 290, Jonathan Blair. 291(t), Ira Block. 291(b), Susan Womer Katzev. 292(t), Louie Psihoyos. 292(b), from the *Anthony Roll;* Master and Fellows, Magdalene College, Cambridge. 292-293, The Mary Rose Trust. 293, Andrew Fielding, The Mary Rose Trust. 294-295, William R. Curtsinger. 296-297, Robert F. Sisson, NGP. 298, Robert M. Campbell. 299(l), John Reader. 299(r), Jay Matternes. 300, ADC, Alexandria, Va. 300-301, Gordon W. Gahan. 302, Jay Matternes. 303-305, David Brill. 305(t), Institute of Human Origins. 306(t), UMP: Otis Imboden, NGP. 306(b), Robert Caputo. 307, Michael and Aubine Kirtley. 308, Jim Brandenburg. 309, John Lee, NMC. 310, Judy Porter, Photo Researchers. 310-311, UMP: Chester Gorman. 312-313, David Brill. 313, ADC, Alexandria, Va. 314, Gianni Tortoli. 314-315, Otis Imboden, NGP. 315, Gianni Tortoli. 316(l), Manolis Andronicos. 316(r) and 317(t), Gordon W. Gahan. 317(b), Spyros Tsavdaroglou. 318(t), James L. Stanfield, NGP. 318(b), National Museum, Aleppo: Gianni Tortoli. 319, James L. Stanfield, NGP. 320-321, David Brill. 321, Adam Woolfitt. 322, Jonathan Blair. 322-323, Robert W. Nicholson and Michael A. Hampshire. 323-325, Jonathan Blair. 326-327, David Hiser. 328, G. N. Fleming, National Archives of Zimbabwe. 328-329, James L. Stanfield, NGP. 330-331, Wolfgang Kaehler. 331, Seth Joel. 332(t), China Pictorial. 332-333, Robert W. Madden, NGP. 333(r), NGPA. 334-335, William Thompson. 335(t), Audrey Topping. 335(b), China Pictorial. 336, Michael E. Moseley. 337, Michael and Aubine Kirtley. 338-339, Werner Emse. 339(t), Georg Gerster, Photo Researchers. 339(b), Thomas J. Abercrombie, NGS. 340-341, Brian Brake, Photo Researchers. 342, Emory Kristof, NGP. 343, John G. Ross. 344-345, Danny Lehman. 345(t), George F. Mobley, NGP. 345(b), NASA. 346-347, Ira Block. 348-349, David Brill. 349(r), NGPA. 349(b), Ira Block. 350, Ivor Noël Hume. 350-351, Richard Schlecht. 351, NGPA. 352-353, Joseph H. Bailey, NGP. 354-355, Georg Gerster.

THE PAST ON DISPLAY

The museums of the world house the tangible evidence of some of humanity's greatest achievements. Many artifacts featured in *The Adventure of Archaeology* are on display for you to enjoy. A sampling from around the world follows.

UNITED STATES

California. Santa Barbara Museum of Natural History, Santa Barbara. Chumash canoe built by J. Harrington.

Colorado. Denver Museum of Natural History, Denver. The Folsom point unearthed near Folsom, New Mexico, by a museum expedition.

Florida. Florida State Museum, Gainesville. A copy of part of the Maya murals from Bonampak.

Illinois. Oriental Institute, University of Chicago, Chicago. Near Eastern artifacts collected by James Breasted. Cuneiform tablets from Nippur.

Massachusetts. Peabody Museum of Archaeology and Ethnology, Harvard University, Cambridge. Mica face found in Ohio by a Peabody expedition. Jade carving of a warrior, recovered at Chichén Itzá by Edward Thompson.

New York. The Metropolitan Museum of Art. Funerary boat models spotted by Herbert Winlock in Meketre's tomb near Deir el Bahri. Egyptian pots discovered by W. M. Flinders Petrie.

Ohio. Ohio Historical Center, Columbus. Stone effigy pipes excavated in the Ohio River Valley.

Oklahoma. Stovall Museum of Science and History, University of Oklahoma, Norman. Engraved shells and other artifacts from Spiro.

Pennsylvania. The University Museum, University of Pennsylvania, Philadelphia. Cuneiform tablets collected by Herman Hilprecht at Nippur. Artifacts found in Ur's Royal Cemetery by Leonard Woolley.

Virginia. James Anderson House, Williamsburg. Artifacts excavated at this capital of colonial Virginia.

Yorktown Victory Center, Yorktown. Artifacts recovered from British ships scuttled in the York River.

Washington, D. C. Smithsonian Institution. Zuni fetishes collected in New Mexico by Frank Cushing.

OTHER COUNTRIES

China. Hebei Provincial Museum, Shijiazhuang. Princess Dou Wan's jade burial suit, found near Shouling.

Hunan Provincial Museum, Changsha. Bronze vessel of the Shang period, excavated in Ninqxiang Xian.

Museum of Qin Dynasty, Xian. Life-size clay figures from the tomb of Qin Shi Huangdi at Xian.

Cyprus. Crusader Castle, Kyrenia. Wreck of the Kyrenia ship, excavated by Michael Katzev off Cyprus.

Denmark. Forhistorisk Museum, Moesgård. Well-preserved remains of Grauballe man, studied by P. V. Glob.

Nationalmuseet, Copenhagen. Ole Worm's collection. Artifacts dug up in Denmark by Jens Jacob Worsaae.

Silkeborg Museum, Silkeborg. Head of Tollund man, studied by P. V. Glob.

Egypt. Egyptian Museum, Cairo. Queen Ahhotpe's jewelry, presented to Egypt's ruler by Auguste Mariette. From Deir el Bahri the cache of mummies removed by Émile Brugsch. Treasures from Tutankhamun's tomb, found in the Valley of the Kings by Howard Carter and Lord Carnarvon. Funerary boat models spotted by Herbert Winlock in Meketre's tomb near Deir el Bahri.

France. Centre de Documentation de la Préhistoire Alpine, Grenoble. Flint dagger and other Stone Age artifacts retrieved from Lake Paladru.

Lascaux II, near Montignac. A full-size reproduction of Lascaux cave and its Stone Age paintings.

Musée Boucher de Perthes, Abbeville. Stone tools that Boucher de Perthes found in the Somme Valley.

Musée des Antiquités Nationales, Saint-Germain-en-Laye. Stone tools discovered by Boucher de Perthes in the Somme Valley. Artifacts unearthed in French caves and rock-shelters by Édouard Lartet and Henry Christy.

Musée du Louvre, Paris. Assyrian bas-reliefs and sculptures taken from Khorsabad by Paul-Émile Botta. The zodiac relief removed from the temple at Dandara. Treasures spirited out of the Apis tombs at Saqqâra by Auguste Mariette. Diorite statues of Gudea, excavated at Telloh by Ernest de Sarzec. Artifacts found in Jerusalem by Félicien de Saulcy.

Musée Guimet, Paris. Statues brought back from Preah Khan, Cambodia, by Louis Delaporte.

Germany, East. Islamisches Museum, East Berlin. The Great Altar removed from Pergamum by Alexander Conze and Karl Humann.

Germany, West. Ägyptisches Museum, West Berlin. Limestone bust of Queen Nefertiti, spirited from Tell el 'Amârna by Ludwig Borchardt.

Rheinisches Landesmuseum Bonn, Bonn. The skull and other bones of Neandertal man.

Greece. Archaeological Museum, Samothrace. Sculptures recovered on the island by Alexander Conze.

Archaeological Museum, Thessaloniki. Artifacts from the tomb of Philip II of Macedonia, found in Verghina by Manolis Adronicos.

Herakleion Museum, Herakleion, Crete. Minoan artifacts unearthed at Knossos by Arthur Evans.

National Archaeological Museum, Athens. Treasures from Mycenae, uncovered by Heinrich and Sophia Schliemann. Artifacts dug up at Akrotíri by Spyridon Marinatos.

Old Archaeological Museum, Olympia. Sculptures unearthed at Olympia by Ernst Curtius.

Israel. Museum of Ancient Art, Haifa. Artifacts excavated at Caesarea Maritima by the Caesarea Ancient Harbour Excavation Project.

Shrine of the Book, Jerusalem. Dead Sea Scrolls discovered in caves at Qumrān, Jordan.

Italy. Antiquarium, Pompeii. Plaster casts of bodies made on site by Giuseppe Fiorelli.

Museo Archeologico, Florence. A reconstruction of an Etruscan tomb found near Volterra.

Museo Archeologico Nazionale, Naples. Artifacts retrieved from Herculaneum by Rocque Joaquin de Alcubierre. Karl Weber's plan of the Villa of the Papyri at Herculaneum.

Museo Nazionale di Villa Giulia, Rome. Etruscan sarcophagus with reclining couple from Cerveteri.

Jordan. Jordan Archaeological Museum, Amman. Plastered skulls found by Kathleen Kenyon at Jericho.

Kenya. National Museums of Kenya, Nairobi. Hominid fossils discovered at Olduvai Gorge, Laetoli, and Koobi Fora by the Leakey family.

Mali. Musée National du Mali, Bamako. Artifacts excavated by Susan and Roderick McIntosh at Jenne-Jeno.

Mexico. Museo de Antropología de la Universidad Veracruzana, Veracruz. Olmec stone heads found by Matthew Stirling at San Lorenzo.

Museo Nacional de Antropología, Mexico City. Maya mosaic uncovered by Sylvanus Morley at Chichén Itzá. Sculptures collected in Mexico by Matthew Stirling. Reproduction of and artifacts from Pacal's tomb at Palenque, discovered by Alberto Ruz Lhuillier.

Templo Mayor, Mexico City. Stone carving of Coyolxauhqui, found here by a utility worker.

Nigeria. Ife Museum, Ife. Statues discovered at Ife by Frank Willett.

Norway. Vikingskipene, Oslo. Viking ship excavated at Oseberg.

Pakistan. National Museum of Pakistan, Karachi. Harappan artifacts dug up by Mortimer Wheeler at Mohenjo Daro and Harappa.

Poland. Muzeum Archeologiczne, Biskupin. Artifacts recovered from this sunken, 2,300-year-old village.

Sweden. Wasavarvet, Stockholm. Wreck of the warship *Vasa,* located in Stockholm harbor by Anders Franzén.

Switzerland. Schweizerisches Landesmuseum, Zürich. Artifacts recovered from Swiss lake dwellings.

Tanzania. National Museum of Tanzania, Dar es Salaam. Remains of *Australopithecus boisei,* discovered by Mary Leakey at Olduvai Gorge.

Thailand. National Museum, Ban Chiang. Jewelry, pottery, weapons, and other artifacts unearthed at Ban Chiang by Chester Gorman.

Turkey. Aphrodisias Museum, Aphrodisias. Roman sculptures found at Aphrodisias by Kenan Erim.

Bodrum Museum of Underwater Archaeology, Bodrum. Shipwreck artifacts from Serçe Limanı, Cape Gelidonya, and Yassı Ada, excavated by George Bass.

United Kingdom. Ashmolean Museum, Oxford, England. The Tradescant collection.

The British Museum, London, England. The collection of Sir Hans Sloane. Greek vases, 6,000 coins, and other artifacts collected by Sir William Hamilton; also the Portland Vase, which he bought in Rome. The Elgin Marbles, removed from the Parthenon by Lord Elgin's men. The Rosetta Stone, discovered in Egypt by Napoléon's soldiers. Statue of Ramesses II, taken by Giovanni Belzoni from the Temple of Amun-Re at Karnak.

From Nineveh the cuneiform tablets and Assyrian bas-reliefs unearthed by Austen Henry Layard and by Hormuzd Rassam, as well as the Flood Tablet deciphered by George Smith. From Nimrud the Assyrian winged bulls and lions taken by Layard and the ivory plaques recovered by Max Mallowan. Assyrian bas-reliefs and winged bulls and lions excavated at Khorsabad by Paul-Émile Botta.

Marble columns and reliefs from the Temple of Artemis, unearthed by John Wood at Ephesus. Reliefs from Carchemish, discovered by Leonard Woolley. Artifacts found by Woolley in the Royal Cemetery at Ur. Anglo-Saxon treasures from the Sutton Hoo ship burial, excavated by Charles Phillips.

City Museum, St. Albans, Hertfordshire, England. Roman artifacts unearthed at Verulamium by Mortimer Wheeler.

Dorset County Museum, Dorchester, England. Artifacts dug up at Maiden Castle by Mortimer Wheeler.

Kingston Lacy House, Wimborne, Dorset, England. Obelisk taken from the island of Philae by Giovanni Belzoni and Henry Salt.

Mary Rose Ship Hall and Exhibition, Portsmouth, England. Wreck of the Tudor warship *Mary Rose* and artifacts salvaged off Portsmouth by Alexander McKee and Margaret Rule.

Museum of London, London, England. Cheapside Hoard. Sculptures found at the Temple of Mithras in London.

Salisbury and South Wiltshire Museum, Salisbury, England. Artifacts excavated at Cranborne Chase by Augustus Henry Pitt Rivers.

Segontium Roman Fort Museum, Caernarfon, Wales. Artifacts dug up by Mortimer Wheeler at Segontium.

Sir John Soane's Museum, London, England. The sarcophagus of Seti I, removed by Giovanni Belzoni from the Valley of the Kings.

Wiltshire Archaeological and Natural History Society Museum, Devizes, England. Artifacts collected by Sir Richard Colt Hoare and William Cunnington in Wiltshire.

363

WHERE TO GO ON DIGS

The organizations selected for this guide sponsor digs in the United States and abroad, and all of them welcome volunteers. An adult usually must accompany volunteers under 16.

To find out about projects close to home, you can also contact a natural history museum or the archaeology or anthropology department of a college or university in your area. They can tell you how to reach your state archaeologist as well.

Credit - Academic credit for students
Local - Digs in the local area
Regional - Digs in the state or region
World - Digs worldwide
Bulletin - Bulletin or newsletter available; may be a subscription fee
Fee - Participants must pay a fee

Alexandria Archaeology
105 North Union Street
Alexandria, VA 22314
(703) 838-4399
Credit, Local, Bulletin

American Anthropological Association
1703 New Hampshire Avenue, N.W.
Washington, D. C. 20009
(202) 232-8800
Credit, World, Bulletin, Fee

American Archaeology Division
15 Switzler Hall
University of Missouri
Columbia, MO 65211
(314) 882-8273
Credit, Local

American Indian Archaeological Institute
Post Office Box 260
Washington, CT 06793
(203) 868-0518
Local, Bulletin, Fee

American Schools of Oriental Research
4243 Spruce Street
Philadelphia, PA 19104
(215) 222-4643
Credit, World, Bulletin, Fee

Archaeological Institute of America
Post Office Box 1901
Boston, MA 02215
(617) 353-9361
Credit, World, Bulletin, Fee

Archaeology Abroad
31-34 Gordon Square
London WC1H 0PY, England
Credit, World, Bulletin

Baltimore Center for Urban Archaeology
800 East Lombard Street
Baltimore, MD 21202
(301) 396-1866
Credit, Local, Bulletin

Carolina Archaeological Services
537 Harden Street
Columbia, SC 29205
(803) 254-3996
Regional

Center for American Archeology
Kampsville Archeological Center
Kampsville, IL 62053
Credit, Local, Bulletin, Fee

Center for Archaeological Studies
232 Bay State Road
Boston, MA 02215

(617) 353-3416
Credit, World, Bulletin, Fee

Center for Southwestern Archaeology
23390 County Road K
Cortez, CO 81321
(303) 565-8975
Credit, Local, Bulletin, Fee

Council for British Archaeology
112 Kennington Road
London SE11 6RE, England
(01) 582-0494
Credit, Regional, Bulletin

Desert Research Institute
Social Sciences Center
Post Office Box 60220
Reno, NV 89506
(702) 673-7303
Credit, Regional

Division of Historic Preservation and Archaeology
202 North Alabama Street
Indianapolis, IN 46204
(317) 232-1650
Regional

Earthwatch
Post Office Box 127N
Belmont, MA 02178
(617) 489-3030
Credit, World, Bulletin, Fee

Islands Archaeological Programs
Post Office Box 398
Horseshoe Beach, FL 32648
Regional, Fee

Ministry of Education and Culture
Department of Antiquities and Museums
Post Office Box 586
Jerusalem 91000, Israel
(02) 278-603
Credit, Regional, Bulletin

Minnesota Historical Society
Archaeology Department
Fort Snelling History Center
St. Paul, MN 55111
(612) 726-1171
Credit, Local, Bulletin

Mitchell Site
National Historical Landmark
Post Office Box 621
Mitchell, SD 57301
(605) 996-5473
Credit, Local, Bulletin, Fee

New Hampshire Historical Society
30 Park Street
Concord, NH 03301
(603) 225-3381
Credit, Regional, Bulletin

Ontario Ministry of Citizenship and Culture
Archaeology Unit
77 Bloor Street West, 2nd Floor
Toronto, Ontario M7A 2R9, Canada
(416) 965-4490
Regional

South Carolina Underwater Archaeological Research Council
1924 Blossom Street
Columbia, SC 29205
(803) 799-8677
World, Bulletin

University Research Expeditions Program
University of California, Desk K5
Berkeley, CA 94720
(415) 642-6586
Credit, World, Bulletin, Fee

Withlacoochee River Archaeology Council
110 North Apopka Avenue
Inverness, FL 32650
(904) 392-1721
Local, Bulletin

INDEX

365

Type composition by National Geographic's Photographic Services. Color separations by Chanticleer Co., Inc., New York, N. Y.; Graphic Color Plate, Inc., Stamford, Conn.; The Lanman Companies, Washington, D. C. Printed and bound by R. R. Donnelley & Sons Co., Chicago, Ill. Paper by Mead Paper Co., New York, N. Y.

Library of Congress CIP Data

Fagan, Brian M.
The adventure of archaeology.

Bibliography: p.
Includes index.
1. Archaeology—History. 2. Archaeologists—Biography. I. Title.
CC100.F33 1985   930.1   85-15275
ISBN 0-87044-603-7 (alk. paper)
ISBN 0-87044-604-5 (deluxe : alk. paper)